Finite Media

A CULTURAL POLITICS BOOK
Edited by John Armitage,
Ryan Bishop, and Douglas Kellner

SEAN CUBITT

Finite Media
Environmental Implications of Digital Technologies

Duke University Press   Durham and London   2017

Library of Congress Cataloging-in-Publication Data
Names: Cubitt, Sean, [date] author.
Title: Finite media : environmental implications of digital technologies /
Sean Cubitt.
Description: Durham : Duke University Press, 2017. | "A cultural politics
book." | Includes bibliographical references and index.
Identifiers: LCCN 2016028022 (print)
LCCN 2016028817 (ebook)
ISBN 9780822362814 (hardcover : alk. paper)
ISBN 9780822362920 (pbk. : alk. paper)
ISBN 9780822373476 (e-book)
Subjects: LCSH: Digital media—Environmental aspects. | Digital media—
Political aspects. | Digital media—Social aspects.
Classification: LCC HM851.C7825 2016 (print)
LCC HM851 (ebook)
DDC 302.23/1—dc23
LC record available at https://lccn.loc.gov/2016028022

Cover art: Chris Jordan, *Circuit Boards #2, New Orleans, 2005* (detail)

CONTENTS

vii   ACKNOWLEDGMENTS

1   **INTRODUCTION** Eco-mediation

13   **CHAPTER 1** Energy

63   **CHAPTER 2** Matter

151   **CHAPTER 3** Eco-political Aesthetics

169   **CHAPTER 4** Ecological Communication as Politics

193   Coda on Saturn

201   REFERENCES
237   INDEX

ACKNOWLEDGMENTS

This book is dedicated to my teachers.

Drafts and fragments have appeared in earlier forms in *Theory, Culture and Society*, *Cultural Politics*, and *Media, Culture and Society*. I am especially grateful for my collaborators on the last of these, Robert Hassan and Ingrid Volkmer. The following editors have generously included essays feeding into this project in their collections: Alexa Weik von Mossner, Anil Narine, David Berry and Michael Dieter, Nicole Starosielski and Janet Walker, Larissa Hjorth, Natalie King, and Mami Kataoka, Paul Graves-Brown, Rodney Harrison and Angela Piccini, Ulrik Ekman, Claire Molloy and Yiannis Tzioumakis, Jay David Bolter, Lily Diaz, Morten Søndergaard, and Maria Engberg, Suzanne Buchan, and my collaborators on two anthologies, Stephen Rust and Salma Monani, who have been and remain an inspiration for ecomedia scholars everywhere. I have been fortunate enough (at the cost of a carbon footprint chilling to contemplate) to have talked through aspects of this research with colleagues at Transmediale, Steirischer Herbst, Central Saint Martins School of Art, the Cinémathèque Québecoise, ISEA Istanbul, the Screen Conference at the University of Glasgow, the Lancaster Institute for Contemporary Arts, the London School of Economics, Trinity College Dublin, and the Universities of Cambridge, Central Lancashire, Dundee, Espiritu Santo, Illinois, Johns Hopkins, Massey, Melbourne, Montreal, Oxford, Sao Paolo, St. Andrews, Siegen, Southampton, Sussex, Warwick, and the West of England, and to them all I owe a deep debt of gratitude. Particular thanks are due to Lanfranco Aceti, John Armitage, Jon Beller, Ryan Bishop, Pat Brereton, Elinor Carmi, Jonathan Curling, Catherine Elwes, Jennifer Gabrys, Charlie Gere, R. Harindranath, Adrian Ivakhiv, Roger Malina, Janine Marchessault, José-Carlos Mariategui, Noortje Marres, Gabriel Menotti, Walter Mignolo, Maree Mills, Salma Monani, Jussi Parikka, Janine Randerson, Lisa Reihana, Ned Rossiter, Stephen Rust, Susan Schuppli, Jacob Scott, Gareth Stanton, Sy Taffel, Paul Thomas, Nathaniel Tkacz, Pasi Valiaho, Henry Warwick, Ken Wissoker at Duke, and the generous and insightful reviewers whose anonymous comments remade this book, my colleagues in the Leonardo and ecomediastudies.org networks, and the many more, human and nonhuman, with names to come.

For Alison, forever.

Finite Media

The Story of the Kelly Gang, dir. Charles Tait, 1906; DVD screen grab of the 2006 digital restoration. Source: National Film and Sound Archive of Australia.

INTRODUCTION ECO-MEDIATION

Say not the struggle naught availeth,
The labour & the wounds are vain,
The enemy faints not nor faileth,
And as things have been they remain.
—**Arthur Hugh Clough**

Of the original sixty minutes of *The Story of the Kelly Gang*, shot by Charles Tait in 1906, only seventeen minutes remain, much of it in the poorest condition. The film records a moment of colonial rebellion, the wild Irishman Ned Kelly refusing the yoke of his imperial masters. Often referred to as the world's first feature film, *The Kelly Gang* is a triumph of realism. We see again animals, plants, and geology now buried under roads and buildings. The nitrate stock, brilliant sunlight, and sharp lenses catch all the flickering of background leaves and grass, as characters approach or remove themselves from the scene. Even the armor is authentic: not Kelly's own, but the helmet and breastplate worn by Joe Byrne, a member of his gang, still a living memory at the time the film circulated, to considerable profit, through the Victorian and South Australian goldfields where the Kellys rode and met their end, and around the colonies. Tait's deep focus and his taste for authenticity place the film in a specific aesthetic tradition of pictorial realism, and enough remains for us to understand the main action. Yet what strikes twenty-first-century viewers is the developing chaos of the blistering support and the silver halides sitting on it, as well as the artifacts produced in the archival process and its transfer to the web-ready MPEG-4 codec. *The Story of the Kelly Gang* is not in any simple way about ecology, but it is itself an ecological artifact, one that links human, technological, and organic worlds in the context of colonialism, and so acts as a talisman for the work undertaken in this book.

When we speak of film as a "living medium," we should take the term literally. The nitrate stock *The Kelly Gang* was shot on is formed by adding camphor as a plasticizer to nitrocellulose, also known as guncotton, a close relative of nitroglycerine (the foundation of the Nobel fortune). It is extremely flammable. Even without fire, the stock gradually outgasses, leaving a sticky and unworkable gel. Such decomposition is as much a fact of film as it is of any other living matter. The archivist's task is to preserve the film in a form as close as possible to an ideal master print at an ideal first screening, to conserve light passed from one time to another. Against this preservationist homage to the ideal, from the point of view of the film itself, the filmstrip is a slowly percolating chemical soup, a patch of molecular combination and mutation. The archival life of film (Fossati 2009) includes this struggle between the order of the archive and the entropy of what the archivist understands as decay, but which can also be understood as the evolution of a new artifact from the old.

In this instance, according to Sally Jackson and National Film and Sound Archive of Australia historian Graham Shirley,

> The surviving fragments were digitally scanned by Haghefilm Laboratories in Amsterdam using the DIAMANT digital restoration system. This allowed major cleaning to remove dirt, scratches and other blemishes, and eliminated the jitter characteristic of the original footage. This digital approach also allowed for the re-creation of frame content which had otherwise been lost through physical deterioration. To achieve this, the Haghefilm restorers copied and modified content from adjacent frames to replace missing information in damaged ones. The result is the cleaner, clearer and much more detailed film we have today. (Jackson and Shirley 2006)

This is interesting on two counts: First, commenting on a blog post about this film, Melbourne blogger Carl Looper suggested, "Some of that 'boiling' may be a function of the restoration algorithms"; and second, because it suggests an even closer correlation between chemical and digital intelligence at work in the clip. Such multiply nonhuman mediations raise with even greater urgency the question of mediation itself, the processes that mediate between populations and environments, and in which environments, it now appears, play a significant role. The Diamant system works in precisely the opposite direction to MPEG and other codecs (compression-decompression systems for transmitting video), which compress video signals by removing anything that appears to the algorithm to be extraneous. The principle of capturing the maximum amount of detail is important for the master copy of a film, but for distribution codecs play on the psychological optics of the good enough, trusting the standard observer to skip over damage and fill in visual blanks. Archivists revert to the maximal principle, even at the cost of promoting probability over actuality.

A film, especially in deep focus, has a special claim to actuality in that it records actual motion, or fragments of actual motion. The actual always contains in itself the virtual: Every motion contains in itself the possibility of unforeseen development, only one of which becomes actual in the next frame, but all of which lie latent in the first. The Diamant algorithm, by dint of necessity, extracts from that virtual character of the individual frame an actuality that it interposes in the neighboring frames. The probable substitutes for the virtual in order to produce a new actual—the archival print—that is now what it must in some sense always be, since films as damaged as this cannot be projected. The *Kelly Gang* we see today (NFSA. 2016) is a representation of the film, an idealized representation of an idealized film. Thus, while the film itself slides toward the gel stage, the degradation of its materiality, its restorations migrate toward the Ideal. It is another ironic triumph of the Idea over the existent. It is as impossible to reconstruct the entropic chemistry of decay as to remake the original sixty minutes of *The Story of the Kelly Gang*. The fragments we view are a work of ongoing catastrophe, the work of humans, technologies, and natural processes: time and its space dissolving, the falling apart that is the pixel, the ordering power of reassembling what information we have across frames, the vector of this artifact moving on through time, now and forever pinned to migration from format to format. This is the work of an art which more than any that preceded it owns up to and embraces, if we learn to see, the effervescence of knowing and its perpetual evolutions. That effervescent commonality of human, technical, and natural processes is referred to in what follows as mediation.

Mediations are not communications (though all communications are mediated). Mediating does not require messages, nor even senders and receivers: It would be false to anthropomorphize the nitrate reaction or the semiautomated digital reconstruction as in some way capable of expression or intention. Mediation names the material processes connecting human and nonhuman events—as the nitric acid catalyst mediates between molecules in the decay of nitrocellulose, and that mediation is mediated again by the Diamant algorithm. Mediation is the primal connectivity shared by human and nonhuman worlds.

Only in some limited and extraordinary cases does mediation become communication. Following Shannon and Weaver (1949), we might say that communication is about distinguishing the message as figure from noise as ground. The distinction prioritizes the distinct units of communication from the chaotic cosmic background. If, in Bateson's (1973, 351) aphorism, information is a difference that makes a difference, noise must be indifferent, and without effect. But then, why try to suppress it? Noise is defined by exclusion: It is what is not communication. But if we do try to grasp noise for itself, when we hear in the static the random burbling of the universe, we should recognize in it the basic flux of mediation, enthralling and distracting as the waves of the sea. Ecologies are not networks connecting previously separate things: Every element of an ecology mediates every other. Life mediates nutrients and sunlight, storing, changing, growing, passing, mutating, returning. *The Story of the Kelly Gang* mediates sunlight, lens, film, the chemistry of nitrate, the politics of archives, and the determinations of digital video. When we speak of the media, we tend to refer to the technological media of the last two hundred years; but everything that mediates is a medium—light, molecules, energy. This flux of mediation is logically prior to communication and to the objects we have learned, through communication, to distinguish from the background hum. The flow of mediation precedes all separations, all distinctions, all thingliness, objects, and objectivity. It precedes the separation of the human and the environmental.

And yet, everywhere in the human world, that flow is parceled out, delayed, amassed, ossified. The question is how, and to what purpose. It is not only that things appear to us as things instead of processes, nor that flux is without form or history. On the contrary, the inevitable mutation that necessarily accompanies mediation belongs to time's arrow, and to the increasing complexity of order as well as its opposite. Life is negentropic, perpetually constructing and defending order. The microcosmic density of ecosystems, human societies, and their interweaving moves toward the increasing mutual mediation of all lives, all deaths. The assertion that the world is composed of things is based on a rejection of this connectedness. Such an ontology of objects would be merely metaphysical were it not for the fact that it describes so accurately the way we see and understand the world. The question is how we, especially in the West, came to see the world this way. In turn, this raises a question of whether it is our perception that works like this or whether the world has changed. I see the actors playing out the roles of Ned Kelly and his captors, but I also see the film stock raddled by time and rebuilt digitally. Each of them is self-consistent over time, and so I see them as things, but the coincidence of the seething surface and the filmed events is unique and ephemeral as the file plays on my computer screen. It is exactly this ephemerality that ties these "things" into a single process, a mutual mediation. I have learned to see this way, but I can also imagine or learn other ways of seeing. The same is not necessarily true of human mediation. Parceling out the planetary flow of matter and energy involves egregious inequality: Gold accumulates around one person, trash around another. There may well be an ontological truth, that every process is a mediation, and that reality is the archery of time, but there is no denying that the flow of mediations concentrates in bloated fortresses of control that operate by damming up the generosity of life and the mercy of mortality.

We have strong theories as to why the poor collude in their own oppression, but we lack understanding of why power and wealth still accumulate far beyond the capacity of their owners to enjoy them, long after any historical rationale, even to the point of the suicidal inactivity that has frozen the world's leaders in the oncoming headlights of climate change. Nothing oppresses us more than the idea that as things have been, they shall remain: that the only response to a thawing Arctic is to drill for oil there; that there is no Plan B, no alternative. Belief in the primacy of objects goes hand in hand with stronger belief in the potency of subjects, yet all evidence points toward a human polity without masters, in the sense of people who can control it. On the contrary, wealth accumulates, and the individuals standing at the nexus of accumulation are accidental to the process: The CEO is fired but the corporation lives on. In the modern era, the era of capital, accumulation has become an end in itself, systemically oriented against redistribution. A theme of this book therefore is that from a primal interweaving of all processes, we have arrived at a point where the world appears to us as things that must be ordered and amassed. It offers as a preliminary thesis that this process in turn begins in an original sin that severed humans from their environments: the privilege granted to communication, a necessary survival mechanism that, however, has come to risk the survival of the whole ecosystem.

Communication places us in relations of sender and receiver, object and subject, as it creates the distinction between the sovereign as acclaimed source of authority and "the capillary functioning of power" (Foucault 1977, 198) that communicates it. Capillary disposition creates a hierarchy of channels, the media through which we assemble our polities, and equally in which we construct our technologies, and by means of which we find ourselves confronted by the Other of nature. In the distinctions between polity, technology, and nature are realized their dependence on one another, a dependence that emerges only once the chaos of primal mediation has been organized, as the ancient creation myths begin in the separations of sky from earth, light from dark, sweet from salt water, and land and sea. The foaming surfaces of *The Story of the Kelly Gang*, quite as much as the flickering sheen of the leaves in its backgrounds, recall that primal mediation, yearning for its return. At the same time, as this book sets out to show, even communicating one's love of nature implies damaging it. The corollary of the assertion that every communication is mediated is that every communication is material. Paper, ink, printing presses all require wood, metals, animals, fire, and energy. Mass-circulation print media of the nineteenth century needed steam; the telegraph needed wires and electric generators; photography and cinematography needed silver and plastics from oil and coal. Much of this book is about the deep dependence of contemporary media on energy and materials. To communicate with one another, we also inadvertently communicate our dismissive relation to the humans and natural environments who pay the terrible price for its efficiency, even for its poetry.

But it is also the case that in this mutual dependence of human, natural, and technological there is a utopian orientation toward a future overcoming of their tripartite separation. *The Story of the Kelly Gang* is so emblematic because it presents the mutual mediations of human actors, technological agency, and natural processes. The dominant utopian mechanism today is technology, and its counterfaith is Gaia. It is precisely because that dualism is so potent that it is essential to turn our gaze toward the polity—the assembly of human beings in action—as the site from which might arise any alternative, and therefore by definition any future, since the future is only knowable by its difference from the present and past. It is we ourselves who must become other in order to produce an other world. The correlative is that we must cease to be human, and most of all cease to exist as exclusively human polity, which is the medium of communication par excellence. The road to that goal, however, must lead through the polis, the humanity of humans, and most of all through our communications in order to imagine a way out of stasis.

The decay of archival film is a mirror to the economics of accumulation. Capital gathers, hoards, and invests in a system that claims immortality for itself and dismisses death as something that occurs beyond its purview. *The*

Story of the Kelly Gang speaks intensely of the mortality of the materiality of media. Media are finite, in the sense both that, as matter, they are inevitably tied to physics, especially the dimension of time; and that their constituent elements—matter and energy, information and entropy, time and space, but especially the first pair—are finite resources in the closed system of planet Earth. Because they are finite, media not only cannot persist forever; they cannot proliferate without bounds. There are not enough of certain metals already for everyone on the planet to have the same access to equipment as Western consumers have become used to in recent decades. To create new materials means using up a finite stock of energy sources. The obsessive accumulation of everything that characterizes our era has limits.

For many ecologists, this problem has its origin in overconsumption. For materialists, the source is as likely to be overproduction. The two are difficult to disentangle, but this book leans toward the latter, not only because it offers a more persuasive explanation but because overconsumption is presented to us—politically—as an ethical issue, a matter for individuals, where overproduction is a political matter involving us as social beings. We are all worn down with the almost impossible moral obligation to shop ecologically, and to persuade others to. Ecological crisis, it is argued here, is not the fault of individuals but of the communicative systems, most of all the tyranny of the economy, of money as the dominant medium of twenty-first-century intercourse between humans and our world.

Communication is inextricably bound up in the concept of the commons. As we will see, the idea of common land, and of the open seas and later outer space as commons has a long, divisive history. In 1609, the great jurist Hugo Grotius took as his premise the following thesis:

> Now, as there are some things which every man enjoys in common with all other men, and as there are other things which are distinctly his and belong to no one else, just so has nature willed that some of the things which she has created for the use of mankind remain common to all, and that others through the industry and labor of each man become his own. Laws moreover were given to cover both cases so that all men might use common property without prejudice to any one else, and in respect to other things so that each man being content with what he himself owns might refrain from laying his hands on the property of others. (Grotius [1609] 1916, 2)

The seas fell into the category of things "common to all," but the "all" disguised a deeper belief in who exactly might lay claim to the freedom of the seas. Grotius, in the first flush of the Dutch Republic's contestation with Portugal for access to the East Indies (Vieira 2003), was contesting the Portuguese claim to own access to the Spice Islands. For Grotius, the regulation of the seas fell under the law of nations. Colonized lands had a different destiny. Where there was evidence of "the industry and labor of each man," there too was evidence of property rights; but since the colonies gave the appearance of unworked lands, they were open to the "improvements" of clearing forests and establishing fields, and therefore to expropriation by the colonizers, regardless of the very different forms of working the terrain and its resources practiced by indigenous peoples. Grotius on this basis made a distinction between *terra nullius*, land that belonged to no one, and *res nullius*, the seas that belonged to all nations.

There thus appeared two forms of commons. In the case of the sea, "Grotius was not basing his argument on the traditional rights of the commons, which tended to be customary rather than codified, but on the limited notion of *res communis* found in Roman law" (Mirzoeff 2009, 292), a legal doctrine defining public goods as property of the *res publica*, the state. In the case of the land, the commons referred not to legal definition but to customary practice, specifically to territory to which everyone had access. As we will see, the contest over what status custom has in law, which precise features of the world can be considered the property of one or many states or one or many individuals, and under what conditions common goods can become private property has been a key feature of environmental history. In our times, the idea of a global commons is offered by influential writers like Hardt and Negri (2009) not as a return to the past but as a future, grounded in tradition but now applied not only to land, water, and air but to knowledge, genetic material, and many other new domains. In what follows, the idea of a return to the commons goes beyond Hardt and Negri in insisting that the new commons cannot be solely human, and that therefore our understanding of what it is to be human needs to change. That task is political, but it is also aesthetic, and deeply engaged in the mediations between humans and their environments, natural and technological.

Three key terms describe what happened to the commons, both in Europe and in colonialism: enclosure, environment, and externality. The enclosure of common land and parceling out of common goods, including the geology lying under the land, the air and the radio spectrum carried through it, the sea and the rivers and waters running into it, was a historical moment, but is also an ongoing process. In many senses, modernity begins with the enclosures that for Marx lay at the beginning of capital, but which also began the alienation of people from land that created the modern conception of nature (Thomas 1983), and created what we now know as the environment. Environments environ: surround, encircle, circumscribe. They become environments by being excluded from the communicative community alienated from them by enclosure. There is a strange contradiction here between enclosing and excluding. It is made only more complex in a third term, externality. An externality is, in economics, anything that can be used without cost. Workers, land, and machinery have to be paid for, but air is free. Firms can use as much of it, and dump as much waste into it, as they wish, without having to pay. Today, legislation applies a cost to the use of common goods like water, and to polluting common benefits like the atmosphere, but those costs are often minimal compared to profits, and treated accordingly. Nature, natural reproduction of species, and harvesting wild foods and medicines require investment in everything except the natural processes they rely on. These are the environments that become economic externalities. Enclosure makes something property: under Grotius's principles, what is not property is there to be exploited by anyone who cares to exploit it. The fate of communication in the modern world is tied up in the translation of the commons through enclosure, environmentalization, and externalization. These processes are not only historical but major features of the contemporary geopolitics of ecology, features that make it essential to consider the aesthetics of media and communication in direct relation to contemporary forms of colonialism. Following in the footsteps of the work done, among many other eco-critical thinkers of the materiality of media, by Grossman (2007), Feilhauer and Zehle (2009), Gabrys (2010), Maxwell and Miller (2012), and Parikka (2015), eco-politics and eco-aesthetics must be thought through in the context of post- and decolonial movements. Media and mediation cannot be separated from their environmental impacts, but for that very reason they are privileged tools in creating a future other than our dark now.

The archived footage resurrected in *The Story of the Kelly Gang* might be considered a microcosm of this potential: The film has grown and changed with its material substrate as that went through its secret and inhuman chemical afterlife. An environment and its inhabitants coevolve. A species does not discover an environment waiting for it. It cocreates that environment by acting in it, eating, excreting, building, reproducing, dying. Ecology is a science of relations and mediations, in which innumerable interactions must constantly re-create the end points "environment" and "inhabitant." These termini do not originate communications: The buzzing, blooming, interconnected flows of mediation come first, construing as needed from the materials at hand the partners, from cells to ecosystems, that will be so mediated. This is the environmentalist account not just of natural but of human history. Too often we presume that the nonhuman has autonomy from human affairs, save only when anthropogenic processes threaten natural cycles. It is a direct consequence of such thinking that gives precedence to preserving wilderness over relationships between the human population and the environing world. Such anti-anthropocentrism reflects an ideal, not the actual circumstances. The aesthetic of mediation is political to the extent that it is mediated through public administration and never exists as pure immanence. If eco-critique is to have a political role, it must address the human as well as the organic, the environment of data centers, Tijuana maquiladoras, the recycling villages of southern China, and the habitat of London's North Circular Road quite as much as Antarctica.

The first chapters start from the premise that the Earth has finite resources, and that mediation depends upon them and their limits. They address in turn energy and matter. The first chapter engages with energy use and transmission, and then with the sources of energy in fossil fuels, nuclear power, and hydropower projects; and the second with materials, manufacture, and recycling. The environmental and human consequences tell a dark tale of colonialism, genocide, devastated ecologies, toxicity, extinctions, and a shameful legacy that will take more than decades to make right. Together these chapters advance the thesis that we are already ruled by cyborgs, vast biocomputer hybrids characterized by their lack of shame, their obsession with profit, their inhumanity, their suicidal tendency, and the integration of waste into their life cycle. They pay special attention to the burdens placed on the poor, in the megacities of the Global South, and among indigenous peoples. The intellectual and spiritual obligations owed by the green movement to First Nations is immense, but has not altered the ongoing destruction of indigenous lands and cultures. The price they pay for our media is a recurrent theme. The emphasis in the chapters on energy is on the scale of human suffering involved in environmental catastrophe, not in the future of climate change, but in the present and immediate past of energy generation and transmission, resource extraction, manufacture, and toxic waste.

The stories of heroic struggles, and some rare successes, against those who would despoil them is heartening (EJAtlas.org 2015), but does no more to resolve the structural problem of media's ecological impact than the injunction to consumers to save power. Chapter 2 therefore addresses supranational governance structures and attempts to understand how it is that they can organize sophisticated global structures to enable communications, but cannot make a decision about energy and other ecological topics. This too is a sad tale. The failure of political elites and the cyborg corporation to provide a decent living for the majority of the world's population, while destroying the very bases of the wealth they crave, would be a tragic spectacle, if it were the story of a human being.

The last two chapters turn toward the second great theme of the book, ecology as mediation. Inspired by pioneers of eco-critical humanities including Dipesh Chakrabarty (2009), Nicholas Mirzoeff (2014), the contributors to Tom Cohen (2012) and Henry Sussman's (2012) critical anthologies, and Joanna Zylinska (2014), these chapters take up McKenzie Wark's (2015) challenge: "Let's take this world-historical moment to be one in which to reimagine what the collective efforts of everyone who labors could make of the world, and as a world." The third chapter looks at how mediation between human population and environment defines politics, and has always been conducted through the capillary organization of technologies, in the first tools, the earliest rock art, and the oldest poetry. This "originary prostheticity" (Stiegler 1998, 98–100), the technology that is always human and the humanity that is always technological, is composed of media, from rituals to scientific instruments. These mediating technologies that are at the same time instruments of government divide and recombine relations between humans, and between humans, their environments, and the mediating technologies themselves. What environs us today, the environment of the twenty-first century, is no longer only what we call nature but the secondary environments of technology and data, with the human body in the process of also becoming an environment. Assessing potential economic, social, and political resources for change, it becomes apparent that the conditions under which we find ourselves demand a revolution in communications, a fundamentally aesthetic politics.

When Marx (1974, 820) wrote of the "realm of freedom" that "begins only where labour which is determined by necessity and mundane considerations ceases," he might have been speaking of the eudaemonistic ethics endorsed in this book, an ethics whose goal is the good life, a terrestrial paradise pursued through and realized in open communication of and between differences. Environmental criticism requires an elaborated theory of mediation, a concept that this book attempts to refine by testing it against the story of the materials that media are made of. Where other disciplines and professions take as their goal a specific good—health, shelter, justice, knowledge, wealth—the arts, humanities, and the best of the social sciences undertake to debate these values and the weighting we should give them. When social science and humanities scholars remember this calling, we do our true work, which is to discuss what is the good life and how we are to live it. How are we to balance the claims of equality and wealth, freedom and justice, security and discovery? What is the value of harmony or peace? Can the aesthetic values of truth, beauty, and the good inform a realistic politics today? These questions may not be answerable, or not now. Where other vocations work toward solutions, the humanities' unhappy brief is to unearth problems. Environmentally informed critique is especially rich in problems. Our situation is appalling, our prospects bleak. The object of eudaemonistic politics is the collective good life, a life and a collectivity that is aesthetic and which, if the arguments in the first section are correct, must of necessity embrace more than the human privilege. Political aesthetics must recognize the desperate conditions we are in, if it is to create a meaningful alternative or identify signals from the internal contradictions of existing conjunctures and from new forms of cultural, political, and economic practice. Methodologically it embraces three tools: consideration of the complex interacting factors that produce a situation, event or instance; wonder at their extraordinary results, prepared to believe the evidence of its own eyes against habits of thought; and hope for the building of a good life for all, without exception and without favoring our own species. Not rescued from ruin but rescued as ruin, *The Story of the Kelly Gang* demonstrates that another and more inclusive commons is possible, but that it must be built out of the wreckage of the past.

CHAPTER 1 ENERGY

In a poem addressed "To Those Born Later," written in exile from Nazi Germany on the eve of world war, Bertolt Brecht (1979, 318) asked, "What kind of times are they, when / A talk about trees is almost a crime." Today it is almost criminal not to talk about trees.

Ostensibly weightless and friction-free, computing had already in 2008 outstripped the carbon emissions of the airline business and was growing, at conservative estimates, by at least 15 percent a year (Climate Group 2008). Yet the dream—the marketing as well as the political quest—of a marriage between consumer capital and environmentalism keeps us looking for that perfect product that "takes only memories and leaves only footprints," in Chief Seattle's admonition. What we imagine, in short, are consumer goods that have no history: no mines, no manufacture, no freighting, and no waste. Like the myths of information and communication technologies for development (ICT4D), of sustainable development, and of endless economic growth, this chapter argues that there is a myth of immaterial media, and that it is our job to crack it open.

We speak too easily of the infinite resources of human creativity and nature's capacities. Since the publication of the Club of Rome's *Limits to Growth* (Meadows et al. 1972), the idea of a finite planet has fluttered in the peripheral vision of our culture. The "green revolution" of the 1960s (Gaud 1968), that massive industrialization of agriculture and conversion to cash crops and monoculture based on global trade in fertilizers, seemed to get around such limits until the crisis of 1973. Subsequently, the expansion of computing to its current level seemed to repress any similar anxieties again by opening up vast reservoirs of business opportunities. The global financial crisis that engulfed the world in 2008 allowed the idea of finite resources to swim once more into focus. We have come to treat the infinite as our familiar: the infinite productivity of engineering or of mathematics, for example. Technically it may well be the case that we can continue to elaborate new utterances out of old tongues, but there are limits to the quantity of technical media we can employ as we do so. The world is composed of matter and energy, and though they can be converted from one form into another, they cannot be increased by a gram or a joule. We know too that in any physical process there is an informational quotient: that it takes energy to maintain a structure, and that energy and order tend to dissipate toward entropy. Any physical process will produce waste in the form of heat and noise. As we will see, some vital materials are in very short supply. We might be able to fabricate new ones, but that will take energy, and energy is also a finite resource. We might get more material and energy from asteroids, but it will take vast amounts of both to get there. This is the meaning of the term *finite media*.

The second theme occupying this chapter is that we are not all in this together. Indigenous people have borne the brunt of the digital boom, and gained least from it. The global poor suffer far more from pollution and environmental loss than the global rich; and much the same is true for the local poor and the local wealthy. This chapter tries to politicize outrage at environmental crime by making as plain as possible the connections between wealth and toxicity. The first of its four sections addresses energy and the inhuman or cyborg nature of the energy market and its players. The second turns to one human capability meticulously excluded from the world of mining, the experience of shame, and the resulting exclusion of the unaccounted. The third addresses a theme implicit in the first two, integral waste, as it emerges in the fabrication and manufacture of digital machines. The final section articulates the integration of degraded populations and integral waste into the consumer discipline of the new mode of destruction, most of all in the moment of disposal of superseded goods.

The question of how we are to live well rests on the question as to whether we can live at all. The purpose of the chapter is not to wag a moral finger at consumers, but to argue that the political elite has failed to respond to either global poverty or global environmental destruction, and for a single reason: the obscene dogma of profit, no longer a human vice but the sole motivation of inhuman forces now dominating what passes for global politics. Environmentalism is a materialism. It demands that we understand what things are made of, and their connectedness, but also their disconnections. At times this research has felt like a litany of disaster. The reader may share that feeling. The positive side is that no modern ecological tragedy has ever been perpetrated without resistance, and that from this resistance we can begin to acquire some sense of how to make politics matter again. It is not a question of either people or ecologies; nor is it necessarily a project of sacrifice. It is a question of how we are to live well, and therefore a question that requires not only a political answer but an aesthetic one; a question, that is, concerning both perception (the root meaning of *aesthesis*) and art, the techniques of mediation and communication in which we construe our relations with one another and the world. In the twenty-first century, communication implies digital media whose environmental footprint we must therefore analyze before we can ask how communication, which is the material bearer of political life, and perhaps also its goal, can contribute to living well. To find how we can properly ask the question how to live well, we must first confront how it is that we live so badly.

A power cut is an instructive event: It allows us to understand not only how much of daily life is dependent on electricity supply, but how useless so much of our equipment is without power. A future archaeologist approaching the ruins of a contemporary city might be mystified at the ubiquitous devices, from servers to handhelds, scattered amid the debris. Like Stonehenge or the caves of Lascaux, these relics would reveal that they were meaning-making machines, but in the absence of electrical power, there would be few sources to guide an understanding of what they were for and how they worked. Without electricity, the archaeologist will have no way of understanding operating systems, protocols, mark-up languages, codecs, instruction sets. The principle that things connect with one another will be as clear as it is in a woven cloth, but no more so. Even if, say, the principles of routing were decipherable from the physical properties of routers, the nature of what was routed will be lost. Optical and magnetic storage media are notoriously short lived: There will be no records other than those saved on paper. In the absence of power, the archaeologist might be the first to actually read the manuals, knowing, however, that she has no machines on which to implement their instructions. Energy is finite: It can only be changed from one form to another, but in those changes it enters history. We have a very long-term energy source in the sun, and another, lesser source in geothermal heat from the molten core of the planet: All other energy sources derive from them; most have taken geological epochs to form; and all can be squandered. Digital media are unthinkable without the energy needed to produce and run them; therefore we begin this investigation with energy. Energy is a universal principle, but it is also subject to entropy, the inexorable equilibration in which its useful form gradually diminishes. As such it embodies the principle of irreversibility, the physical foundation of history. Thus although it is a universal, energy distribution and use are also deeply historical. We begin therefore with distribution.

Energy Supply
DATA CENTERS, SERVER FARMS, AND CLOUD COMPUTING

According to the U.S. Department of Energy (2008), "Data centers used 61 billion kWh of electricity in 2006, representing 1.5% of all U.S. electricity consumption and double the amount consumed in 2000. Based on current trends, energy consumed by data centers will continue to grow by 12% per year." The same agency reported in 2011 that "information technology and telecommunications facilities account for approximately 120 billion kilowatt hours of electricity annually—or 3% of all U.S. electricity use," double the figures of a scant five years earlier. The 2011 report continues, "Rapid growth in the U.S. data center industry is projected to require two new large power plants per year just to keep pace" (U.S. Department of Energy 2011). In 2008, Boccaletti, Löffler, and Oppenheim at consultants McKinsey estimated that IT manufacture and use was responsible for 2 percent of global carbon emissions—like the Climate Group (2008), noting that this was the same amount as the much-criticized airline industry—and was heading for 3 percent by 2020, when it would be responsible for the same amount of carbon as the United Kingdom produced in 2008. The authors argued that "the fastest-increasing contributor to emissions will be growth in the number and size of data centers, whose carbon footprint will rise more than fivefold between 2002 and 2020" (Boccaletti, Löffler, and Oppenheim 2008, 2).

One of the drivers in this movement is the switch from broadcast media to Internet as the preferred delivery mode for rich media like films and television, including legal transmissions, illegal file sharing, and quasi-legal forms like user-posted video on YouTube. Media corporations are increasingly using video-sharing platforms to entice purchasers of tickets or discs, or using similar technologies on their own sites and content aggregators like Apple's QuickTime trailers portal, while the games industry is moving toward free-to-play models involving millions of users in media-rich interactive network services with complex business models involving substantial record maintenance and updates. The engineering solution on offer is cloud computing, the use of remote servers to store files and the software needed to access them. Best known through consumer services like Amazon s3 and Google Docs, many companies also provide bulk storage and handling of corporate, public service, and government data (see the list of companies provided in the appendix to Carr [2009, 235–44]). The theory is that end users no longer need a complex and expensive computer with ecologically damaging hard drives and CD-DVD players, or memory- and power-hungry local software. In place of full-blown computers, for all but highly professional or necessarily secure uses, a "thin client" will be sufficient. This is the fundamental design of netbooks and tablets with little more than a flash drive for boot-up, connection, and RAM, but which can be linked instantaneously and constantly to remote data centers, also known as server farms, where all their software, documentation, and files can be securely stored and accessed.

As so often in Internet matters, it is difficult to assess how many servers are involved, since any computer can act as a server once connected to the network. However, millions of dedicated servers constitute the backbone of the Internet. They are typically robust machines that are rarely if ever switched off and rebooted, and which have no other function than to provide services to remote clients. Server numbers reflect the kinds of content they serve, the desire for redundancy in case of failure, and the cheapness of building servers. The Domain Name System for Internet addressing is controlled by 376 root servers. Multimedia files, requiring far more memory, require far larger numbers of servers. Blizzard, the company behind the popular massively multiplayer online role-playing game World of Warcraft, was already estimated to have around five hundred servers before the boost from tablet and smartphone users (GamePlanet.com 2008). According to Wowiki, World of Warcraft has 229 recognized private servers in the United States and at least as many again worldwide running additional realms, supporting non-English-speaking players, and providing community services associated with the game's 7.7 million subscribers. Media-rich cloud services like YouTube, Instagram, Tumblr, and Flickr employ huge quantities of memory. Amazon has been estimated to run up to 1 percent of the Internet from its servers, with other shopping and auction sites not far behind. E-mail, ftp, World Wide Web, bulletin boards, and other remnants of the early web use far less computing power, but as they become increasingly media rich, they require more server space, or the equivalent power use associated with torrent and file-sharing technologies such as Skype. There are almost certainly millions of servers associated with the Internet. Mesh networks like BitTorrent provide one possible alternative, but many major companies like Apple are not persuaded. Cloud computing, providing bulk document storage for industry, financial services, medical records, academia, and government, is likely to remain a significant and growing part of the overall load of Internet server traffic. Cloud storage has the immense benefit of allowing service providers access to the metatags, if not the files, of users, information they constantly commodify and sell in what Vincent Mosco (2015) calls "surveillance capitalism." However, the most intense new usage will come from the expansion of dashboards, offering real-time abstracts from massive datasets (Bartlett and Tkacz 2014), the move to mobile apps that work by drawing down and interacting with cloud-based software and data (Goldsmith 2014), and the Internet of things connecting, according to one influential estimate, fifty billion smart devices by 2020 (Evans 2011), all of which will vastly expand the demand for mass server farms.

With an 82.7 percent share in June 2013 (according to Netmarketshare .com), Google dominates the global search market. In a post to Google's official blog, Urs Hölzle (2009) proposed a figure of 0.0003 kWh of energy per search, equivalent to about 0.2 grams of CO_2 (the post was a response to a London *Sunday Times* story of the same date suggesting a larger figure; Leake and Woods 2009). Multiplied by the billions of search queries entered daily, that is already a vast amount of power. But Google's activities extend far beyond search: AdSense, AdWords, and DoubleClick advertising services, Google Maps and Google Earth, Gmail, Blogger, YouTube, Google Books, Android, Chrome, and Google Docs. These services all devolve on the index Google maintains of the trillion-plus pages of the Internet, an index by their estimate of over 100 million gigabytes (Google 2015). Google has become the world's largest manufacturer of computers, albeit exclusively for use in the server farms needed to keep this empire alive.

Typically, 1,160 servers will fit into a shipping container, complete with batteries, power, cabling, water cooling, and fans. Each container draws as much as 250 kilowatts of power. The containers themselves, in one facility dating back to 2005, are stacked and networked in buildings holding forty-five containers, each drawing down 10 megawatts apiece (including additional cooling and water pumps), which now has three such buildings. The design was the subject of a patent applied for early in 2008. Since then, Google has been building server farms across the United States and globally, but does not publish the number or their locations to minimize vandalism. Each data center draws power either from the grid or from specially constructed power plants, backed up by generators and lead-acid batteries to ensure there are no interruptions to service or loss of stored data. There is also massive redundancy. The Internet root server authority ICANN (*Internet Corporation for Assigned Names and Numbers*) admits that its servers duplicate one another, all of them copying the basic logical structure of a mere thirteen servers. Other major server users like Amazon and Facebook are less forthcoming, although both Facebook and eBay have released figures on their energy efficiency, and Facebook has launched a project with industry-wide ambitions (Open Compute Project, opencompute.org), open-sourcing its designs in an effort to share best practice and crowdsource new efficiency ideas, to which it hopes to attract the industry's main body, the Open Data Center Alliance, which specializes in security and interoperability, rather than sustainability.

On the positive side, Google has invested heavily in the design of power linkages, and tends to site facilities close to energy sources like hydroelectric dams and more recently wind farms, while Apple has resorted to building biomass generating plants at the sites of their new centers. The common measure of energy use is the power usage effectiveness index established by Green Grid, a membership organization for the server industry, but the measurements used have proved controversial, partly because they measure only infrastructure, not the efficiency of the IT devices used. However, even when stressing the importance of IT efficiency, consultants tend not to mention the massive redundancy of network storage, although they do advocate that "new data centres should locate in areas with ample free cooling and/or low-carbon electricity grids" (Masanet, Shehabi, and Koomey 2013, 630). Cheap energy has been part of the history of cloud computing. In 2008, Google registered patents for floating wave-powered server farms (the floating part is significant because of the quantities of water required to cool the servers down). This may well be a better solution than, for example, building a farm in Lithuania, 98 percent of whose power is nuclear, according to a brief but damning report in *Harper's* (Strand 2008). It has, however, garnered some political opposition from BRIC countries (Brazil, Russia, India and China), especially China, who note that where several Asian nations in prime server territory—notably Singapore—have only two-mile territorial waters, such farms may well fall outside national jurisdictions, and therefore outside the ambit of the International Telecommunications Union (ITU), China's preferred agency for future Internet governance. Other companies have initiated strategies that may also be more economically sustainable, such as Microsoft, which announced plans in 2008 to build a farm in Siberia to solve the cooling problem, said to absorb at least 20 percent of the energy used by server farms. Energy costs, however, seem to be the main driver in these pursuits, rather than sustainability in its own right (Carr 2009, 132). Warming snow in Siberia is still warmth in the global heat budget.

Large outfits with reasons for discretion like the U.S. military run their own server farms of unknown size, although the scale of National Security Administration (NSA) monitoring must require immense resources (estimates vary from 12 exabytes upward; Hill 2013), representing only a part of the cyberwarfare capacity of the nation. Popular services like Dropbox, Facebook, Twitter, Amazon's S3, EMC's Mozy, and Apple's iCloud are creating new business models not only from storage and transfer but from monitoring and marketing knowledge of user behaviours in an industry set for major expansion with the entry of telcos into provision of on-demand online utilities for business and domestic users. As industry insider Joe Weinman (2009) blogs, clouds may be "reducing total resource requirements through statistical multiplexing. Fewer resources imply less manufacturing, and less electricity consumption for power and cooling." But this requires a parallel reduction in in-house computing resources, for which there is precious little evidence. Much use of the cloud is for backup of locally produced and maintained files, implying an increase rather than a decrease in the quantity of storage and therefore the amounts of energy required both to store and to transport files. A major investigation by the *New York Times* suggested that in 2012 there were 30 million server farms connecting millions more laptops, desktops, tablets, mobiles, smart TVs, and game consoles, with only a brief blip in growth occasioned by the global financial crisis, growth that requires increasing amounts of electricity, in turn dependent on fossil fuels, hydropower, and nuclear power.

Perhaps the most intriguing, even ominous, aspect of near-future scenarios is ubiquitous computing, combining the Internet of things with the increasing integration of mobile wireless and Internet media. Biochips (Thacker 2004), RFID tags (Hayles 2009), and a variety of wireless devices can be installed in anything from fridges to mousetraps, pets to monitoring devices for health, immigration, and prisoners, creating a vast demand for new storage and communication services. The arrival of portable formats for books, games, music, and feature films, the inclusion of increasingly sophisticated cameras and recording technologies in handhelds, and the arrival of mass-market wearable devices will increase both the quantity of and the traffic in data over the foreseeable future. That increase has been measured in a number of ways (see, for example, Lyman and Varian 2003). One remarkable finding is that "the amount of information created, captured, or replicated exceeded available storage for the first time in 2007. Not all information created and transmitted gets stored, but by 2011, almost half of the digital universe will not have a permanent home" (Gantz 2008). Estimating the current size of the digital universe at close to 300 billion gigabytes, Gantz's team at consultants IDC do not make extravagant claims for growth. But as television, for example, moves toward both high definition and on-demand network delivery, the quality as well as quantity of media involved in net traffic is likely to expand with no clear end in sight. The question is whether this is a sustainable future.

THE ECOLOGY OF STANDARDIZATION AND INTELLECTUAL PROPERTY

Any answer will have to address the ecological impact of the general economy, embracing not only information and communication technology but the rest of our uses of power and resources (Koomey 2007). Autodesk's Stewart and Kennedy (2009) argue in the pages of *Environmental Leader* that "if designers, architects, engineers, general contractors, energy auditors, land use planners and policy makers are able to access services that use vast sets of dynamic, complex and otherwise un-integrated data on the cloud for pennies a minute, think of the massive impact this could have on buildings, infrastructure, land use and urban design and policy-making." This avenue for savings in the physical economy through advances in IT rests on the premise that informatic infrastructure will be less costly than the building works it replaces. In the 1980s, it was widely held (for example, during discussions of the Cable and Broadcasting Bill in the UK) that telecommuting would be the wave of the future. Though at that stage rather dimly imagined, many believed computer networks would remove the need for massive city-center headquarter blocks and the obligation to commute into them. The arrival of the Internet as a popular medium in the wake of the introduction of the Mosaic browser in 1993 has not had this effect. On the contrary, coworkers now communicate by e-mail even when they are on the same corridor. There has been no reduction in commuting or in the importance of corporate headquarters in the ensuing years. Likewise, the promised efficiencies of the paperless office have yet to be realized, and substantial data pointing toward decreasing efficiency in networked offices dates back to at least the early 1990s (Sproull and Kiesler 1991). The argument that increased efficiency in the general economy as a result of network computing will balance the books involves a second premise: that the data required will be accessible and ready to be integrated into disparate, evolving local systems, and will not simply duplicate them.

One challenge is that "software is reduced too often into being simply a tool for the achievement of pre-existing neutrally-formulated tasks" (Fuller 2001). The notion of task-oriented engineering is based on a problem-solving conception of design, where problems are likely to be established through profitability measures, rarely judgments of social or environmental good. Packages like Microsoft Office offer a host of functions, large numbers of which rest unused. The phenomenon of software bloat leads to ever fatter, slower, more energy- and memory-hungry applications, in turn leading consumers to trade in their old machines for new ones capable of dealing with the new demands of new software generations. Despite this redundant functionality, proprietary software standardizes the experience of working, and in almost all cases forbids modification of the software. Standardization is equally central to cloud computing, where remote software is even less open to tinkering and modification than is the case with software installed on local hard drives. The engineering perspective is that common standards make data interoperable: If we all use the same software, the data we store will be available in principle to anyone using the same software. If, however, it is the case that spreadsheet, presentation, and word processing software constrain and guide the kinds of work users do, and therefore the kinds of data they store, predictability begins to slip from a useful tool for sharing knowledge toward the homogeneity created when data itself becomes predictable. Information is by definition something new and to a degree unexpected. Common software, as a shared system for handling data, tends toward repetition, even where incoming data are new and significant: This is the upshot of Tufte's (2006) critique of PowerPoint. Software solutions to this problem largely devolve toward different ways of presenting the data, described by one industry observer's blog as "a fresh array of flashy visual effects that encouraged us to hide our data behind a thick layer of cheap makeup" (Flew 2009). Standardization of cloud software thus may encourage communication while at the same time reducing the quality and quantity of information communicated.

Adding to the increasing energy demands of cloud computing is the extension of intellectual property regimes, led by the United States, unsurprisingly given that its major exports are now entertainment, software, pharmaceuticals, and military technology. Without a test for originality (as required if not actually enforced in patent law), copyright is wielded as a critical legal provision for monetizing Internet communications. Cloud computing has developed in the commercial, military, and government sectors under regimes of strict confidentiality, using firewalls, encryption, passwords, and subscriptions as means of keeping data from unlicensed users. Users themselves demand security and privacy for their materials. While scientists and academics struggle for open-access publishing, corporations and government agencies often see such publications as intellectual property that should be commercialized in the interests of profit or, in the public sector, to be secreted away from prying eyes and restricted to expert functionaries.

The redundancies of grid, local, and battery power at data center sites is mirrored by redundant storage of multiple copies on multiple local and remote hard drives. The burden of multiple copy storage is only increased by the extension of copyright to longer and longer periods and the use of licenses rather than outright sale that began with software (where licenses restricted access to source code) and now embrace games and audiovisual content. Sharing is at best borderline legal. Therefore each consumer ends up either storing one or several copies of the same Kanye West album, or accessing it through streaming services from cloud servers. It has been clear to archivists for several decades that complete and permanent recording is an idle dream. Choices must be made as to what is saved and what is not. That problem now spills out of libraries and media archives into public space. Information is not free but pay per use, often kept by statute (and in such vast quantities only other programs can mine it), and immensely energy expensive to preserve. The laws of physics make an equation between energy, time, and information: Information, like order, can only be maintained by expending energy. We now face an interesting challenge: to decide what we leave to the "gnawing criticism of the mice" and what we deem worthy of maintaining. This strategy will, however, work only if we can find a way to leave behind our proprietorial leanings where information is concerned.

Cloud computing has tended to serve monopolization, specifically through patent and copyright, and to produce information silos and their associated carbon emissions. The case has often been made that cloud computing reduces the energy signature of local computers. This ignores both the use of the cloud for backup copies rather than unique instances, and a business model that relies on connection to millions of personal devices including mp3 players, cameras, consoles, GPS devices, and the Internet of things as well as varieties of desktop and mobile computers. Due credit should go to initiatives oriented toward reducing carbon emissions in the cloud industry, but as we will see in later chapters the materials used to power and serve the cloud also require huge amounts of energy to extract and manufacture, while the efficiency gains in IT envisaged by the Open Compute Project are measured as much by profitability as by environmental metrics, and to that extent may slow but do not halt or reverse the inexorable growth of server energy use. Excess storage, redundant systems, overrobust power supplies, overproduction of information, obsessive duplication, and the inherent obsolescence of electronic media all entail increasing energy usage as the irreconcilable by-product of unregulated competition, as well as of the consequent unregulated monopolization.

Some movements at the consumer end have already made a difference: Weber, Koomey, and Matthews (2009, i) argue that "purchasing music digitally reduces the energy and carbon dioxide (CO_2) emissions associated with delivering music to customers by between 40 and 80% from the best-case physical CD delivery, depending on whether a customer then burns the files to CD or not." One way of furthering such developments might be to develop file-sharing technologies, in which individual computers allocate parts of their cycle to processing messages passing between other computers, routing around the large centralized server farms on which cloud computing is premised. But the successful prosecution of Napster in 2001 by the Recording Industry Association of America for copyright infringement demonstrates how Napster's centerless sharing, a user-driven, grassroots solution, was closed down in the interests of intellectual property rights and corporate profit. Solutions are not in the interests of industry, as the story of the Phoebus cartel, immortalized in Thomas Pynchon's *Gravity's Rainbow*, makes clear. In 1924, a group of electric lightbulb manufacturers, including GE, Philips, and Osram, established an international agreement that shortened the life span of lightbulbs by up to half, a move that invented planned obsolescence, and against which consumers were powerless (Krajewski 2014). Consumers may be persuaded to ease their use of media-rich files, or to amend their habits in terms of power usage, but this individualist approach shifts the burden of toxicity away from industry toward consumers, in a move that parallels the shifting of debt and austerity from failing economic and political elites to the already overburdened poor.

Some initiatives already point in related directions, such as The Green Grid initiative (http://www.thegreengrid.org/) campaign, which recommends simple consumer steps such as power management and unplugging devices when not in use. But such consumer-led actions, while laudable, do not provide the large-scale savings required when confronting not only the current scale but likely future expansion of power usage in ever-larger server farms. Electorates are notoriously ready to push environmental issues down the list of priorities when elections loom, so that national initiatives are likewise constrained in their attempts to ameliorate the problem. Problems of this scale require not one but many tools for their resolution. Consumers may be persuaded to ease their use of media-rich files, or to switch off devices in default stand-by mode, just as many have learned to use ad blockers and antiviral software on a regular basis. Governments may take the message of Kyoto and apply it to their information and communications infrastructures. Civil society bodies may be able to persuade manufacturers, service providers, and governments to synchronize their activities on this front. But it is clear that the solutions are not exclusively about these familiar sectors of the political economy. What digital media have demonstrated is that a different type of economy is possible (Mason 2015), one grounded in collaboration (Scholz 2008) and peer-to-peer systems (Bauwens 2005), most familiar in the examples of the Linux software environment and Wikipedia. Equally, it is clear that proprietary solutions will benefit only sectors of a global network, not the whole system. For that, we require social as well as economic reactions to the emerging energy crisis of information.

Supranational initiatives are therefore bound to be a major part of the solution for these problems. The failure of the UN's COP15 climate change summit in Copenhagen in 2009 and COP18 in Doha in 2012, alongside the much trumpeted but non-binding and unenforced results of COP21 in Paris in 2015, suggests, however, a deep lack of political will or economic commitment to change. China and its BRIC allies have been arguing since the UN's World Summit on the Information Society (WSIS) in Tunis in 2005 that current nongovernmental governance of the Internet should be replaced with a more nationally oriented body such as the ITU. At such junctures, movements to curtail emissions run up against the clash between the civil society institutions that have traditionally managed the technical infrastructures of the Internet, the commercial interests who have increasingly entered into governance bodies since WSIS, and the rising geopolitical power of rapidly developing economies whose "growth at all costs" strategies often include weak environmental regulation and enforcement.

The proliferation of new consumer technologies is integral to maintaining growth, the sine qua non of capital. It seems therefore important to ask whether the cloud-based Internet is less or more damaging to the environment than the alternatives. Film requires oil for plastics and minerals for chemical processing and printing, while print production depends on both timber (and the loss of natural forests and their dependent species) and paper milling with its notorious history of pollution. Professional equipment like typewriters, filing cabinets, and movie cameras have, however, product life cycles far longer than equivalent electronic kit, and use significantly less power. Unfortunately, the comparison is not usefully measurable. The reason is not simply that the comparisons are between unlike systems (an analog-based media industry in the twenty-first century would be just as prone to environmental catastrophe). It is also undecidable because we can no longer return to the era before easily accessed information. In 2013, Google senior vice president Urs Hölzle observed during a discussion of the booming demand for data storage and delivery services that "five years ago, you basically didn't have an iPhone, you didn't have app markets. YouTube was much smaller. Facebook basically didn't exist. . . . It was just a radically different world. So who am I to say that I can know how the world five years from now is going to be radically different?" (McMillan 2013).

It seems that the one thing that can be assured after WSIS and the Paris summit is that there will be no binding international, intergovernmental resolution; and that the pursuit of profit will continue even in the face of catastrophic consequences. A central reason why this is so lies in the dependence of digital media on the energy market.

FORMATION OF THE ELECTRIC ENERGY MARKET

Introducing his history of electrification in the United States, David E. Nye argues that "it is . . . fundamentally mistaken to think of 'the home' or 'the factory' or 'the city' as passive, solid objects that undergo an abstract transformation called 'electrification.' Rather every institution is a terrain, a social space that incorporates electricity as part of its ongoing development" (1990, x). The linear vision of senders, channels, and receivers of communications media is a cultural proposition premised on the distinction between producers, transmitters, and users of electrical energy. As the electricity market has evolved, consumers now buy from retailers, while generation and transport disappear into vague background. The sociality of electrical power is thus reconstituted in a three-way interaction between sellers, users, and the technology itself. It is this technology that now appears to us, much as factories did to our forebears, as massive agencies whose logic exceeds human scale, understanding, or control.

The lightbulb did not make Edison's fortune: Providing an electric network to power it did. In New York, Edison's capitalization of the electrical supply was soon so large as to constitute a major barrier to entry for any potential competitor. Such natural monopolies, common in utility markets, also help sustain colonial legacies. In the introduction of electric supply to

Madras prior to 1947, "apart from the introduction of technological artifacts, the colonial power often introduced certain new organizational methods, institutions and trajectories which are as lasting in the colony as the technology itself" (Rao and Lourdusamy 2010, 51). Such organizational legacies, not exclusively in Madras, include dependence on imported equipment rather than self-sustaining networks, and an absence of R&D in the colonized territory, techniques that keep the regional power companies in thrall to larger global corporate networks of goods and services. While these transnational networks are more competitive, the imbalance of competition between municipal providers in poor megacities like Manila or Dakar, and corporations of the size of Siemens and GE, is considerable and constraining.

During the 1970s and with increasing virulence in the 1980s, the natural monopolies, especially those integrating generation, transmission, and supply aspects of the electricity industry, were the targets of pro-competition regulation. Publicly owned services were increasingly supplanted by investor-owned corporations. Two facets of this separation are important to the present context: the introduction of markets for power in the megacities, and the cultural differences that emerge from the separation of the dirty business of generation from the clean image of energy consumption.

Consistently advertised as hygienic, toxin-free, and clean since its initial competition with sooty and humid coal gas, contemporary electric power in the developed world separates use from production. This is in part an industrial strategy, designed to centralize generation, which encouraged the initial monopolies and the new speculative markets. Typical white goods hide as much as possible of their operations from users, while generators are either geographically remote or, during the early decades of the last century when losses of power per mile of transmission were greater than today, built as spectacular cathedrals of modernity like London's Battersea Power Station. Dependent on extraction and transport of fuels, however, urban generator plants were always vulnerable to strikes, a threat that ultimately sealed the fate of Battersea under the Thatcher government. Remote plants can be hidden unless, as in the case of Three Mile Island or the Three Gorges hydroelectric scheme, they turn critical or become otherwise controversial. The cabling and pylons required to deliver power over great distances are by now so familiar as to have disappeared into the background of perception, especially when contrasted with the resistance to wind farms, solar farms, and tidal barrages. The enormously high voltages required to reduce current (and therefore loss of energy to conducting materials) make overhead bulk power transmission a far more attractive option, at an estimated $10 per foot, than underground cabling, which requires insulation as well as installation costs, at between $20 and $40 per foot at 2010 prices. Even so, the U.S. electricity supply industry loses 7 percent of generated power in transmission (EIA 2012), discharged as heat, hum, and radiation. The environmental costs of this are as much geopolitical as they are aesthetic: Much of central and eastern Europe acquires its electricity from Russia, which uses its position to secure political advantage. Meanwhile, the low energy and economic cost of overhead transmission makes the Boston–New York–Washington megacity an electrical province of Canada. Both scenarios have had unfortunate results in recent years.

In Latour's (2005) actor-network theory perspective adopted and updated by Jane Bennett (2010), electricity grid failures in megacities—she discusses the northeastern blackout affecting the Boston–New York and Great Lakes conurbations in August 2003—can be traced to the chaotic behavior of electrical flows in complex grids. Like Virilio (2007), she sees the very existence of the power grid as an intimation of its collapse (Bennett 2010, 27), and argues that the energy trading corporation on whose lines the disaster began, FirstEnergy, was not responsible for what happened, suggesting that humans should not be regarded as privileged by their capacity for action apart from "the order of material nature." Instead, Bennett argues, "Autonomy and strong responsibility seem to me to be empirically false, and thus their invocation seems tinged with injustice. . . . Individuals [are] simply incapable of bearing *full* responsibility for their effects." Bennett's critique of naively personalized claims of causality is powerfully argued, even while she acknowledges the proximity of her argument to the defensive position of FirstEnergy, avowing that, despite the temptation, she finds it "hard to assign the strongest or most punitive version of moral responsibility" to energy traders. Nonetheless, it is important to emphasize in analysis the interconnection of this chaotic network with the chaotically deregulated energy market of the United States in the 2000s.

It is illuminating to compare the 2003 blackout with another case of megacity outage in the United States. The now-shamed Enron Corporation had used campaign funds to pressure California legislators to deregulate the state's energy market. Before deregulation, there had been only one serious rolling blackout: from the deregulation of December 2000 to its reregulation in June 2001, there were thirty-eight (Public Citizen 2001). In August that year, Enron's share price began to tumble, resulting in its filing for bankruptcy in November. There is no clear connection between the collapse of California's energy market and that of Enron. It is true, however, that ascribing the collapse of both to human greed is inadequate. Equally, Bennett is correct in saying that the electrical network, the medium through which these crises occurred, provided the affordances necessary to drive them into collapse. The collapse, however, was exacerbated by changes in network goals. As David Nye writes in his history of U.S. blackouts, the 2003 event "was what one could expect from an under-regulated utility system, relying on outmoded monitoring equipment and inadequate transmission lines to meet rising demand" (2010, 161), conditions clearly encouraged by prioritizing shareholders over customers. Missing in Bennett's analysis is the interaction between two systems, the public utility and the market. It was this interaction that created the new network behaviors which provided the necessary if not the final causes of the crises (Healy and Palepu 2003; see also Eichenwald 2005; Fox 2003). The third system involved is real-time automated trading in electricity spot markets, reliant on computers, which themselves not only depend on an electricity supply but have been core to the steadily rising demand for power in the years leading up to 2003, when at least 13 percent of the total power generated in the United States was used to run the Internet and computers (Nye 2010, 186).

FirstEnergy, like Enron close to the Bush administration (chief executive H. Peter Burg had a seat on Bush's energy transition team), had quite a record. It owned GPU, the New Jersey generating company that ran Three Mile Island, and in February 2002 had its own Davis-Besse reactor in Ohio shut down at the brink of another nuclear disaster. The investigation into the blackout found FirstEnergy at the heart of the four causes (a term they found suitably problematic) of the disaster: FirstEnergy's systemic failure to address problems in its network, specifically of voltage levels; its inadequate situational awareness; its failure to manage trees under its power lines; and persuading its public oversight body not to inspect its systems and practices. While it is difficult to demonstrate that FirstEnergy was shifting power in and out of the region affected by the blackout, as Enron had done in California, the combination of software bugs and a flashover caused by overheating power lines sparking against untrimmed trees do demonstrate the argument that when share price is the only value, energy companies abandon safe, clean, and reliable supply (Bratton 2002).

This is not an example of emergent properties in a chaotic network: It clearly arises when one value (the provision of energy) conflicts with another (the extraction of profit), in the California instance not from retail sale but from speculative trading in real-time energy futures, and in the northeastern from taking immediate profit at the expense of the long-term profitability or even feasibility of the operation. These outcomes of clashes between service and profit are even more visible in the developing world. Thus in Lagos, Nigeria, under the auspices of the World Bank and IMF during the Babangida regime in the 1980s, the national electricity provider was privatized at knockdown prices, enriching the elite while discouraging investment in the service. The absence of public utilities led to widespread tapping into privatized electrical lines, resulting in frequent blackouts and electrical fires (Packer 2006, 6–7). According to Francisco Bolaji Abosede, Lagos Commissioner for Town Planning and Urbanisation, "By 2015 Lagos will be the third largest city in the world but it has less infrastructure than any of the world's other largest cities" (IRIN 2006). The National Electric Power Authority (NEPA), now renamed the Power Holding Company of Nigeria (PHCN), is accused of long-standing corruption. The World Bank has, however, provided $100 million to aid in its privatization, despite vigorous opposition from power unions and others. Also, NEPA was signatory to a contract with Enron that locked it into a guaranteed purchasing agreement that had become unsustainable by 2005. Unions implied that Enron's successor, AES, was not supplying the agreed amounts of power, and the whole contract was embroiled in a legal battle alongside the political battle over splitting NEPA into eleven smaller companies prior to privatization and deregulation (Hall 2006, 12). As Bennett suggests, such intricate networks are subject to chaotic storms and sudden, violent collapse; but such emergent behaviors cannot be understood apart from the political economy of capital and the specific ideologies of neoliberalism that power them.

ENERGY ECONOMIES AND COUNTERECONOMIES

A different issue with similar causes afflicts Mumbai, where "every slum I see in Jogeshwari has a television" (Mehta 2004, 125), even though the power is likely again to be stolen, in this case from overhead cables. The utility company serving the area, Reliance, is in partnership with USAID to provide up to 6 million slum dwellers with legal electricity; given that what they have is illegal, unpaid, and dangerous. Leaving aside whether it is necessary to make the supply legal, the problem lies in the marketization of energy. Reliance supplies areas of the city not served by the municipal authority Brihanmumbai Electric Supply and Transport Undertaking, and both buy their power from Tata. But Tata has its own distribution company, one that has been growing swiftly, and as a result the generation arm is no longer prepared to sell electricity at below-market rates to Reliance, which it now sees as a competitor. The regulatory body for the state of Maharashtra had to intervene to persuade Tata not to cut supplies while legal processes went on (Rebello 2010), demonstrating the vulnerability of the system to profiteering.

The application of neoliberal structural adjustment in developing nations dates back to the privatization of the Chilean electricity industry in the 1980s. Surveying five years of data on attitudes to utility deregulation in Latin America, Checchi, Florio, and Carrera discuss what they refer to as "the regressive welfare impact of reform through price changes" (2007, 347). It is not only the poor in Latin America who feel cheated by the Washington Consensus: "Less developed domestic financial markets and inadequate human capital imply that quick divestiture of utilities need foreign capital and management, so that denationalisation was often coincidental with the transfer of assets to foreign ownership. This rules out or decreases the possibility of sharing with part of the middle classes the quasi-rents of divested utilities" (Checchi, Florio, and Carrera 2007, 347).

Even where problems seem least, there are always reasons to be cautious. In La Paz, 60 percent of electricity comes from geothermal energy and 40 percent from hydroelectric. The right-wing Baker Institute, however, decries Bolivia's failure to drill new oil wells since the Morales government came to power on a wave of protests against the extraction and export of natural resources, especially natural gas (Baker Institute 2008, 2). The neoliberal crushing of an older development paradigm based on import substitution, state enterprise, and control over trade and capital flows clearly is not enough for some factions in Washington: States should also cede control over exploitation of their resources to market forces and extraterritorial expropriation.

In this light, it is especially distressing to see Bennett cite approvingly Garrett Hardin's (1968) "Tragedy of the Commons," an essay that argues for the marketization of the environment on the grounds that "freedom in a commons brings ruin to all." Hardin argues that naturally occurring competition between humans will always exhaust any resource held in common. His liberal apologia ignores the historical reality: Common land was for centuries, in some regions millennia, sustained and nurtured. It was only after enclosure that monopoly owners began to clear forests and to make sustainable livelihoods gleaned from coppicing, hunting, or gathering illegal. Enclosure was also responsible for the divorce of energy production from consumption: Forbidden to gather fuel in once-common woodland, the peasants were forced to buy it from specialized producers of timber and later coal, gas, and electricity. As we can understand from this genealogy, as utility, energy is a use value, like common land. It is only when marketized that the classic free-rider problem emerges: If I cannot be excluded, I have no reason to pay, and therefore a private market has no motivation to provide the public good (Dahl 2004, 4). As is the case with the effective (albeit illegal) expropriation of public land for construction by slum landlords, a common good becomes subject to rent. Such rents, regarded in neo-Ricardian economics as "a pre-capitalist legacy and an obstacle to the progressive movement of capital's accumulation" (Vercellone 2008), are now being read increasingly as the very basis of capital. The expropriation of the commons, whether environmental or intellectual, and the rents charged on the privatized results are the recourse to which capital increasingly turns when faced with the collapse of labor value in the declining manufacturing sector (Marazzi 2011). Rather than celebrate the electricity network's capacity for chaos, it makes far more sense to imagine a revivification of the ancient commons, in the sense at least of challenging rentier capitalism by increasing the number of agents capable of acting within the network. This indeed is the activity of the gray energy economy in megacity slums (see Graham and Marvin 2001).

Stealing power from the grid is a way of exacting justice, whether among squatters or in defiance of privatization: an act of network justice in the era of global conglomerate control over amenities. Yet it is also the case that stealing power—and some forms of local production of power including small oil-powered generators—is dirty, dangerous, dishonest, for what that is worth, and dependent. Theft requires the conglomerate production of grid electricity and fails to challenge it, merely taxing it for traversing popular space. Burning fossil fuels to provide light is a better use than setting them alight to drive cars, but is typically polluting, smelly, and noisy. These are survival mechanisms, but like the circulation of stolen water through shantytowns, risky to life and to homes: Live electricity channeled through handmade switches and ring mains with little or no insulation or protection from the weather is a constant danger to its users. In many respects, these relations of antagonistic dependence are the result of the colonial legacy of power supply in megacities (Rao and Lourdusamy 2010).

Being without electrical power, being condemned to darkness after nightfall, is a great deal worse than having dodgy supplies. In 2010, the UN Human Development Program adopted for the first time a set of measures, the Multidimensional Poverty Index, that, in addition to economic poverty, measures indicators including access to electricity. Countries with the lowest access to electricity are for the most part rural, like Burkina Faso; but a striking 53 percent of Nigeria's population lives without access to electrical supply, and other states with megacities like Bangladesh (59.3 percent) have similar statistics (UNDP 2010, 218). In rural areas, there is no electric power to steal. In the megacities, theft is a response to centralized and marketized supply. The real alternative is local production of power. Distributed electricity generation is a potent symbol for the exit from capital. Wind and sun are ubiquitous, rivers and streams common: Small-scale turbines and photovoltaics are increasingly cheap to produce and easy to maintain. They secure independence from corporate capital and municipal corruption alike; and in many respects the distributed model already holds in slums far more than in wealthy districts where mains power is more likely to be installed, if not reliably, and where politics concerns itself with securing privileged access to centrally owned or operated networks. But it is precisely this struggle for control of the center that hampers the development of a distributed commons of electricity generation.

The inventiveness of slum dwellers makes local energy production a critical support industry for the local economy and culture. *New Scientist* reported that diesel generators and solar panels, a response to unreliable grid electrical supply, were in widespread use across northern India during the blackout of July 2012 (Hodson 2012), which affected at least 600 million people, several times more than the previous worst in Indonesia in 2005. Here the poor are ahead of the rich in developing distributed generation in microgrids, especially illegal ones, or grids run on cheap or stolen fossil fuels (Indian government subsidies for diesel for farmers are often seen as contributing to the failure to invest in power infrastructure). The poor cannot sacrifice the power to act. They use electricity to extend their productive days and increase conviviality. Unlike the monopoly generation and distribution corporations (Hausman Hertner, and Wilkins 2008; Hughes 1983; Lagendijk 2008), the poor live amid the consequences of their stolen or locally generated light: the fumes and roar of diesel generators, burns and shocks from jury-rigged connections. When McLuhan described electric light as a medium without a message, he was right phenomenologically but wrong historically. He wrote at a time when disguising appliances and hiding wiring became design fetishes, and when light was severed from the vast hydropower schemes that were transforming the Canadian hinterland. Such dematerialization does not hold today in the slums where light is fought for, at the scale of the local reseller of stolen power or of the East Fourteenth Street Con Edison power station in Lower Manhattan exploding into flame at the height of Hurricane Sandy in October 2012. The chaotic system of deregulated electricity markets separates generation, distribution, and bulk and retail sales into discrete enterprises competing to extract profit, not to provide a public good.

In one sense at least, Bennett is right to underscore the inhuman principles at work in electricity networks. Fantasy cyborgs look like human beings with technological implants. Actually existing cyborgs are huge agglomerations of technologies with human implants. Corporations like Enron and FirstEnergy are such cyborgs, composed of nonhuman actors with human biochips embedded to carry out specialist tasks like those involving human resource management and public relations. Corporate cyborg agency is distributed but not communal, not least in electrical grids connecting aggressively active users (who can scarcely be caught in the term *consumers*), the unmanaged turbulence of deregulated and automated markets, and the inhuman drive for corporate profit. Such actor networks are realized sociopolitical agencies whose other-than-human standing is confirmed by their lack of shame. Frankenstein monsters created out of the logic of advanced capital, their sole motive is profit, regardless of all other consequences. Their environment is not the physical world but the financial, a world where human affairs appear only as inputs and price fluctuations. As we will see in greater detail in chapter 2, the corporate cyborg not only risks the future of humanity and its environment but its own future in actions which, in a human being, would be deemed suicidal. For example, both fuel and asphalt prices spiked in April 2012, the period of the greatest intensity in the uprisings in Syria, Bahrain, Tunisia, and Egypt. The two prices are locked because once oil reaches a certain price, it becomes economically feasible to mine the Athabasca tar sands and other sources of low-grade shale oil, otherwise usually used as bitumen for road building, for fuel. The fact that cars without roads are useless does not compute in the profit-driven model of the cyborg corporation, any more than the degradation of the environment, air pollution, black carbon particles, or any other nonfiscal feature up to and including rendering their own life cycle as profitable enterprises impossible. Yet despite their manifest irrationality, these corporations rule. The Fortune Global 500 top ten companies listing for 2015 includes six petroleum, two automobile, and one energy company, plus Walmart. This fact alone might explain why, in a polity obsessed with GDP as the sole measure of success, no political player is willing to speak up for environmental regime change.

Energy Sources

Electricity is perhaps even more central to contemporary societies than fossil fuels, a significant proportion of which are used for electrical power (50 percent of EU and about 67 percent of U.S. electricity generation; EIA 2016; Eurostat 2015). The marketization of electrical power involves highly centralized generation and supply models built on globalization, actively opposing alternatives using locally generated power, especially those based on communal principles. Centralization leads to geographical separation between energy sources and energy users. Fossil fuel extraction, refining, and use in generation typically occurs away from population centers, despite the waste of energy inevitable in its transmission. Hydroelectric schemes are rarely close to population centers, and all too often, as in the northern Quebec dams that provide most of the energy supply to the eastern seaboard of the United States, are built at the expense of indigenous populations already displaced from their homelands by colonial expansion in the eighteenth and nineteenth centuries. Equally, oil wells in traditionally nomadic desert areas or in the fishing grounds of traditional Arctic peoples show the link between electricity supplies and colonialism. When we add the energy required by server farms to the demands of domestic and office equipment usage, and to them the energy costs of extracting materials, manufacturing digital equipment, and recycling it, we begin to understand the scale of the environmental footprint proper to digital media. The electrical foundation of electronics anchors our uses of digital media in both global trade patterns and colonial relations to people, lands, and nonhuman agents. This chapter traces the energy challenge posed by digital consumerism, capital growth strategies, and energy security considerations, and their impacts on air and water pollution, destruction of human and animal habitat, and climate change.

OIL

Markets in electricity depend on fuels derived from an irreplaceable fossil heritage whose chemical potential is still not fully understood, on hydroelectricity from dammed rivers, and on uranium. The hunger for oil replaced that for coal, whose resources are far closer to the metropolitan centers of energy consumption, and which were variously exhausted or subject to organized labor that challenged the raw greed of the market. The search for a replacement expanded into territories formerly regarded as inhospitable. These include seabed exploration, but also wilderness areas—often the result of clearances that drove indigenous peoples out in favor of preserving some remnant of the aboriginal flora and fauna—and land deemed useless for farming, deployed in settler colonies like the United States and Australia as reservations for the displaced human remnants of wilderness clearances and the genocide of indigenous peoples.

The foreign policy of the European powers, and to an even greater extent the United States, has been driven by demand for combustible materials. In November 1910, locked out of the collieries by their owners, miners in the South Wales coalfield went on strike. The Home Office sent in police and later cavalry to break the strike, resulting in something on the order of five hundred injuries (Evans and Maddox 2010). Though his role is much debated, the home secretary at the time was Winston Churchill. In 1913, as first lord of the admiralty, Churchill led the conversion of the Royal Navy from coal to oil as its major energy source, a decision driven in large part by his experience of the power of miners and by the equal power of unionized coal heavers responsible for loading the fuel onto naval ships. This new dependence on oil in turn fired a series of diplomatic moves, culminating in the formation of the Anglo-Persian Oil Company in 1915, with a British government share of 51 percent argued for and won by Churchill. This company would in time become British Petroleum (BP; Ewalt 1981). The concentration of energy source, national security, and energetically geopolitical diplomacy is not only historical. The *Washington Post* nearly a hundred years later ran a story celebrating Estonia's determination to exploit its oil shale reserves as a move against energy dependence on Putin's Russia, with the opinion, "Thanks to the liberation of these Eastern European nations from Soviet dominance, they are beginning to develop economies based on economic freedom" (Tapscott 2014). As we shall see, oil shale is one of the dirtiest forms of hydrocarbon, a quality not mentioned by the *Post*.

If the twenty-first-century neoimperial foreign policy of the United States and its allies in the European Union is driven by oil, so too is resistance to it and the wars and corporate occupations that it has relied on to secure a stable energy supply for the maintenance of its economy and power. Even if it was in a sense halfhearted (Harman 2009, 273–74), nonetheless the invasion of Iraq, replacing a dictator originally put in place by the United States in the late 1960s with a weak puppet government, was an attempt to secure Middle Eastern oil supplies, fix oil prices apart from the operation of the OPEC cartel's more unfriendly members like Hugo Chavez, and reduce the competitive (and therefore political) power of Putin's Russian oil and gas fields. (That the invasion demanded immense state expenditure on military supplies and fuel, transferring more state assets to corporations and weakening the public sphere in favor of the corporate, was an additional driver.) In the 1950s, Shell geologist M. King Hubbert first proposed the thesis of peak oil, the idea that at some point in time, the rate of extraction of oil would surpass the amount of oil reserves left in the ground (Hubbert 1956; see also Campbell and Laherrère 1998). Drawing on Hubbert, Midnight Notes describe the fallout from this kind of global strategy on the ground: "In the

Niger Delta, . . . there is now an ongoing war of appropriation waged by groups like the Movement for the Emancipation of the Niger Delta (MEND); such groups are demanding that the people of the Delta be recognized as communal owners of the petroleum beneath their soil, against the Nigerian government and the major oil companies. Indeed, there is a political limit being reached in oil exploration and extraction that Steven Colatrella has aptly called a 'political Hubbert curve'" (2009, 7).

Much of the anger of the Arab Spring revolts of 2011 came from disgust at the handling of oil wealth in countries like Libya and Bahrain. The continuing civil war in Iraq can also be understood in part as triggered by the conduct of the oil trade under Saddam Hussein and subsequently. Maghrebi insurgents, allied with Islamic fundamentalism, who seize Western hostages at Algerian desert oil installations do not fit the western Left's model of freedom fighters, but the failure of the oil industry to provide for the physical and spiritual well-being of desert peoples is surely a direct cause of the violent insurrections in the Sahel and across Syria and Iraq.

Oil transportation is as militarized as the oil fields themselves. The Suez Crisis of 1956 that in many respects marked the end of British Empire concerned control over the key avenue for transporting Persian Gulf oil to the UK and Europe. More recently, much of the worsening relations between China and Japan, which many see as an early indicator of the rise of China as a global superpower, focus on the Taiwan Strait, the shipping channel through which 80 percent of import-dependent Japan's oil arrives. The ambitions of this book concern the environmental impacts of digital media, not geopolitics, but geopolitics will always haunt the exploitation of mineral resources in the age of globalization. Nor does it dwell on the financial arrangements that follow the oil industry. Yet it should not be forgotten that the new wealth flowing to OPEC countries after the quadrupling of oil prices in the early 1970s was largely banked in the United States, which loaned the money to developing economies like Brazil and Poland, investments that locked them into global oil consumption and then became crippling debts. Finally, the nationalized industries and the cartelization that characterize the oil business form an ongoing contradiction with the neoliberal dogma espoused by the Washington consensus and central to neoliberal economic globalization. Oil is the dominant commodity of the early twenty-first century, without which we could not have the existing information society, cognitive capital, or semiocapitalism ("a form of social production which is essentially focused on the production of signs. . . . I know that shoes and cars and houses are produced too. But everything is more and more translated into signs. Everything is more and more replaced, on the economic level, by a semiotic form of production" [Berardi 2012]). Its underpinning financial, manufacture, and transport networks would be unthinkable without oil. At the same time, the oil industry is the exception to every rule, and in times of crisis to every law. All too often, those who suffer most are the indigenous peoples whose courageous defense of land and culture so taunts the consensual silence over the energy and material infrastructure of contemporary media.

Wars are only the most publicized fatal feature of the fossil fuel industry. Road traffic causes 1.24 million deaths (and about twenty times as many injuries) each year, placing it in the top ten causes of death worldwide (WHO 2013). Even before air, water, soil, and noise pollution, we should also consider the deaths, injuries, and sickness, human and animal, associated with oil production and transport, and the losses suffered by those whose lands have been occupied by petroleum extraction. According to one tanker industry body, 5.7 million barrels of crude oil have been lost in maritime spillages since 1971 (ITOPF 2012). They note that the vast majority of spills are less than seven barrels, and that statistics on them are hard to come by and not included. If we add to these therefore almost certainly conservative figures spills from oil rigs like Deepwater Horizon, and land-based spills and leaks from pipelines, drilling rigs, refineries, and events like the Lac-Mégantic tanker train derailment of 2013, the losses are almost certainly at least triple. More energy is wasted flaring gas, without including the energy required both to drill and to clean up and store waste products: A NOAA survey for the World Bank estimates 150 to 170 billion cubic meters of flared gas a year, representing 27 percent of U.S. consumption or $40 billion, adding about 400 million tons of carbon dioxide to the atmosphere each year (World Bank 2007). The ordinary volatility of fossil fuels exposed to the air, transport costs and the drips, leaks, and accidents associated with them, and the endless small wastage from inefficient generators and end use in factories, public space, and homes continue the sorry tale. It includes the energy frittered away in lengthy transmission cables, and in the transport mechanisms used to carry the organized electricity of digital messages. The amount of light thrown uselessly upward by street lighting makes the night sky invisible; Pylons generate waste radiation, as do mobile phones and computers. The world's biggest and most strategic industry, intimately involved with water, agriculture, industry, finance, and creativity, is founded on throwing away vast quantities of energy. Every time matter or energy are moved or converted into different forms, the first law of thermodynamics tells us that no energy is lost, but the second tells us that it degenerates from energy that can do work into heat or noise, by which the industry understands energy too dispersed or at temperatures too low to be useful. The unwillingness to capture this low-level energy—for example, to use waste gas to power drilling operations, or to provide local energy needs—is typical of the profligacy integral to the energy cycle as it operates under capital. We ought to be, but are not, surprised that the same profligacy extends to the environments and people living closest to the major energy production sites and transportation routes.

Robert Vitalis's (2006) work on the impact of the oil business on what is now Saudi Arabia details the role of oil exploration and drilling in creating the authoritarian House of Saud: the elimination or bribery of local landowners and nomadic Bedouins, the racist segregation of local workers, the destruction of water tables, and the brutal suppression of strikes and claims for social justice. Central to Vitalis's account is the Arab American Oil Company, and his story, especially during the crucial 1940s and 1950s, parallels the emergence of the United States as player in the oil-rich Middle East, an engagement that has borne especially bitter fruit since the invasion of Iraq in 2003. The caricature of democracy that the United States has attempted to import or ascribe to national governments, themselves geographically defined by colonial-era decisions, derives, according to Timothy Mitchell, from overcoming the democratic gains made by workers in the era of coal. In the coal era, "the coordinated acts of interrupting, slowing down or diverting [coal's] movement created a decisive political machinery, a new form of collective capability built out of coalmines, railways, power stations and their operators," key sites and practices where workers could strike for wages and rights (Mitchell 2011, 27). Oil, a far more distributed and nonmetropolitan energy source, was never as vulnerable, and for Mitchell, "in fact, oil pipelines were invented as a means of reducing the ability of humans to interrupt the flow of energy" (2011, 36). Criticized for his overly determinist account and his elision of oil strikes that did indeed exploit vulnerabilities in the distribution of oil for democratic struggles (Labban 2013), Mitchell nonetheless demonstrates a key factor in the globalization of energy production (and the globalization made possible by energy flows): that democratic rights, already vulnerable in the increasingly corporatist state typical of the developed countries, have historically been entirely ignored or violently repressed in the kingdoms and dictatorships sponsored by the oil giants. A combination of factors including ethnic and religious factions, extensive corruption, easy supplies of migrant labor, and the close connection between oil and arms economies must be added to any detailed analysis of the oppression of indigenous Arabs, as for example in Beinart and Hughes's (2007, 251–68) account of the British involvement in the Kuwaiti oil industry. As Halliday (1974, 1997) maintained, oil was always at the heart of the region's polity and must take the lion's share of blame for foreign complicity if not for every passage in the tormented political history being lived through from Pakistan to the Mediterranean today.

After the eighty-seven-day spill from the Deepwater Horizon rig in the Gulf of Mexico that began on April 20, 2010, killing eleven people and damaging coasts from Louisiana to Texas, BP established a fund of $20 billion for individual claimants, was fined $4.5 billion, and paid for a $594 million early settlement fund, although total costs of the cleanup are obscure, and other parties to the spill have also contributed or been asked to contribute large amounts. By contrast, in a January 2013 ruling, a Dutch court found Shell not guilty of pollution in the Niger Delta, blaming saboteurs. Two years earlier, a UN report (UNEP 2011) found groundwater and air pollution (largely from flaring natural methane, which Shell prefers to burn and pay fines for than to clean for practical use) at exceptional levels in Ogoniland, an area where oil drilling ceased in the wake of the Ogoni Nine killings over a decade previously. According to the Centre for Constitutional Rights (2009), "an estimated 1.5 million tons of oil has spilled in the Niger Delta ecosystem over the past 50 years. This amount is equivalent to about one 'Exxon Valdez' spill in the Niger Delta each year." Royal Dutch Shell offered $15.5 million to the families of Ken Saro-Wiwa and the Ogoni Nine in a "humanitarian" gesture following the oil protesters' deaths in 1995. Shell, who admitted liability after the UNEP report in 2011, was still to begin paying four years later, citing ongoing poaching from their pipelines and corruption in government (Vidal 2015). No other major payments have been recorded, in part because Shell operates through a Nigerian subsidiary, but in great part because there is no political muscle, as there is in the continental United States, to demand payment. Most of all, it would appear that the value of lives, livelihoods, and environments in Rivers State are worth far less than those of U.S. citizens. Billions of dollars' worth of oil have been siphoned out of Nigeria since the 1950s, with little for Nigerians to show except a wealthy clique composed of members of the largest tribes and a well-equipped army largely devoted to guarding oil installations.

Ken Saro-Wiwa's (2005) own account of the campaign for indigenous rights and environmental justice and of his imprisonment in *A Month and a Day* gives voice to a people blighted by the hunger for clean electricity and the freedom of the car. In the twenty years since his death, however, the spree has continued there and elsewhere. The catalog is long and bitter, but does include some stories that bring at least a ray of hope. In June 2013, Petroecuador announced that a landslide had ruptured a pipeline, sending at least a million and a half liters of crude oil into the headwaters of the Coca River. A few days later, the slick had polluted drinking water in the city of Coca (population eighty thousand), and had flowed into other Amazon tributaries in Peru and Brazil. The problem is rather older, and more ingrained, in the Lago Agria oil field, which Petroecuador, the national oil company, took over from Texaco after the Frente de Defensa de la Amazonia (ChevronToxico, chevrontoxico.com), a coalition of indigenous Amazonians, took out a lawsuit against the American company in 1993. Nineteen years later, Ecuadorian courts awarded damages of $8 billion against Chevron, who had taken over Texaco. Chevron, however, declared that they were not liable, that Texaco had settled all cleanup costs to the satisfaction of a previous government, that Ecuador had no legal rights in the matter, and that since they had no assets in Ecuador, they were in a position to refuse to pay. Their lawyers immediately lodged an appeal in the United States, which succeeded in March 2014 after a trial that many commentators saw as seriously flawed and lacking jurisdiction to overthrow the Ecuadorian decision. Campaigns continue despite a substantial public relations war against the campaigners and their lawyers (Legal Team for the Ecuadorian Communities 2014).

Not only is legal delay a typical corporate strategy; even the attempt to place a cash value on environmental vandalism, the better to walk away from the consequences, is insulting. It places the environment of the Quichua, Cofán, Secoya, Shuar, Siona, and Huaorani indigenous peoples inside a regime of exchange values that is entirely incommensurate with their beliefs and values. Even were the cash forthcoming, and especially if the current socialist government were to be replaced by a more U.S.-friendly one, the money would by no means necessarily flow into the hands of those most affected, nor would it be able to replace the world destroyed by Texaco in its decades of malpractice. The pressures on developing nations to continue pumping oil, and to do so with the same level of carelessness as their colonial predecessors, are immense and continuing, as are the aftereffects of spills, leaching into soil and water decades after the first leakages: the characteristic heritage of the resource curse (Auty and Mikesell 1993).

The resource curse can also be traced in the increasingly desperate, even suicidal determination to continue extracting even the most dangerous of hydrocarbon geology. In the case of the Athabascan tar sands in Alberta, as in the Ecuadorian Amazon, indigenous peoples and their legal teams have laid claim to the principle enshrined in the UN Declaration on the Rights of Indigenous People, whose Article 29 states, "Indigenous peoples have the right to redress, by means that can include restitution or, when this is not possible, just, fair and equitable compensation, for the lands, territories and resources which they have traditionally owned or otherwise occupied or used, and which have been confiscated, taken, occupied, used or damaged without their free, prior and informed consent" (United Nations 2008).

The Canadian government is a signatory to the declaration, however with a proviso: that they did not accept the principle of free, prior, and informed consent (FPIC). On this basis, Canadian First Nations have no recourse, despite the damage done to them and their traditional lands, for the prior and nonconsensual extraction of oil shale from their land. Extracting usable fuel-grade oil from the bitumen sands in which they occur in Alberta requires melting them sufficiently to flow using heat generally supplied by steam. The water for the steam comes from the Athabasca River, and the contaminated water from the process, ostensibly held in waste lakes, is believed by local people to be returning to the water table, poisoning the fishing and hunting on which they depend, and resulting in cancer rates among local indigenous Canadians 30 percent higher than in the general population. Like oil shale, oil sands are very poor grade, and require far more energy to extract and refine than ordinary oil, which accounts for their greater expense and dependence on continuing high prices for oil. The by-products of refining include airborne nitrogen and sulfur oxides responsible for acid rain as well as particulate matter that has serious effects on animal and human respiration, while the clearance of boreal forest—the world's largest carbon sink—and ancient wetlands that will take hundreds if not thousands of years to recover forms a further reason to cease (Hrudey et al. 2010). Protest, however, was not welcomed by the Harper government in Ottawa: According to a report from the Aboriginal Peoples Television Network, a March 2011 strategy document obtained by Climate Action Network Canada under a freedom of information provision labeled First Nation leaders "adversaries" in a tally of stakeholders, allies, and opponents of the government's crash course in developing the bitumen industry (APTN National News 2012).

Albertan shale oil production, currently running at 1.6 million barrels a day (with provision to expand to as much as 9 million), needs an efficient transport system to reach its core markets (efficient in the sense of economically viable). The prime contender is the thousand-kilometer Enbridge Northern Gateway pipeline and tanker project, taking liquified bitumen from a base at Edmonton across the Rocky Mountains to the Pacific port of Kitimat, where up to two hundred tankers a year would carry the product south and east (CAN Canada 2012). The prime aim of the Northern Gateway is to access the Chinese market, although it is unclear whether this is merely a diplomatic gambit to pressure the United States into accepting the alternative route south toward Texas and the refineries serving the midwestern states, the immensely controversial Keystone. This alternate oil transport system takes dilute bitumen (DilBit) from northern Alberta, eastward across Saskatchewan and Manitoba before heading south to refineries in Nebraska, Illinois, and the Gulf Coast of Texas. Keystone XL is the fourth phase of the project, which takes a more direct route south to Nebraska. In 2012, President Obama refused to sign permissions allowing the new route to begin construction; in 2013, the governor of Nebraska signed an approval; at this writing, however, the route is still awaiting its first stages of construction.

The key problem concerns the nature of the fuel to be transported. The chemistry of DilBit is unlike that of fuel oil, which is self-lubricating. According to a Natural Resources Defense Council report, "DilBit contains fifteen to twenty times higher acid concentrations than conventional crudes and five to ten times as much sulfur as conventional crudes. It is up to seventy times more viscous than conventional crudes. The additional sulfur can lead to the weakening or embrittlement of pipelines. DilBit also has high concentrations of chloride salts which can lead to chloride stress corrosion in high temperature pipelines. Refiners have found tar sands derived crude to contain significantly higher quantities of abrasive quartz sand particles than conventional crude" (Swift et al. 2011). The sulfur content is acidic and, according to the same report, corrosion due to these acids, abrasives, and salts has resulted in the Alberta pipeline system having up to sixteen times as many spills as conventional pipelines in the states. The combination of heat needed to maintain fluidity in the severe northern winters and the remoteness of much of the territory passed through increases the risks, although governments have not added any special regulations to cover safety under these special conditions.

The history of pipeline integrity is not encouraging. According to the Alberta Energy Regulator (2013), there have been over fifteen thousand leaks and 880 ruptures in Alberta pipelines since 1990. But as one news account of these figures points out (Young 2013), as we saw with tanker spills, incidents are only reported when they are of significant size (in this instance, larger than two cubic meters). Nor does it include the larger pipelines crossing the U.S. border, which fall under the jurisdiction of the National Energy Board, whose website indicates that it only began to gather data on pipeline performance, excluding shorter routes, in 2012: Their website does not offer any report on the results (the Alberta regulator offers a database for $300). Both bodies rely on self-reporting on the part of companies. Inspections are only triggered by accidents, often serious, and the chair of the board at the main provincial regulator was founding president of the Canadian Association of Petroleum Producers, feeding concerns over the independence of the regulator from the industry it is charged with regulating, and adding to worries that it has inadequate resources to inspect the infrastructure.

The idea that information concerning oil production and transport is commercially sensitive or covered by military secrecy laws is as old as the secret diplomacy of Churchill's Persian adventures a hundred years ago. The murk under which the oil industry plies its trade necessarily breeds suspicion, especially when it replays what used to be called the military-industrial complex. Friends of the Earth alleges extensive abuse of the Washington lobbying system by Transcanada, the major operator of Keystone XL, including an allegation that Transcanada "tainted" the State Department review of Keystone (FOE 2013), while *Mother Jones* reported that the consultants hired to undertake the report, Environmental Resources Management, included a number of staff previously employed by Transcanada (Kroll 2013). As Pope Francis (2015, para. 26) writes in the encyclical *Laudato Si'*, "Many of those who possess more resources or economic or political power seem mostly to be concerned with masking the problems or concealing their symptoms." The amounts that appear to have been spent on marketing Keystone would have been better deployed elsewhere.

One major player on the Keystone project, Transcanada, has adopted a strong stance toward indigenous Canadians: "Our Aboriginal Human Resource Strategy was developed to increase Aboriginal employment accessibility and to support our respectful and inclusive work environment. Our Aboriginal Contracting Strategy provides opportunities for Aboriginal businesses to participate in both the construction of new facilities and the ongoing maintenance of existing facilities" (Transcanada 2014). Elsewhere on the pipeline's proposed route, indigenous people have rejected such approaches. At the Lakota reservation at Pine Ridge, North Dakota, "Unemployment . . . hovers around 80 per cent and only one in ten graduate from high school. Women live an average of 52 years, men 48. Half the population over 40 has diabetes and one in four children is born with some kind of foetal alcohol disorder." Nonetheless, Native leaders organized to block pipeline company trucks trying to cross tribal lands, on the grounds that water, land, and wildlife were under their protection (Oakford 2014). Athabasca Chipewyan First Nation protested that regional hydrocarbon mining "has caused significant damage to the ecosystem, including the disappearance of bugs, decline in the numbers of migratory birds, elevated rates of certain types of cancers, and the possible extinction of caribou herds" (Cardinale 2013). Eriel Deranger, spokesperson for the Nation, told reporters that the jobs the oil industry brought were by no means unmixed blessings. While wages and health care were welcome, drug and alcohol abuse were spiraling: "We are seeing increases in the cases of post-traumatic stress disorder because they are watching the destruction of their ancestors. And this is why we are seeing an epidemic of substance abuse. . . . They are trying to numb that pain" (Baker 2013). Across the world, the corporate and military competition to control resources after peak oil leads to "the drive to the margins to find 'new' oil. . . . All the horrors of the primitive period of the oil industry are returning. Indigenous people must be driven from their lands; previously uncontaminated waters and lands must be polluted" (Caffentzis 2005, 168). At the same time, from the Lakota to Chiapas, from the Ijaw of the Niger Delta to the mujahedin of the Sahara, scmetimes in civil disobedience and sometimes in desperate armed insurrection, indigenous people resist the despair that the oil corporations visit on them. The resource curse rebounds on those that operate it.

The resource curse recurs in the Arctic Circle. Controversy over the development of oil fields in northern Alaska is among the more public instances. Here the complexities of global trade, politics, and security are matched by the ecological understanding of the indigenous people. In spring, female caribou in calf trek hundreds of miles to give birth. The planned pipeline will pass through this area.

> When caribou arrive at the coastal plain, a type of nutrient-rich cotton grass returns to life after the long winter. The caribou feed on it, build up milk, nurse their calves, and slowly begin their return migration. The Gwich'in call the caribou calving ground "IIzhik Gwats'an Gwandaii Goodlit" ("The sacred place where life begins"). However, the coastal plain is not part of the Gwich'in traditional homeland. Instead, it is the traditional homeland of the Iñupiat. The Gwich'in do not inhabit the coastal plain, they do not go there to hunt, they do not even walk there, and yet they are making a claim for its protection. (Banerjee 2013)

The difference between the Gwich'in who do not walk on these plains and the corporations that equally never visit them is that the Gwich'in admit the codependence of their livelihood and culture with the remote area. The Arctic, with local increases in average temperatures on the order of 3 to 5 degrees Celsius, is one of the regions where the effects of climate change have been most strongly felt. Ironically, it has also made it increasingly economical to drill for oil as the summer ice cap recedes. Few things illustrate the suicidal tendency of the corporate cyborg more than the Arctic oil rush. The little coverage the prospect has received focuses on the likely destruction of wilderness in the inevitable event of accident. Cleanup in the long dark of winter at temperatures around 50 below zero, when oil acts in very different ways, will be patchy at best. The effect of swaths of black oil in place of snow will be to increase warming: of course, freeing up more space for underwater drilling, more warming, and more profits. The first to feel its effects are once again the indigenous people. Russian Sami in the Murmansk area have been campaigning against mineral extraction since the 1990s: Now, like their cousins in northern Scandinavia, they face losing their reindeer pasture and migration routes to oil installations and pipelines. Partly because of the extreme conditions, and partly because the sites are so far from centers of control and oversight, Russian pipelines are especially prone to leaks. No official figures are available, but excluding floating rigs, according to Greenpeace (2013), "The Russian oil industry spills more than 30 million barrels on land each year—seven times the amount that escaped during the Deepwater Horizon disaster," of which 4 million barrels makes its way down thawing rivers into the Arctic Ocean. The Arctic is home to 4 million indigenous people, dependent on herding, hunting, and fishing, all of them not only threatened but actively in decline due to oil and gas exploration. Life expectancy is dramatically shorter than among comparable populations in those areas like the Yamal Peninsula, described by Vladimir Putin as "the world's storehouse" of gas and oil (Ferris-Rotman 2009)—the world's in the sense that the results of Arctic extraction have worldwide implications; the world's, but certainly not the storehouse of the Nenets, whose traditions have them here for over five thousand years.

URANIUM

For ten times as long, fifty thousand years, indigenous Australians have lived in the Northern Territory. The Kakadu National Park is a UNESCO World Heritage site of escarpments of scrub highlands peppered with natural caves overlooking a vast billabong system. When the first Australians walked here across the land bridge from New Guinea and saw these small savannas overlooking an endlessly stocked larder of plants, fruits, fish, and animals, they must have felt they had at last reached home after their long wandering out of Africa. Their rock art has been maintained alongside traditional means for preserving and hunting the land ever since. But the discovery of uranium in the 1950s led to agreements signed by the traditional owners, the Mirrar people, to extract uranium at sites at Jabiluka and the open-pit Ranger Mine, both nominally outside the park though surrounded by it. As the geopolitics of power moved toward nuclear weapons, the geopolitics of proxy wars and puppet regimes placed oil supplies increasingly in jeopardy, while risking the kind of price spikes that triggered the global financial crisis in 1973. Uranium became a strategic resource in the Cold War, and remained strategic in the fight for energy security that has followed it. At first the mighty atom was presented as the ultimate in hygienic modernity, an inexhaustible and clean fount of energy. Even before the dark shadow of mutually assured destruction, that promise was already being revealed as a lie in the uranium colonies of the Southern Hemisphere.

The Jevons paradox states that whatever more efficient means we discover for generating power, we will always waste the newly cheap and abundant resource (Polimeni et al. 2008). The same can be said of digital media. It is a brutal fact of the expansion of Internet and mobile communications that the more bandwidth we have available, the more traffic we generate, in terms of increased numbers of messages and increasing complexity of media-rich communications, and the more power we use. While much of the political attention has been focused on fossil fuels, because of their contribution to global warming, politicians in countries with fewer petrochemical resources have turned back to nuclear power as a major alternative. Environmentalists are rightly concerned that this nuclear turn may, and indeed almost certainly will, lead to extremely long-term radioactive waste disposal problems. But it is also the case that mining radioactive minerals is already causing environmental damage, and that that damage is in an unholy alliance with internal colonization.

After two decades of protest (see Fowler et al. 1991), the $63 billion project to build a nuclear waste site at Yucca Mountain, Nevada, on traditional lands of the Western Shoshone and Southern Paiute nations, was abandoned. That leaves the United States with a sole long-term repository for their waste product, the Waste Isolation Pilot Plant (WIPP) near Carlsbad, New Mexico. The plant is intended to be sealed within seventy-five years, once filled with waste, and to remain so for ten thousand years, the half-life of the most toxic materials buried there. In a bitter twist, the panel of linguists, archaeologists, and anthropologists gathered to advise on warning signs that would still be comprehensible over these time scales included recorded messages in the six official tongues of the United Nations, plus Navajo, the language of the people whose traditional lands have been seized for the purpose. There is a savage irony in this choice of language to address the far future. A generation of nuclear mining and testing in the area (Brugge, Benally, and Yazzie-Lewis 2006; Solnit 2000) constitutes an effective continuation of the assault on indigenous Americans during the westward expansion of colonial capitalism. The chances of their language surviving this ongoing genocide are limited.

On the positive side, the WIPP facility is buried 600 meters below the surface, and dug out of solid salt, whose geological and chemical properties will help stop seepage, even if not over the time scales envisaged. The Ranger Mine, one of four major uranium mines in the Alligator Rivers region in Australia's Northern Territory, is rather less secure. Australian government debates on uranium mines in the World Heritage Kakadu National Park, listed unusually for both environmental and culturally unique qualities, are surprisingly few. The result is captured in an Australian Senate report:

- Potential damage to the ecology of the Park from contaminated water from the mine site
- The disposal of tailings and the leaching of uranium from the tailings into the water system of the Park
- Threats to the health of workers and the local population from radiation
- Threats to the cultural heritage of the Aboriginal population, including possible damage to significant art, archaeological, and sacred sites
- The potential for damaging social impacts on Aboriginal people and culture (Senate Environment, Communications, Information Technology and the Arts References Committee 1999)

The park is studded with warning signs at the sites of abandoned mines from as early as the 1950s. Conditions there must have been hard: intense heat and humidity, isolation, backbreaking work with primitive machinery, and precious little protection for health and safety. The leavings of these sites still carry warnings not to camp, wash, or eat nearby. The situation was so bad that the Australian government barely headed off a move by UNESCO to declare the park "in danger," resulting from a working group report that found "potential danger" in faulty hydrological mapping, failing practices for securing tailings, and impacts on catchment areas.

Four years after its 1998 report, the Senate committee returned to the issue. In the deliberate language of bureaucracy, they noted:

Authorities and mine operators acknowledge that there has been contamination from mining activity but argue that even though there have been hundreds of incidents, the number is not significant and that, in any case, environmental damage has not been proved.

It is the case however that a pattern of underperformance and noncompliance can be shown. The Committee also identified many gaps in knowledge and found an absence of reliable data on which to measure the extent of contamination or its impact on the environment. (Senate Environment, Communications, Information Technology and the Arts References Committee 2002, ix)

They further observed that "the Mirrar People, although Traditional Owners, have no direct role in the regulatory system and power of veto was removed in 1976 over both the Ranger and Jabiluka mining rights for the Mirrar and the NLC [Northern Land Council]. This was despite Justice Woodward's statement in 1974 that 'to deny to Aborigines the right to prevent mining on their land is to deny the reality of their land rights'" (Senate Environment, Communications, Information Technology and the Arts References Committee 2002, x). The exclusion of those most affected by mining from decision making is a typical form of environmental governance. It makes clear that indigenous populations can be treated with the same disdain as the natural environment, while simultaneously revealing that the "local" indeed comprises both people and place.

In 2003, however, a Senate committee noted concerns of the Mirrar people, whose traditional land has been seized for the Ranger and Jabiluka mines, that 13.6 metric tons of radioactive tailings were being held in aboveground dams, with a view to burying them in the pit left by the first excavation, Pit #1. The Gundjeihmi Aboriginal Corporation's submission to this particular enquiry noted that the top of the waste material will only be "20–35 m[eters] below ground surface" and that "the approvals process for tailings deposition into Pit #1 led to ERA not being required to line the pit with an impermeable barrier, such as clay" (Commonwealth of Australia 2003). The climatic context here should be borne in mind: Average wet season figures at Jabiru airport, a few kilometers away, show more than a meter of rain falling over three months; and the mine gives onto a vast floodplain running from the Arnhem Land escarpment to the sea. A history of ill-conceived expeditions to mine uranium since the 1960s litters the local landscape with cairns announcing, in English, local soil contamination and warning hikers away. The Mirrar and Gundjeihmi peoples warn that the extraction of huge amounts of water for ore processing, its disposal, and the disposal of waste and low-grade ore as well as nonradiological hazards like heavy metals and by-products like acids are as inadequately treated now as in the recent past; that climate change threatens heavier rains and bigger storms in typhoon season in the future; and that far more toxic material is seeping into surface waters and subterranean aquifers (in a basically gravelly local geology) than mine managers ERA, a Rio Tinto Group company, are prepared to admit. The effects on health and ways of life through the mortality or mutation of local food sources are intensely local, but the traditional owners recognize their global connectedness. Writing to Ban Ki-moon in the wake of the Fukushima disaster, senior traditional owner Yvonne Margarula was saddened that uranium from her lands now contaminated Japan, requesting that Jabiluka, abandoned as an active mine after years of protest, be returned to the park (Murdoch 2011). This is a level of global solidarity unthinkable in the public relations departments of corporations like Rio Tinto.

If the mines are not able to protect their local environment to the satisfaction of local people today, then ten-thousand-year planning for safe storage is unlikely to be better, neither for the seventy-thousand-year half-life of thorium, also present in the tailings, nor for the half-million-year half-life of its by-product, radon. A 2007 report by Klessa and colleagues indicated that measured radiation among workers did "not exceed 5% of the annual worker dose limit of 20 mSv" (millisievert: the UK safe dosage requirement is currently 1 mSv). The authors admit, however, that this is an average, and that workers in some parts of the plant show higher dosages, though still within legal limits. If, however, that dose is multiplied by the scale of the environment into which these materials are leaching and by ten thousand years, given bioaccumulation of radioactive materials and their specific action on the reproductive system, then the genetic as well as biochemical consequences of mining the Kakadu are chilling. We should note too that the "permissible dose" has a specific history (Walker 2000) and a contemporary politics, marked by pressure from the U.S. Environmental Protection Agency to raise the permissible dose threshold as a result of then-recent radiological leaks, allowing far more lax cleanups after spills (PEER 2013); a relaxation very similar to that attempted by the Japanese government in the wake of the Fukushima disaster.

The 2013 release of *Utopia*, a documentary by Alan Lowery and journalist John Pilger, gave some international airtime to the shocking 2007 military intervention ordered by then Australian premier John Howard into traditional communities in the Northern Territory. Ostensibly motivated by reports of child abuse (which turned out to be no more prevalent than in suburban Sydney), the armed intervention and brutal policing that followed (Manderson 2008) gave a clear signal to its international customer base that Australian uranium supplies would be secured at all costs, starting with reneging on native title to the lands where the ore is extracted. On the one hand, this established for potential investors the Australian government's readiness to withdraw constitutional guarantees to its citizens—including suspension of the Racial Discrimination Act—in order to protect inward investment, provide overseas customers with unregulated access to a neoliberal market in energy (Hinkson 2008), and allow politicians in uranium-consuming nations to announce that by going nuclear they had provided their economies, in turn, with energy security, of the kind they had failed to achieve through invasion and corruption in Libya, Iraq, and Saudi Arabia. Just as the increasingly dangerous rainfall in the Kakadu is a global responsibility, so is the market in energy that drives its mining. At the heart of this process, which lies at the heart of the energy requirements of the digital economy, is the continuation of colonization.

The UN Human Rights Committee determined in 2009 that the Australian government, which had acted with bipartisan support, had breached the terms of the International Covenant on the Elimination of Racial Discrimination, specifically with regard to the Northern Territory: "The Committee notes with concern that certain of the Northern Territory Emergency Response (NTER) measures adopted by the State party . . . are inconsistent with the State party's obligations under the Covenant. It is particularly concerned at the negative impact of the NTER measures on the enjoyment of the rights of indigenous peoples and at the fact that they suspend the operation of the Racial Discrimination Act 1975 and were adopted without adequate consultation with the indigenous peoples" (OHCR 2009, para. 14).

The Northern Territory can be frightening, a unique wildlife habitat for saltwater crocodiles and venomous reptiles, fish, and insects. Navigable in great part only by boat in the wet season, and arid rock in the dry, it was never coveted by the settlers who cleared the first inhabitants from more fertile land further south. But the discovery of lucrative minerals has led to further incursions on the remainder of otherwise unprofitable land onto which indigenous Australians have been herded. The case is sadly not unique, nor even unique to Australia: A 2009 European report disclosed that "70% of the World's uranium resources are located beneath lands inhabited by indigenous peoples" (European Commission 2009, 8). The Gundjeihmi traditional owners of the mined area organized a successful campaign to end mining at the nearby Jabiluka site, although current owners Rio Tinto maintain that they will resume uranium extraction once the Ranger is mined out. Major spillage incidents in 1995, 2004, 2007, and 2010 led UNESCO to require long-term monitoring of the health of local people (WISE Uranium 2013). Sadly, indigenous Australian health and life-expectancy statistics are among the worst in the developed world, and the possible impacts are masked by deaths from other causes, including but by no means limited to background radiation from the geological deposits.

The mining of the Kakadu stands out because of the anomalous position of the mine in a UNESCO World Heritage Site, but it is far from unique in its relation to indigenous peoples. Marginally the largest share of the global market in uranium oxide (23 percent to Australia's 21 percent) belongs to Canada, centered on three mines in northern Saskatchewan whose impact on native Canadians has been every bit as damning (Harding 2007). In the third and fourth largest producers, Kazakhstan and Russia, mining takes place disproportionately on indigenous and nomadic traditional lands (as indeed is the case with petroleum extraction in both countries). The World Information Service on Energy points to new uranium mines in Namibia, one of the largest of the next tier of producers, which includes Greenland, Kenya, Tanzania, Andhra Pradesh, and Mongolia, among others. The consequences of Arctic mineral and petroleum exploitation are already well known, though their impact on indigenous peoples is less so. The record of oil well safety in the Niger Delta is a sufficient pointer to the likely care to be taken by global corporations in Africa.

Australian deposits of high-grade uranium ores, which are cheaper to process, are the largest in the world by a considerable margin; exports were valued at US$1.1 billion in 2011, when the Fukushima disaster softened prices in the world market. Its major markets are in the United States, Japan, and the European Union, notably the UK, though new bilateral deals with China and India (in negotiation at time of writing) may change that balance (WNA 2013). A signatory to the Nuclear Non-Proliferation Treaty, Australia has strict protocols on its nuclear exports preventing direct military use. What cannot be controlled is the further processing of exported uranium, for example in depleted uranium weapons, a by-product of the enrichment process undertaken at power plants, whose use in the first Iraq war has proven highly controversial (Hooper 1999). Moreover, it is clear from the security arrangements at the Ranger Mine itself and at ports handling refined uranium from the mine (though not necessarily on roads carrying haulage of radioactive materials) that all nuclear facilities are considered potential targets for terrorism, and to that extent, like the waste products from mining and processing, a permanent and ongoing risk. The rhetoric of safe nuclear power comes at the price of eternal vigilance, a vigilance however not applied to the human and nonhuman inhabitants of the land where mines are situated and mine tailings are dumped.

Though not itself a militarily nuclear power, Australia has a history of allowing testing of British nuclear weapons at the Maralinga testing range near the RAAF base at Woomera, a desert area formerly visited by indigenous Australians on seasonal treks. Maralinga suffered from the legal doctrine of terra nullius, which declares "empty" any land that does not bear the traces of prolonged human development. The continuing legally null status of Woomera should be inferred from the fact that between 1999 and 2003 it housed a detention camp for migrants deemed to have arrived in Australia illegally: a null place for null people. Migrants were detained after being denied the refugee status that would grant them human rights, and, since they had no Australian citizenship, neither did they fall under the United Nations' Universal Declaration of Human Rights. It should be recalled that indigenous Australians were excluded from citizenship until 1967, and still suffer some of the worst social conditions in the developed world (AHRC 2008), including the suspension of the Racial Discrimination Act associated with disputes over mining rights on traditional lands mentioned above. The exclusion of both first peoples and migrants from membership in the state indicates that the ongoing state of exception (Agamben 2005) operated, not only in Australia but almost everywhere that economically valuable geology lies under traditional lands.

The exclusion of first peoples is the test case for the exclusion of many others from the calculus of risk. Some of the world's richest uranium deposits lie in the landlocked country of Niger, which lies north of Nigeria between Mali and Chad. On its liberation from the French, Charles de Gaulle enforced agreements under which Niger received French protection in exchange for preserving French mineral rights. As the world's second-largest consumer of uranium after the United States, France had a special reason for maintaining in power the kleptocracy of Niger's dictator Mamadou Tandja until he was finally ousted by military coup in 2010. The state-owned French company Areva derives a third of its uranium from Niger, on terms including almost complete exemption from tax, and a royalty of 5.5 percent of the value of the minerals, far below the 50-plus percent paid to other source countries like Australia and Canada (Reuters 2014). Even so, Tandja was not satisfied, and invited in Chinese companies brokered by a network of shell companies and middlemen who use their connections to siphon payments to corrupt regimes like Tandja's, just as the Europeans had done before them (Burgis 2015, 132, 139). Of the billions of dollars of uranium revenue extracted from Niger's mines, hardly any has returned to the people whose homes have been destroyed, and whose land is now, as in the Kakadu, contaminated with radioactive tailings, effectively forever. Payments for signatures on undisclosed contracts keep dictators in power, removing the necessity to raise taxes locally and therefore accountability to the people who pay them. Meanwhile the revenues ensure that the local currency is inflated by investors, making it impossible to create export industries out of the wealth created, even if that wealth did percolate beyond the ruling elites (Burgis 2015, 140). Meanwhile, the mines leach water from pastoral land and gardens; radioactive dust from the open-pit mines settles over the parched landscape; and the air itself is laden with it (Greenpeace 2010). The people of mining towns like Arlit, with daily mean temperatures in the 30s Celsius for six months of the year, and their succeeding generations, have been excluded from health, wealth, and happiness, and some from life itself, to provide France, and more recently China, with cheap energy.

The state of exception extends beyond the land into nonstate territory of the open sea, which enters the narrative of uranium in a particularly poignant manner. After lifting its prohibition on uranium mining in 2012, the Queensland government's Uranium Implementation Committee opened discussion on how to transport the ores. An island continent, Australia must send this kind of bulk export by ship. Attempts to build a new port serving the Mary Kathleen mine at Mount Isa were frustrated by international campaigns, so in the first instance, ores were to be freighted thousands of miles interstate to Adelaide and Darwin, the only ports currently licensed for uranium. Plans to build a new port are currently on hold, so licensing of Queensland's two major northern ports, Cairns and Townsville, became a priority. Elections held in 2015 restored a Labour government to the state, who swiftly rescinded the reopening of Queensland's uranium mining, but in the longer term the demand for uranium (and the rich deposits of rare earths accompanying it) will be a constant threat, not least because it is the cheapest way of dealing with the millions of tons of tailings left by the mine's previous operators. Townsville and Cairns are the state's major access to the Great Barrier Reef, another UNESCO World Heritage Site, already under threat from coral bleaching, agricultural runoff, climate change, rising sea levels, and spillage from other maritime traffic using the narrow passage between the reef and the coast, or actually passing through the reef itself (Tanquintic-

Misa 2012). The record of oil tanker safety does not bode well for transpacific or Indian Ocean maritime transport of nuclear ores; nor does the history of piracy in Philippine and Somali waters. The International Tanker Owners Pollution Federation note a rapid reduction in oil spills to a mere thirty-three incidents involving over 700 tons in the 2000s (ITOPF 2012). Uranium shipments form a far smaller proportion of maritime transport than oil, but a single 700-ton spillage, given ocean and wind currents, would be a disaster on a global scale. The International Chamber of Commerce's International Maritime Bureau reports 206 incidents of piracy and hijacking at sea in 2013 (ICC 2013). Again, the chances of a victim vessel being a uranium freighter is small, but the consequences significant. The freight itself might be of little value, and simply dumped, on land or at sea, or sold under far less stringent health and safety controls than normally applied.

The lessons of Three Mile Island, Chernobyl, and Fukushima are yet to be learned. Edwin Lyman (2011) of the Union of Concerned Scientists argued to the U.S. Senate that in the United States, "We have 23 plants of the same design. We have plants that are just as old. We have had station blackouts. We have a regulatory system that is not clearly superior to that of the Japanese. We have had extreme weather events that exceeded our expectations and defeated our emergency planning measures (Katrina). We have had close calls (e.g., Davis-Besse) that were only one additional failure away from becoming disasters." The reference is to a 2002 incident at FirstEnergy's Davis-Besse nuclear power plant in Ohio, where dangerous corrosion was found in the reactor chamber. In its analysis, the Nuclear Regulatory Authority noted, "In the past ten years, we have had two significant precursors—the Wolf Creek drain down event of 1994 when operators inadvertently transferred water from the reactor coolant system to the refueling water storage tank and the Catawba Loss of Offsite Power event of 1996 when one emergency diesel generator was unavailable. Since 1979, we have had 18 events that would be classified as significant precursors under today's guidance. Of these 18 events, four had risk measures higher than this condition at Davis-Besse" (Baranowsky 2004).

FirstEnergy attempted to replace the faulty reactor head with a used unit from another reactor, but in 2006 it began leaking radioactive acids. Davis-Besse also suffered from a computer virus attack in 2003, a tritium leak in 2008, cracks in the containment vessel in 2011, and leakage from reactor coolants in 2012. FirstEnergy's Davis-Besse plant sits at the southern end of Lake Erie, less than forty miles from the Canadian shore and a quarter of a million people. The exposure zone in case of emergency is defined as ten miles, considerably less than that assayed and failed at Fukushima. More than 2 million people live within a fifty-mile radius of the plant. It is always possible that regulatory systems will improve, that leaks and spills become things of the past, that the legacy of historic damage might be cleaned up. The fact of risk remains unalterable and for some intolerable. For others, the risk is precisely tolerable: within tolerances, if it secures the excess of energy we have grown accustomed to, and the levels of profit that corporations allege their shareholders demand of them.

Uranium is used in cancer treatment and the food industry because of its lethal properties: targeting cancerous cells or irradiating food to kill germs and other pests so foodstuffs will last longer and be able to join the international circuit of the food trade. Industrial X-ray equipment used in manufacturing to check for faults in metal parts also uses uranium, which remains of interest in laser technology, the basis of the global fiber optic network. It is also valuable in transmission electron microscopy, where it is used to stain ultrathin samples. These uses, along with historical applications in glass, glazing, dyeing, and photography, indicate the functions of uranium in media. Both enriched and depleted uranium weapons should also be understood as communications media: Weapons are blunt communications, but they communicate. Like any commodity, uranium also acts as a medium in circuits of exchange linking miners, processing and power plant workers, end users, and indigenous peoples in networks of power and poverty. Even when we artificially restrict "medium" to the technological media, many telecommunications satellites in Earth orbit rely on radioisotope thermoelectric generators (RTGs) for their power, both for maintaining orbit and for boosting relayed signals. The plutonium 238 isotope typically used in RTGs is produced in the decay of uranium in nuclear power plants, ensuring uranium's position not only as a key energy source powering the Internet and the manufacture of its material infrastructure, but in the physical plant that cycles telecommunications via orbital as well as terrestrial channels.

The power source of choice for long-life satellites is also RTGs, including three aboard Voyager 1, which passed the heliopause and left the solar system on September 12, 2013, the first human artifact to enter interstellar space. The implication is that orbital, solar system, and interstellar space are treated legally as of a kind with indigenous lands: open for colonization, and, like the high seas in international law since Grotius, open for the disposal of waste (including, until 1993, radioactive waste; Milun 2011, 119). The utopian science fictions of what was once announced as the Atomic Age were rapidly abandoned in the interests of Cold War militarization and first world commercialization of transatmospheric space (Beebe 1999). Heidi Keefe, in the 1990s, observed the utopian dimension of early space law: "Space would not be divided up, as were the land masses on earth, through conquest and colonialism. Rather, the vision for space was one of humans working in harmony to better the lives of all mankind by exploring and possibly exploiting space resources for the good of all, in the spirit of cooperation and harmony" (1995, 346). However, she concludes her argument by asserting that mining even the near planets is too costly to be viable unless property rights can be asserted in some form, proposing an organization empowered to lease extraterrestrial mines "once a settler or investor can demonstrate to the organization that he/she has either occupied the outer space area, or improved it (including establishment of a resource extraction scheme)" (Keefe 1995, 370). Keefe is not untypical of the legal discourse addressing outer space in exactly the language once reserved for colonial expropriation of the commons, down to the brutal description of resource extraction as improvement. Uranium proves itself a power source in all senses of the word.

Uranium is also a medium in that it communicates between geological and anthropological categories. Like other radioactive materials, as the name suggests, uranium is also a transmitter in the radio spectrum (Kahn 2013), a contributor to that noise which engineers like Shannon and Weaver have striven to overcome in cybernetically efficient systems but which remains perpetually integral to the very nature of the radio spectrum as inhuman commons. In its geological and technological forms, uranium as toxin and noise demonstrates a feature that environmentalism often likes to overlook: the nonhuman world can also be antihuman, and indeed antilife. Yet we should also note that naturally occurring radioactivity must also have contributed to the mutations driving evolution, and to that extent forms part of the genetic commons that contemporary bioengineering is attempting to privatize. Uranium reminds us of the foundational imbrication of human and nonhuman.

Uranium circuits, from geology to extraction and processing, through transportation, use in electricity generation, and applications in telecommunications and satellite technology, demonstrate the dependence of the electronic media and the energy they use on the principles and actuality of colonialism. As Milun (2011, 13) argues, "A colonial spatial imaginary created the law of the seas and the international law of colonial nations. That spatial imaginary supports the dispossessive agenda in the global commons." From the Kakadu via the Great Barrier Reef to the nuclear plant at Sandusky, Ohio, and the waste dumps of New Mexico, even beyond the outer reaches of the

solar system, what once was commonwealth, common land, common geological heritage enacting the ancient compact between living and nonliving
in the evolutionary matrix is now subjected to a colonial regime of ownership, one that treats land, organic life, and people as cost-free resources, extending that principle, through Voyager's freight of plutonium batteries, to
the universal scale.

The central character of one of the most significant artworks to take on
the role of uranium in the twentieth century, Peter Greenaway's *Tulse Luper
Suitcases: A Personal History of Uranium*, is perpetually imprisoned. It would
be a crude metaphor to describe *Luper* as imprisoned by uranium; it is, however, a tempting analogy. Certainly, for those whose homes and lives have
been blighted, incarceration seems at least a partial description of the loss experienced, at its most intense among indigenous peoples, from Yucca Mountain to the Alligator Rivers, paralleled by the Dene, Inuit, and Siberian in-
digenes now being displaced by oil, and the Iroquois and Cree displaced by
hydroelectric dams. The doctrine of terra nullius allowed colonizers not only
to remove but to slaughter whole populations, and to treat the remainder
as economically external, left out of accounts both fiscal and political. That
same externalization applies to colonized land, seas, and space. We should
recall that the UK and the United States fiercely protested their right to dump
nuclear waste at sea right up until international protests led by Greenpeace
forced a ban through the Basel Convention in 1993 (still not ratified by the
U.S.). The ocean was regarded as nullius, and the sea floor as desert, and is
still described as such by some dissenting voices even after the discovery of
deep-water reefs and thermophile colonies endangered by the practice (Ringius 1997). While capitalists claim their expectation to be paid for the risks
they undertake, the real risks are externalized, and many of them privatized,
much as debt has been, so that the risks of the nuclear cycle are borne by
miners, people living near mines, seamen, processing plant workers, and the
flora and fauna of the areas most affected by the trade. This economic externality extends beyond what once were commons, whose real tragedy is that
they only become overexploited when colonized by capital, to include significant and often culturally unique human populations. In this corporate dis-
avowal of human responsibility, the corporations demonstrate that it is they
who are truly imprisoned by the cultural logic of uranium.

A central task of ecocriticism in media is then not only to extend analysis to the materiality of media but to ensure that abandoning anthropocen-
trism does not mean abandoning our shame at the fate of indigenous and

other colonized peoples resulting from our communications technologies. This case study of uranium has sought to demonstrate that eco-critics also need to readdress the real abstraction of exchange. Exchange, under conditions of capital, is inevitably unequal. The depths of that inequality have been extended both by neoliberalism (Harvey 2010) and by the continuing process of colonization. Moreover, neoliberalism's ever more efficient use of externalities to displace any brakes on growth has made ever clearer that the society of exchange can no longer be understood as exclusively human. If we understand by "nature" everything that is excluded from the economy, then eco-criticism must embrace the exclusion of indigenous peoples, just as it embraces the nonhuman, even the antihuman. As legal and nuclear cultures extend to the ocean floor and into deep space, so too must eco-criticism. These are lessons to take from the study of uranium's role in mediation.

HYDROELECTRICITY

The idiocy of countering climate change with nuclear power is less comprehensible than meeting energy demands through hydroelectric power. Rob Nixon (2011, 150–74) devotes a chapter of his pioneering work on environmentalism and colonialism to a comparison of the "uninhabitants" of land taken for nuclear tests and for dams. That denial of habitation is contested in the protests around China's Three Gorges Dam. The Chinese government's official statistics for internally displaced populations associated with the development of the Three Gorges alone stands at 1.3 to 1.9 million people (Chao 2001), while even Xinhua (2007), the official news agency, reports that pollution, silting, erosion, and poorly understood meteorological effects of replacing agricultural land with vast reservoirs are taking a serious toll on the Yangtze. The Chinese sturgeon is one of several fish species threatened, along with the livelihoods of traditional fisherfolk. Water-borne disease is an increasing hazard on the banks of the stagnant reservoirs, and the natural flood defenses guarding Shanghai from the sea, created by outflows of silt into the delta, are diminishing rapidly, making the city vulnerable to storm surges and corrosive salt water (Peryman 2013).

The Chinese hydropower scheme is matched by the massive dam-building program that the Indian government has commenced, with loosened legislation for corporate and overseas investment and exploitation, in the name of neoliberal economic development. Arundhati Roy (1999) is one of many activists to demonstrate that this development does not include those displaced by these megastructures and their environmental fallout.

Writing in 2013, Grumbine and Pandit count 292 dams under construction in the Indian Himalayas, and a further 129 dams in neighboring Himalayan countries destined to supply India. Previous dam building in India has displaced anywhere between 16.4 and 40 million people (Negi and Ganguly 2010), almost all of them in the so-called tribal areas, with massive loss of forest and animals as well as the diversity of human cultures. The record of protests aimed at preserving wilderness in the midwestern United States, or of historical artifacts at Aswan on the Nile, has scarcely been matched in the case of the massive displacement of the poor in projects like the Narmada River dams in India.

Both Indian and Chinese hydropower schemes depend on Himalayan glaciers: "The long-term effects of glacier melt under climate change include reduced river flows that will reduce supply to downstream countries and dry up some perennial sources of potable water and irrigation. The glaciers of the Himalayas, which regulate the water supply to the Ganges, Indus, Brahmaputra, Mekong, Thanlwin, Yangtze and Yellow rivers and provide water supply to hundreds of millions of people in these water basins, are vulnerable to global warming" (UNESCAP 2012, 8).

Climate models from the IPCC agree that the total flow from the Himalayas will fall by between 10 and 20 percent by 2050. This is prior to any assessment of the environmental impact of damming the hundreds of rivers flowing down to supply water to half the world's population. Power supplies for the electronics and communications manufacturing centers of East, Southeast, and South Asia compete with agriculture and drinking water as well as electric light and utilities in the region's megacities for a resource already diminishing as a result of climate change. As Mike Davis (2004, 14) pointed out a decade ago, when the numbers were much smaller, the five megacities of South Asia alone (Karachi, Mumbai, Delhi, Kolkata, and Dhaka) "contain about 15,000 distinct slum communities with a total population of more than 20 million." As well as the tribals displaced by the proposed orgy of hydroelectric construction, 80 percent of Bangladeshi farmers depend on water flowing through India; India in turn is increasingly dependent on water that originates beyond Indian territory; and China's program to build a hundred dams in the Himalayas and Karakoram will deflect much of that flow into hydropower schemes and away from the south.

A major 2008 report neatly summarizes the risks associated with the Indian, Pakistani, Nepalese, and Bhutanese projects: "Submergence of lands, homes, fields and forests on a large scale will displace hundreds of thousands of people. Damming and diversion of rivers will severely disrupt the downstream flows, impacting agriculture and fisheries and threatening livelihoods of entire populations. Degradation of the natural surroundings and a massive influx of migrant workers will have grave implications for the culture and identity of local people, who are often distinct ethnic groups small in numbers. As the entire region is seismically active, these dams face high risks of catastrophic failures due to earthquakes" (Dharmadhikary 2008, 4).

These dark tales could be duplicated in many more regions where the resource curse has rebounded on local, especially indigenous, peoples. Adding the grim details of sickness, perinatal mortality, and habitat and species loss can only make the tale darker still. It is hard to believe that the blame can be placed on bad men. Most seem to act in the interests of abstractions: the corporation itself, and in some instances the phantom alibi of shareholders. These decades-long acts of slaughter would require wickedness of an extremity that is not properly human at all. Such acts have historically been done in the name of God, race, or country, grand abstractions whose role is now supplemented by action in the name of the company. Corporate functionaries thus do not act in their own interest but according to the logic of the firm, that is the logic of profit. When they sacrifice their own humanity and risk ungodly effects of their actions, they cease to be human, and become instead operative functions, biochips, of the vast and inhuman cyborg corporation. It is hard to believe that because lawyers defend Texaco-Chevron, they would be prepared to poison a child themselves. Only the machinery of profit legitimizes such violence. Only profit makes it seem rational to describe the number of leaks of radioactive material as "insignificant," to describe local toxin levels as "sustainable," or toy with the statistical definitions of acceptable risk. The monopoly tendency—the slide of capitalism toward vast conglomerates owning and running whole markets—is nowhere more marked than in the market for energy. There is an obvious solution, even to the otherwise irrational dislike of wind farms (why not protest the pylons and motorways that scar the landscape?). That solution is devolved and distributed local power generation: domestic wind turbines on the roof alongside the TV aerial, a return to local wind and water mills. This has the added attraction that lighter domestic windmills do not require the neodymium magnets used in industrial-scale wind turbines for their high power-to-weight ratio. Neodymium, which is also used in hard drives, is a rare earth whose extraction from monazite ore has attracted some environmental criticism (Arvesen and Hertwich 2012)—though accounts are muddied by rivalries between renewable and fossil fuel industries. Despite the market rhetoric of individualism, the decline of self-reliance and matching dependence on centralized services is an integral part of capitalist socialization. The grave fear that greets us at the entrance of this particular Inferno is not that there is no hope, but the belief that there is no exterior to the combined cyborg grids of fossil, hydroelectric, and nuclear fuels, electricity markets, and globally networked digital media.

CHAPTER 2 **MATTER**

Materials

The Russian city of Chita, a center of uranium and gold mining since the 1960s, ends a distressing list of mining and processing disasters presented by Saskia Sassen (2014, 155–82). Radiation from waste piles and tailings at the Krasnokamensk mine, which produces half the civilian and military uranium requirements of Russia and profits in the hundreds of millions for owners TVEL, is believed to account for the extreme numbers of children born with disabilities as well as cancer rates well above the national average, despite official denials (Belton 2006). In such accounts there is a stylistic and ethical challenge. On the one hand, environmentalists are used to conducting arguments through statistics, which, however, almost always translate into ordinary language as "big," and, couched in the type of abstract policy discourse used by our masters, aims at convincing a corporate audience that is incapable of responding to them. On the other, the alternate humanist strategy runs the risk of sentimentalizing individual cases, failing to take responsibility for the telling anecdote of a child or family suffering the effects of toxins. The horror of a troubled and painful pregnancy undertaken only to deliver an infant missing a limb or an eye or suffering debilitating learning difficulties, of a life lived with a bloodstream in which circulates the very chemistry of which our workplace and consumer media are built: These can be as distant from us as the coldest data set. In what follows, I have elected to write without such stories. The horror that we confront in addressing environmental disaster and its human consequences is not easy to convey or convincing for those not already converted. The purpose of this chapter is to deepen the stakes against which a proper aesthetic response might be made, by presenting the case that, as Sassen argues rather differently, the contemporary ecological catastrophe is tied to the specific mode of capitalism operating in the early twenty-first century.

BULK METALS

While the intensity of pollution is greatest where it is produced, recent figures indicate that global pollution is now a greater killer than tuberculosis, malaria, and cancer combined, with the greatest concentrations among the global poor (GAHP 2013). The rich, however, are not immune. Toxins leaching from mines and mineral processing swiftly reach river systems that frequently lead through more densely farmed and populated areas, while mineral dust, once airborne, circulates well beyond the locales where it is generated. In the first century of the Industrial Revolution, territorial demarcations separated wealthy suburbs from polluted extraction and manufacturing zones. With the scale and velocity of pollution now involved in producing and powering the digital tools with which the wealthy extract and consume value, geographical distance is no longer trustworthy protection. The market dynamics that network Australian uranium to global power generation and financial markets are paralleled by global atmospheric and water cycles, competing with any life-form that depends on air or water. As is the case with climate change, "environmental costs and benefits are often distributed so that those who already suffer other socio-economic disadvantages tend to bear the greatest burden" (IPCC 2014, 15), but even the lesser burden born by wealthy populations is risky and unpleasant. As we will see, this rising tide swamps as many boats as it floats.

One way for the wealthy to mitigate the effects of environmental change is to monetize them. The commodification of water is one such tactic. Since mineral extraction in most circumstances requires large quantities of water, its commodification is genealogically linked with mining. Lithium is one of the affected metals. It has its use value as a mineral widely employed in electronics. It has an exchange value: Traded prices for lithium hydride more than doubled between 2005 and 2007 and, after a brief blip at the height of the global financial crisis, have been rising steadily since. A commodity, according to the classic definition, "is nothing but the definite social rela-

tions between men themselves which assumes here, for them, the fantastic form of a relation between things . . . endowed with a life of their own,
which enter into relations with each other and with the human race" (Marx
1976, 165). In our analysis we will have to acknowledge a further quality: that
the commodity is that exchangeable object that disguises the real relations
between humans and their environment. The lithium-ion battery is a "social
hieroglyphic" (Marx 1976, 167) of this kind: an ostensibly innocent artifact
in which is disguised a world of complex networks that, however, present
themselves to humans in "the form of a movement made by things, and these
things, far from being under their control, in fact control them" (Marx 1976,
167–68), we in the wealthy part of the world no less than the global poor.
It is not just industrial design but the commodity form that constrains and
determines industrial design, which serves to mask the global networks of
corporate crime, human suffering, and suicidal assaults on the environment
buried in the hieroglyphic forms of our communications hardware.

Overuse and pollution of both surface water and subterranean aquifers
has become a critical concern for global development (UNDP 2006), and a
source of bitter competition between traditional users, mainly farmers, and
new superusers like the mines that produce the metals needed to build electronic devices. Commodification of water has become a major biopolitical
tool in enforcing the regime of the corporate cyborg. In 1997 and 1999, at the
insistence of the World Bank (which subsequently adopted commodification
as policy), the Bolivian government privatized the water supplies of La Paz
and Cochabamba. Neither of the companies involved was popular, but the
U.S. firm Bechtel, who operated the Cochabamba franchise, was especially
hated. After protests against rising prices and failure to guarantee access to
drinking water, during which at least one teen was killed, both franchises
were renationalized (Assies 2003; see also Hailu, Osorio, and Tsukada 2010).
Karen Bakker (2007) argues that public-private partnerships also failed because of water corporations' fear that they would not recover profit in adequate amounts from the poor of these and similar cities, noting that similar
renationalizations have occurred in Buenos Aires (which has one of the
world's most polluted waterways in the the Rio La Matanza-Riachuelo; Di
Filippo 2011), Jakarta, Manila, and even in Atlanta, Georgia. The real money
to be made, without the risks associated with recognizing the right to water
upheld by nongovernmental organizations (NGOs), is in industrial supplies
and extractive industries like fracking.

Water is especially scarce in the high Andes, and most of all in the environs of the great salt lakes that form the lithium triangle: the Salar de Ata-

cama in Chile, the Salar del Hombre Muerto in Argentina and, richest of all, the Salar de Uyuni in Bolivia. Formed in the gigantic continental uplift that stranded them millennia ago and raised them to extreme heights, these inland lakes persist in areas of extremely low rainfall, but over substantial underground water tables formed by melting snow. In the Salar de Atacama, "mining already consumes 65% of the water" (Tahill 2007), leading to angry disputes with local communities whose wells run dry, and whose crops are afflicted by runoff from the ponds of saline solution from which the lithium salts are garnered. Similar protests met an earlier attempt to extract lithium further north: "In 1990, US-based Lithco had planned to invest $46m in Salar de Uyuni, but hunger strikes and massive protests forced the company out, despite pro-capitalism former Bolivian president Jaime Paz Zamora's protests. Lithco eventually set up operations at Argentina's Salar de Hombre Muerto, and eventually became part of FMC [the U.S. company Food Machinery Chemical]" (COHA 2009).

Reporting from the Argentinian mine is scattered, but there are many reports of protests against the overuse of water by the mines and loss of it for agriculture and living. The Bolivian disaster of privatized water and the increasing pressure on the country to permit international corporations to start extracting lithium from the Uyuni may have inspired the Bond movie *Quantum of Solace* (2008), whose plot revolves around the newly discovered wealth to be had from water monopolies. Given international distrust of the proindigenous and pro-poor socialist government in Bolivia, director Marc Forster's tale of espionage and destabilization is all too believable.

Lithium's strategic significance lies in its two most appealing features: It is the lightest of all the metals and is an extremely good conductor of heat and electricity. Its lightness finds it a place in aeronautical engineering, but by far the largest use is in batteries, especially lithium-ion (Li-ion) batteries. First developed in the 1970s in the context of the oil crisis, lithium-ion technology research was initially supported by Exxon, who dropped it as the crisis receded, and the baton was picked up by Sony, with an eye to portable consumer electronics like the Walkman. The development of portable media (cameras, phones, laptops, and tablets especially) expanded from specialist uses, for example in the media industries, to become the essential tools of internal communication and distributed working practices in the new horizontal and nomadic management structures adopted by business in the 1980s. These workplace media are one of the biggest markets for Li-ion batteries. Today the expanding market in electric and hybrid cars, driven once again by rising oil prices, is the hungriest competitor for lithium, drawing Exxon and the U.S. energy giants back into the game (Levine 2010).

The major component of Li-ion batteries, lithium, is the mineral next to sodium in the periodic table. An estimated 75 percent of the world's extractable reserves are in the Andean lithium triangle, and there are already signs that the two southern lakes are heading for depletion at the accelerated rate of demand driven by the new desire for batteries. At Uyuni, indigenous Aymara, supported by President Evo Morales, have been fighting off attempts to extract the mineral by foreign companies. Writing for the London *Daily Mail*, a paper with few left-wing sympathies, journalist Dan McDougall (2009) casts light on why this resistance has arisen with this description of the Chilean operation: "In the parched hills of Chile's northern region the damage caused by lithium mining is immediately clear. As you approach one of the country's largest lithium mines the white landscape gives way to what appears to be an endless ploughed field. Huge mountains of discarded bright white salt rise out of the plain. The cracked brown earth of the site crumbles in your hands. There is no sign of animal life anywhere. The scarce water has all been poisoned by chemicals leaked from the mine."

The *Daily Mail* coverage goes on to record a visit by a Chilean delegation led by Guillen Mo Gonzalez to the Bolivians living near the Salar, warning them of similar environmental degradation, and especially of the loss of water, evaporated in huge quantities in the mining process. Because Li-ion batteries are also crucial for electric and hybrid cars, the large reserves available are even now being parceled out among hungry corporations planning for the changes in energy use after peak oil. Covering the Chilean industry, *Forbes* magazine, like the *Mail* not known for left-wing sympathies, notes that "nothing grows in the heart of the Salar de Atacama" (Koerner 2008). Salt lakes do not naturally harbor vegetation and the wildlife that accompanies it, but the function of salt in the landscape, leaching out for millennia into the surrounding country, is unexplored and remains so as long as the mineral is valuable to corporations. The possible function of solar reflection from lakes like the Uyuni, the size of Northern Ireland and spotted by Neil Armstrong on his space flights, is left out of account. The sheer geological beauty of the place, the culture of the indigenous people who live by its shores, and the high likelihood that extraction will take place in third world conditions involving dispensing with vast quantities of the chlorine with which the lithium is bonded are similarly unaccounted for. The Atacama is the driest region on the planet. Water has to be pumped up to it to dissolve the lithium salts. The rest of the lake is ordinary sodium salt with some potassium and iodine salts mixed in: Traditional salt collection has benefited from the iodine, an essential dietary supplement, and has for centuries provided locals with a living. The by-product of industrializing lithium extraction is massive amounts of corrosive salt water, a commodity with no commercial potential, much of which has been allowed to flow into the surrounding area, killing everything it meets.

Li-ion batteries lose about 20 percent of their efficiency per year of life, so that resource-rich areas are under pressure to admit the miners to replace the spent metal. One example reported in *New Scientist* in October 2012 is the Inuit-owned Nunavut Resources Corporation, which "hit Wall Street asking for $18 million to help prospect half-a-million square kilometers of the Kitikmeot region in northern Canada. They expect to find gold, diamonds, platinum and lithium" (Pearce, Reardon, and Brahic 2012). Their hope is clearly to preempt an open season on traditional lands. Lithium prices tripled between 2000 and 2012, in a billion-dollar market powered by the success of tablet computers and hybrid cars (Riseborough 2012). Controversy rages over how much lithium is in the ground, the scale of future demand, and the likelihood of running out. Generous estimates backed by Ford suggest a hundred-year supply (Gruber et al. 2011): Others estimate depletion of mineable stocks by 2020 (MIR 2008). Scarcity will drive up prices and will only increase pressure on governments like Morales's, already a hated figure in U.S. foreign policy circles for his alliance with Ecuador and Venezuela and his socialist and indigenist policies at home.

Study of the Salar de Uyuni reveals a typically complex ecological network. Far from the lifeless zone it has been depicted as by proponents of the terra nullius doctrine, the salt lake is home to a famed population of flamingos. An experimental reduction in their population in the 1980s led to a significant increase in cyanobacteria, food to the birds but lethal for humans and other plants and animals. Mining cannot but drive off the birds, making the region toxic. The abuse of water management increases the likelihood of the cyanobacteria entering groundwater reservoirs, increasing the existing environmental risks of PCBs from polyethylene used in drying tanks, and the diversion of drinking and agricultural water to industrial use (Wanger 2011).

Ribera (with Requena 2011) reports that "in mid-2010 the Bolivian government reversed a decree to create a state-owned lithium extraction company after a civic group in Potosí, where the Uyuni salt lake is located, complained that the company had been established without citizen consultation and was intended to be based in the country's capital rather than in the affected region." The fear that benefits would flow to the urban elite reflects the history of the extractive industries in Bolivia since colonial times, and of Chilean lithium mining's control by the deregulated Sociedad Química y Minera (SQM). It is reflected in the considerations driving the decision of the Nunavut Resources Corporation to attempt to establish and control their own mines. But as Ribera also notes, this by no means guarantees environmental protections or environmental health regulation. Rising prices and increasing demand will mean more temptation to bribe chronically poorly paid public officials, a tale all too familiar in resource-rich developing nations whose public service numbers and wages have been radically diminished by structural adjustment programs, one would say precisely in order to make them compliant with bribing corporations. Morales declared on his reelection in 2009 that ending corruption was the most urgent task of the presidency (Hollender and Schultz 2010, 49), but the corporate and political interests at home and especially abroad with money to spend on bribery cannot be regulated in the same way as local functionaries. Julio Ponce, the head of SQM, is regularly described as a billionaire. The poor are not to blame for poverty, nor are corrupt officials guilty of bribery: They only accept bribes; the criminals are those that offer them. And as Michael Goldman asks, introducing his study of the World Bank, "What if governments and development agencies prosper financially and politically from a project, what if their professional staffs are all 'on the take' in the sense that their salaries depend on the idea of development and its premises? What if a region's capitalist class invariably becomes enriched and empowered through development projects? What if this thing called 'corruption' is not the exception but the rule and as such defines the political economy of development?" (2005, x).

Between development discourse and institutions, market pressures, international interventions, treaty obligations, national and local political, cultural, and ethical dynamics, the effort to control the health and environmental consequences of mining the Salar de Uyuni involves an ecology of wealth and exploitation at least as complex as that of the cyanobacteria.

Wanger (2011, 2) notes that "lithium is not considered for recycling because it is still cheap enough to dump old batteries and to mine the virgin material." The politics of corruption are immediately bonded to the economics of waste: Keeping the price down is matched by ensuring that demand remains steady or increases in order to maximize profits. This is not entirely true of all metals. As we will see below, copper and other widely used minerals are still targets of recycling. But the accelerated demand for electronic devices and infrastructure still places enormous strain on the landscapes unlucky enough to cover them. Iron, copper, and aluminum are among the most plentiful minerals on Earth, and the most extensively used: Nearly 19 million tons of copper were mined in 2012, for example (Copper Development Association 2013). Australian exports of bulk minerals to Chinese and Indian markets have to be freighted by sea. Against storms of controversy, the federal and Queensland governments have determined they will approve the expansion of port facilities, notably at Abbot Point. Though the Queensland government has now stopped the practice, dredge spoil was being dumped in some cases mere tens of kilometers from the Great Barrier Reef, already stressed from rising temperatures and salinity, the coral predators these conditions favor, and climate change-induced cyclones. The risk of bulk carriers running aground on the reef is expressed as a statistical unlikelihood. One spill, however, would be enough.

Bulk metals mining is crude, dangerous, and today quite unlike the romantic picture of pick-and-shovel digging or panning for gold. Strip and open-pit mining remove vast quantities of earth, strip out, if only in a preliminary way, the principal ores sought for, and dump the rest eventually back into the pits, but now in far looser aggregates than the original rock, so that water runs through, dissolving other loosened elements into the water table. In Zambia's vast copper pits, for example, not only has the landscape been rearranged without regard to wildlife, agriculture, or the course of rivers, but the use of explosives and drills produces silica dust that attacks the lungs, while nearby smelters release large quantities of sulfur dioxide, which falls as acid rain, devastating small farms a hundred kilometers away (Dymond 2007). International business leaders nonetheless criticize the Zambian government for attempting to curtail the worst impacts (Caulderwood 2013). In an account of the previous seventy years of bulk mineral extraction in 1985, the EPA (1985) estimated that, between 1910 and 1981, all types of metallic ore mining and beneficiation in the United States generated a cumulative total of more than 40 billion tons of waste. Copper production accounted for roughly half of this total. As with almost all ores, copper occurs with many trace elements. In addition to airborne dust, the sulfur compounds released during mining and processing often form sulfuric acid that, along with iron oxides, catalyzes the release of other trace minerals that then enter the soil and water. These billions of tons continue to be produced, while the old mounds left by earlier mining remain, still interacting with the surrounding environment decades after they were disturbed.

Bauxite, the mineral form of aluminum, is common throughout the tropics and typically extracted in open-pit mines that deforest the land, drive off the wildlife, and disrupt the hydrology of the region, all of which tend to lead to erosion, flooding, and water pollution. As the desired metal typically occurs in densities of 3 to 5 percent, thirty to fifty tons of ore must be processed to extract one ton of metal. Since transporting raw ore would be prohibitively expensive, the processing needs to be done close to the mines. To get at the metal requires significant amounts of power, due to the high melting point of aluminum, one of its sought-after properties. Given the preeminence of tropical deposits of bauxite, hydro is the preferred source of power. The Tucurui Dam in the Brazilian rain forest was built specifically to provide power for aluminum smelting. The oxygen-deprived water of the vast static lake behind the dam promotes anaerobic bacteria that, digesting the drowned rain forest, produce significant quantities of methane, a greenhouse gas twenty-five times more potent than carbon dioxide. The land taken by this one dam displaced about forty thousand indigenous people and the wildlife, fisheries, and forest they depended on for sustenance and culture, wrecking an important wilderness reserve of biodiversity while also altering flows below the dam to the detriment of subsistence farmers. In similar projects, downstream towns have found their low-lying areas, often those occupied by the poor, waterlogged and, in the wet season, flooded.

Aluminum forms 8 percent of the earth's crust. The next most common mineral is iron. Like both bauxite and copper ores, iron rarely appears alone: open-pit mining typically releases large quantities of allied minerals like asbestos, sulfur, and mercury, all of them poisonous in their native or compound forms. One of the earliest minerals to be mined and processed, iron has not ceased to be used in the electronic era, where it provides structural supports as well as occupying an important place in the construction of infrastructural works like server farms. Its role in the Industrial Revolution, and its relation to charcoal, coal, and later coke furnaces, are well known: The scale of the mess left behind by two centuries of exploitation is less so. Iron and steel are a reminder that the environmental effects of mining are not only for the generation that enjoys the wealth of the mine, but generations afterward. The 60 million cubic meters of polluted water released from iron mine tailings dams into the Rio Doce, Brazil, in November 2015, carrying potentially toxic mud that sets hard as cement into the South Atlantic breeding grounds of the leatherneck turtle will, in the opinion of locals and experts, change the river, its valley and forest, and its wildlife for generations to come (Eisenhammer 2015). In other instances, the effects stretch backward into the past, as in the case of OM Manganese, obliged to pay an AU$150,000 fine for desecrating an Aborigine site at Banka Banka Station in the Northern Territory, an ancestral site whose destruction affects not only living and future generations but the ancestors (Scambary 2013). With annual revenues in excess of $400 million, parent company OM Holdings will find the fine negligible and easily assimilated as a running cost. The fine itself is payable to the Northern Territory government, not to the traditional owners.

This scorning of the ancestral construction of place indicates a second feature of the corporate cyborg: its disdain for the past, not only as a value, but as a responsibility. Sassen notes, commenting on the case of serial gold industry polluter Frank Duval, "This sort of severe ecological degradation and discharge of associated costs through corporate restructuring is the rule rather than the exception" (2014, 159). She is referring to the cunning action of declaring bankruptcy in order to escape legal responsibility for cleanup costs. In the timescale of long-term environmental despoliation, it is rare that any company will survive long enough to deal with the mess it creates. This ability to transform from one configuration to another, like posthuman robot toys, is a characteristic of the cyborg entities that produce the materials of media hardware, as is the use of this inhuman superpower to slough off their own past as well as that of the territories they despoil, and with that past even the semblance of moral obligation to the people and places left in ruins by their actions. The justice system that has created the legal avenues to accommodate this amoral practice of irresponsible transformation is a crucial infrastructure of the cyborg environment and one that, as we will see in chapter 3, extends from lack of protection for indigenous and poor people to the technical regimes governing the design and use of digital equipment.

RARE EARTHS AND PRECIOUS MINERALS

With the turn against lead in electrical goods, tin has become an important commodity. Digital technologies are not the only consumers, but the electronics industry uses up about half of the world's tin production as solder. A tablet computer can hold between one and three grams of tin, a large-screen TV up to five. Much smaller quantities, but still significant, are used to dope indium tin oxide (ITO), a major component of flat screens and the mirrored surfaces of optical media. In many respects, these smaller quantities are the more dangerous because they are so difficult, and therefore expensive, to recover in recycling. Global demand for tin has been increasing at over 10 percent per year in recent years, despite the global financial crisis, with prices at a historical high in 2011 and still averaging about four times the 2000 price.

One-third of global tin production comes from Indonesia, and most of that from two islands, Bangka and Belitung, and the seafloor between them.

Because the dredging used to access marine tin destroys the inshore fishery, while prices for local agricultural produce, mainly pepper and rubber, have been tumbling, locals risk death daily digging cassiterite (tin sand) ore in legal and illegal open-pit mines. Total Indonesian exports for May 2014 were 12,778.8 tons. How much of that originates in illegal pits is unknowable (Hodal 2012; Simpson 2012). China, which has the world's largest production of tin and its largest reserves, is also its largest consumer, so much so that it imports up to 49 percent of its refined tin, the majority from Indonesia, which also supplies Microsoft, subject of a Friends of the Earth campaign against materials sourced through child labor. The irony is that Microsoft, like other solder users, and like the major solder manufacturers, has been moved to source its tin in Southeast Asia in order to avoid accusations of using conflict minerals from the Congo (Shaikh 2014). China's domestic tin mining is largely undertaken in the kind of small, quasi-legal pits prevalent in Indonesia. Ancient mines—evidence dates back to 3000 BCE when the metal was alloyed with copper to give the Bronze Age its name—share with the early modern Cornish and Asian mines the unpleasant proximity, physical and chemical, of arsenic, released during smelting. In colonial times as today, transport costs and the value added by processing encourage mine operators to smelt locally. Processing at the point of extraction aims for the most easily extracted metals. As a result, tailings and mine waste were and are full of toxic impurities: Even today, a hundred years after the peak of Cornish tin mining, tailings from abandoned mines are bereft of biota.

The persistence of the past, ignored by the logic of the corporate cyborg, is evident in other features of mining. The legacy of seventeenth-century colonial Andean mines—the forced labor, the deaths from mercury poisoning (used in the extraction process), lung disease, and accidents (Robins 2011)—is reflected not only in scarred landscapes and broken ecologies. The continuing extraction of wealth at the expense of indigenous miners (whose techniques of high-altitude smelting had already been stolen from them) continued through the revolutionary period to the 1930s and the Great Depression, demonstrating the specific genius of colonialism in extracting not only raw materials and forced labor but the techniques and knowledges of colonized peoples, taken in order to be concretized in machines that would become the effective masters of those who once commanded them. The 1985 collapse of tin prices, which halved its tradable value, increased pressure on the industry. Environmental damage from silted rivers, algae-filled waste pools, and wasted grounds combined with the terrible conditions endured by miners at high altitude extracting ores from exceptionally hard rock to produce waves of unrest that further hastened capital flight from Bolivia. Since his election in 2005, indigenist president Evo Morales has nationalized a number of facilities run down by their overseas owners, some of whom purchased mining rights through earlier corrupt regimes in order, it appears, specifically not to exploit them and in that way to maintain the high prices the commodity has enjoyed in recent years. These high prices allow U.S. corporations to eye up tin reserves in Alaska, enacting a form of cyborg ethnic cleansing by endangering the ecology, poisoning the indigenous Inuit and Dene, or driving them out by destroying their traditional livelihoods. This geographical fluidity has two effects. "Precarization" of labor is the term initially used by sociologists like Pierre Bourdieu (1998) to describe the breakdown of lifelong careers in favor of temporary, precarious, contract work. In the 2000s it was extended to apply especially to migrant workers, but soon after also to the prevailing form of contracts in the digital and creative industries, at which point the specific power of the term was somewhat lost (Casas-Cortés 2014): As Mitropoulos (2005) pointed out, precarity in that case applied to anyone who was dependent on employment to survive. In the case of indigenous peoples faced with the loss of their livelihoods, the term still seems to capture the breakdown of regional cultures, the increasing migration away from affected regions, and increases in poverty, sickness, mental illness, and crime. The second feature of the accelerating geography of mining is the increased volatility in local economies, which further weakens the ability of states to control the predations of capital.

The ultimate destination of much of the metal currently being mined is landfill sites, home to nearly a third of the world's tin where the small quantities in any one device make it expensive to recycle. Throwing the metal away is integral to maintaining the high price of tin and, paradoxically, the low wages and environmental carelessness of existing and future mines. The rarer the mineral, the more difficult it appears to be to recover it from waste. Gallium, for instance, is a vital component in the manufacture of LEDs, the light-emitting diodes used in infrared remote controls and as backlights for electronic screens due to their low heat signature. New uses in solar power cells suggest it may become a strategic metal in the same way that lithium has. The major source is bauxite, aluminum ore. Unfortunately, not all bauxite deposits have much gallium: the richest sources, and the biggest suppliers to the dominant U.S. LED fabrication market, are in China and Ukraine, though the U.S. Geological Survey reports increasing investment in recycling from scrap, since even the most promising U.S. bauxite deposits do not have economically recoverable gallium (Jaskula 2009).

The LED is, like all advanced technologies, deeply embroiled in the glo-balization process and the new terms of struggle, in the era of free trade, for strategic advantage, especially as governments plan for the postoil economy. Each individual diode employs minute amounts of gallium, indium, and ar-senic, used in doping the semiconductor parts, but the quantities delivered to fabrication plants can be in the kilos, and the toxicity, especially of arsenic, extremely high. There is intense competition for indium, whose transpar-ency and ability to conduct electricity makes it an essential component for liquid-crystal display (LCD) screens in the form of ITO. The process for coat-ing these screens is disguised by the delightful name "sputtering," a highly in-efficient process in which only 30 percent of the material reaches the screen, the rest getting mixed with grinding sludge from the target preparation and other residues in the sputtering chamber, a mess from which a handful of companies, usually the screen manufacturers, recycle what they can (Tol-cin 2009). According to a *New Scientist* report (Cohen 2007), world sup-plies of indium may run out as soon as 2017, although this depends on how high prices rise, since there are currently uneconomic reserves in waste from other mineral ores that may be worth extracting, though this will require either intense chemical action (and risks of leakage), or large amounts of energy, or both. It is worth recalling that LEDs require a gemstone substrate, the favored one being industrial-quality sapphires. Madagascar discovered a major source of these gems in alluvial deposits, meaning they were very easy to get to and required little processing. But because in the early 2000s, despite a long cease-fire, Madagascar was officially still in a state of civil war, the sapphires were officially conflict gems and could not be traded on open markets. With the stones thrown into the illegal economy, Madagascar was unable either to get their full value (Duffy 2005) or to use revenues to con-trol wildcat sapphire rushes that have been damaging its unique forests in recent years (Laing 2012). It seems very possible that international interest in securing the sapphires led to the 2009 coup in that country. The discovery of rich deposits of these rare minerals creates desperate temptations for poor countries like Guinea and Kazakhstan, which have some of the world's most gallium-rich bauxite: Resource revenues may replace taxes and therefore the accountability of governments to taxpayers; revenue streams may well find their way into the offshore accounts of national elites; and the poor may bear the consequences without the potential income (Humphreys, Sachs, and Stig-litz 2007). The resource curse impacts minerals quite as much as fossil fuels.

The LCDs in TVs, smartphones, and tablets require other dangerous and increasingly rare earths like selenium and germanium. The levels of penetration of personal devices in the West is not sustainable across the rapidly developing markets of India and China, let alone the remaining portion of the global population living in the underdeveloped world. There will not be enough raw material to reproduce the West's expectation of multiple, individually owned and used devices for each member of the population. The strategic importance of rare earths has sparked fears about China, which produces 95 percent of the world's lanthanides, and has introduced export controls, placing its electronics industries in a powerful position to dominate twenty-first-century manufacturing, either through domestic firms or by forcing transnationals to move their manufacturing to China in order to access the necessary raw materials (Blakely et al. 2012). Though 42 percent of global reserves are outside China's borders, refining capacity is limited, extraction costs are often higher, and in some instances, as with Arafura, an Australian rare earths mining company, China has moved to purchase significant shares (Proactive Investors 2013). The possibility of trade wars on a level with those currently being fought over access to oil may loom for the high-tech industries, and indeed for green technologies: Hybrid cars require up to two kilograms of rare earths for their batteries alone.

In Mongolia, the extraction of rare earths, geologically associated with radioactive mineral deposits, has a particularly unpleasant history, with the *New York Times* reporting in 2013 that "in northern China, near the Mongolian border, radioactively contaminated leaks from two decades of rare earth refining have been slowly trickling underground toward the Yellow River, a crucial water source for 150 million people" (Bradsher 2013), while the *Guardian* reported a year earlier on local conditions in the processing town of Baotou, "The foul waters of the tailings pond contain all sorts of toxic chemicals, but also radioactive elements such as thorium which, if ingested, cause cancers of the pancreas and lungs, and leukaemia," and that locals, no longer able to grow crops or raise animals, are either fleeing to the cities or dying ("Rare-Earth Mining in China" 2012). Both the local impacts and the effects of seepage into the headwaters of a major water supply suggest a cataclysm in the making that will only be intensified by uranium mining. On the other hand, *Le Monde* mentions Baotou specifically as an engine of growth in the then rebounding Chinese economy (Faujas and Pedrelotti 2013), while the World Trade Organization was more concerned with China's allegedly protectionist stance toward exporting rare earths, a highly strategic group of metals in electronics and other sunrise industries including renewable energy technologies, than with controlling the means of their extraction and processing (WTO 2013). Again, the hunger for strategic minerals trumps not only the potential for major environmental disaster in the form of radio-active pollution of drinking water across central China, but the lives and cultural expressions of the indigenous people who suffer from the misfortune of living on top of valued mineral deposits.

Nigeria is one of these countries, as we saw in the case of Ogoniland oil in chapter 1. It has also suffered from climate change, with the southward advance of the Sahara affecting the north of the country. As Aaron Sayne (2011) notes, "Poor responses to climatic shifts create shortages of resources such as land and water. Shortages are followed by negative secondary impacts, such as more sickness, hunger, and joblessness. Poor responses to these, in turn, open the door to conflict." A few months later, the *Africa Review* noted that jihadi extremist group Boko Haram recruitment has been driven by the effects of climate change on the countries bordering the Sahara (Mayah 2012). In recent years, Nigeria has also been afflicted with a new resource curse: gold. Apart from its use as ornament and investment, gold is used extensively in the electronic industry for connectors, especially in high-value uses and extreme conditions, but also to add attractiveness to consumer goods like HDMI cables. The rising price of gold in the wake of the global financial crisis has amplified rushes in areas where the metal is an extremely low proportion of ores, as is the case in Zamfara State in northern Nigeria. Here the ores are especially rich in lead, a powerful toxin. In 2009, Médecins sans Frontières (2012) began treating 2,500 children for lead poisoning traceable to the artisan mines; Human Rights Watch (2012) reports child mortality rates of 40 percent or more in many villages; while Elizabeth Grossman (2012) records lead levels in local soil up to 250 times the safety level set by the U.S. EPA. What is less clear from these accounts is the trajectory that takes the gold from hand-milled ore, via local processing yards, to the international marketplace. Yet such connections are already apparent in the drive felt from climate-fueled rising prices and decaying agriculture that makes these kinds of risks worth taking for the immiserated poor.

It is clear from other cases, such as the rash of mercury poisoning in the gold-processing *entables* of Colombia, that local miners would rather control their own means of production, however toxic, than welcome international corporations, whom they see as closing them down out of self-interest using environmentalism as an excuse, and taking away the meager profits and independence they enjoy now (Siegal 2011). Nigeria can no longer look to agriculture as an alternative to gold mining: Climate change has all but wiped it out. Yet the gold mines are also politically difficult because they lie in the immediate vicinity of the Boko Haram guerrillas. One reason the lead poisoning has been so devastating in Zamfara villages is because, in this devoutly Muslim area, women are largely restricted to family compounds. Crushing ores by hand appears a good way to contribute to family income while look- ing after children. Women and children thus suffer far more from the effects of lead than their menfolk. Boko Haram's 2014 kidnapping of schoolgirls would suggest that this pseudo-traditional separation is also part of the jihadi culture, and likely to continue the exposure to lead dust. Attempts by NGOs to introduce cleaner artisan processing methods are hampered both by the jihadi insurgency and by distrust of the notoriously corrupt officials and government of Nigeria. Some part of the circulation of gold in our electronics owes its origins to this dark trail of corruption and self-exploitation.

EXTERNALITY

How then is it possible to argue that corporate capital is to blame, when the perceived value of gold is more ancient than capitalism, and people have, admittedly in desperation, elected to devote themselves to mining and processing it? Artisanal mining requires the minerals but also the motivation: a high enough price, and the absence of alternative ways to survive. It also requires buyers, typically in a long chain in which the highest profits go to the last handlers. The market for gold will not question the metal's provenance, nor take responsibility for the conditions under which it has been produced. The attraction is all the greater if cheap human labor replaces expensive plants while avoiding health and safety costs and environmental protections. What is experienced as a desperate act of survival in Zamfara is merely subcontracting from the point of view of the market, a subcontract moreover without penalty clauses. What is experienced as self-employment in Zamfara, as freedom from the centuries-long drift to wage labor identified by Wallerstein (1983, 24–25), nonetheless serves capital in the same way as piecework, where costs to the wholesaler are reduced to the price per unit supplied, and with as few protections because this kind of work has never benefited from the historical gains of socialized labor. It is of even greater benefit if the money earned is promptly returned to the global circuit of capital in the purchase of arms for holy or unholy wars.

There are some lessons from history. In a brief, devastating essay, Rebecca Solnit gives a figure of 24.3 million ounces of gold removed in the California Gold Rush by 1857, in a process that left ten times as much mercury in the state, and shifted 13 billion tons of the Sierra Nevada into its rivers, lakes, and San Francisco Bay (Solnit 2007, 115, 117, 118). Gold mining today has to work with far poorer deposits, with far larger environmental consequences

(Frank Duval, whose pillorying by Saskia Sassen was mentioned earlier in this chapter, is one of those eking out gold from old mine waste). Diminishing reserves in the ground make them increasingly valuable. What makes the situation worse is that it is not the current price payable to miners that guides gold's market value but the future price, calculated on the basis of known or estimated reserves and likely demand as established by traders in futures exchanges. These trading houses buy and sell contracts to purchase metals at a specific price on a future date, a gamble on what future prices will be. These contracts themselves can be bought and sold in a secondary gamble. This is what is called a derivative, the kind of financial instrument widely blamed for triggering the global financial crisis. Even when they function well, these markets in future commodity prices ultimately rest on the gold produced at sites like the wildcat mining villages of Zamfara. On one hand, we are able to ignore the realities of mining when we purchase a ring because we do not see the mountains of rubble, the poisoned rivers, the lost fish, the displaced tribes. This is one feature of the commodity as a screen behind which is carried on the relationship between humans and their environment. On the other, once transformed into derivatives, future gold ceases to have even the use values in electronics we have concentrated on in this chapter and becomes pure exchange. In that abstraction, not only does gold, like all the other metals tracked in this chapter, lose its roots in mining: It becomes something quite other. It becomes an abstraction, and one of a very specific kind: It becomes data. As in the case of Enron's Californian energy dealing examined in chapter 1, these data are traded not on the basis of human gambling but of automated or "algo" trading, reliant on the very computers that in turn rely on these metals. Financialization, that ugly neologism that describes the movement of the economy from material goods and services to pure financial operations, has its own ontology. We have to add another ugly neologism. Financialization is datafication.

It was a formative premise of commodity exchange that a commodity had to be an object: a discrete thing that could be counted, so that the numerical count could form the basis of exchange, rather than unpredictable uses. In the financial commodity, further removed from use value, it is not the quantity, quality, or even the object nature of commodities that matters but data about their production and consumption. Like any digital device, the interconnected network of computers forming the global finance market works on inputs of data. This dissociation of data from materiality is intrinsically semiotic. Semiotics distinguishes between signifiers, the letters and symbols we use to carry meanings, and referents, the real-world objects they refer to.

In spoken languages, semioticians claim, meaning is produced by the relationships between signifiers, not by their relationship to real referents. Datafication similarly creates wealth out of the relationships between numerical signifiers (prices) that need have no relationship with their referents (use values). This semioticization of the market also impacts consumption, producing what Baudrillard (1980, 147) referred to as sign value, the perceived value not of a shoe or a shirt but its brand. In this particular semioticization, consumption enacts the final divorce of the finished good from its human and environmental production. When financialization extracts purely semiotic data from the production and consumption of goods, leaving out of account anything not strictly financial, it deals in pure sign values. This dissociation of consumption from environmental impact repeats the central structure of coloniality, which Mignolo (2011, 2) defines as "the underlying logic of the foundation and unfolding of Western civilization from the Renaissance to today of which historical colonialisms have been a constitutive, although downplayed, dimension." The reality of the colony was always hidden from the imperial consumer by the sweetness of sugar, the whiteness of cotton sheets, the brilliance of gems. Orientalism shrouded in its glamour the fetish form of the commodity.

The "environmentalism of the poor" movement has, since the 1980s, contested the idea that environmentalism is a benefit that can only be addressed once abundant wealth has been achieved. On the contrary, activists in the movement argue, the cheap materials and zero-cost dumping of waste are "not a sign of abundance but a result of a given distribution of property rights, power and income" (Martinez-Allier 2002, 3). At the same time, as Quijano argues, mind-sets intrinsic to modernity or coloniality must also be opened and contested: "We have also to do with a colonization of the other cultures, albeit in differing intensities and depths. This relationship consists, in the first place, of a colonization of the imagination of the dominated; that is, it acts in the interior of that imagination, in a sense, it is a part of it. . . . Cultural Europeanisation was transformed into an aspiration. It was a way of participating and later to reach the same material benefits and the same power as the Europeans: viz, to conquer nature—in short for 'development'" (Quijano 2007, 169).

Development agendas espoused since Rostow's "forms of industrial development" model of 1960 (see also Pieterse 2001) have only paid lip service to a concept of sustainability premised on an unquestioned growth model of the global economy. Bundled with that development model, the conquest of nature is exported to the ruling classes of developing nations with the promise that exploiting nature will provide the benefits of not only European wealth but scientific knowledge and the power associated with it. Duménil and Lévy (2004) argue that neoliberalism as pursued in national and international policy has always been a political project to restore and in some cases install ruling-class power, starting in Allende's Chile and, as much by accident as by design, culminating in contemporary China (Arrighi 2007; Harvey 2005), a project that is both national and international and thereby colonial in scope. A political understanding of neoliberalism in crisis is therefore the necessary first step to understanding the stakes in the export of environmental costs to the global poor, and a politics that exceeds the limitations of a consumer strike.

The present global financial crisis has lasted almost a decade already, stretching the definition of "crisis" to the point where the state of emergency becomes normal. Indeed it is apparent that the practices that brought it about are unchanged, that there is no political will to rein in rogue banks and financial services, no justice either for those who benefited or those who paid the price, and no bulwark against continuing or renewed crisis (Brummer 2014). In Marazzi's (2011) analysis, all financial crises are based on the principle of making the future pay for the present: the resolution of one crisis is the genesis of the next. Our crisis is thus the end result of the crisis of the 1970s, which was resolved through offshoring, precarization, and automation; by immense growth in network communications and the accompanying investment in semiocapitalism, the production no longer of goods but of symbols (Berardi 2009a); by self-financing (GM's soft credit for purchasers for example, which rapidly outgrew its automotive revenues) and supplementing profit derived from production with surpluses derived from securitization: debts bundled and sold with the original debtor as effective guarantor.

The 2008 crisis arose from overtrading in securitized debts, future incomes that will never be realized. In the 1970s, short-term stabilization was achieved by crushing wages and squeezing government spending (with the exception of military budgets, essentially subsidies to the aeronautics and weapons industries, including many of the digital inventions they fostered). These policies, however, promoted a new crisis: Precarization (underemployment, economic migration, short-term contracts) led to lower wages and consequent anxiety about spending and therefore to underconsumption. At the same time, automation encouraged overproduction. The global expansion of neoliberal policy since the 1980s was a response to this crisis, drawing in more and more geographical territories while opening up more and more sectors of the economy to private ownership. When this in turn began to fail in a series of regional crises in the 1990s, the new policy of the 2000s was to pump credit into the consumer base of society. The new money was supposed to be spent on the accumulated commodities of overproducing corporations, whose profit margins were, at the same time, diminishing as automation increased the number of items but reduced the prices of each item sold (the "falling rate of profit"). Debtors were effectively given an advance on future earnings so they could spend them on consuming surplus commodities, so making up for the falling rate of profit in the decaying productive sector. The rendering of accounts is always deferred to the future whenever the present cannot produce an adequate return. The definition of adequacy here is a minimum growth of 3 percent per annum, which is to capital what velocity through water is to a shark. There is a fundamental irrationality to the trade in futures (completely opposite to the perfectly informed and rational trader of economic theory). The artificial inflation of debt—in order to finance the consumption of excess product—denies Say's Law, the supposed magical fit between supply and demand. The structural irrationality of an unstable and unpredictable market requires political interventions, like that of the European Union in the Greek Eurozone crisis of 2015, to ensure that the future is foreclosed by debt. Having gained enormous wealth and power in the decades since 1973, financial and political elites are ready to do almost anything to control the emergence of radically different futures.

The artificial creation of debt produced by giving cheap loans to people who could never afford to pay them back is a special instance of an economic phenomenon known as an externality. An externality is any consequence of economic action that is not accounted for in bookkeeping. A positive externality might be, for example, the education of a workforce, which is paid for by local governments or churches, and which a firm benefits from without having to pay for it; the commonest example of negative externality is pollution from a factory that is not factored into its profitability. Externalities are the unaccountable, in the sense that they do not appear in the accounts. The environmental effects of mining examined here convert what once was common land into a resource whose economic value is calculated according to the (future) price of the metals in it, not the (equally future) costs of the residues left out of the accounts. Whatever remains as commons is, in this sense, only what is externalized by the economic cycle, and it is precisely this externality that constitutes the material infrastructure of the information economy: its dependence on physical places that, however, it excludes not only from its promotional materials but from its financial responsibilities.

When continuing colonial enclosure takes over a preexisting commons in order to subsume it into global and universal capital, it is always simultaneously turned into an externality. In Kathryn Milun's (2011) account, that which was legally *res communis*, held in common by everyone, becomes *res nullius*, belonging to no one, and therefore available to be converted into property for division and exploitation at no cost to the one who acquires it. The description of both the Americas and Australia as terra nullius, no-man's-land, opened them up to ownership by the colonists, and gave legal permission for ethnocide, since definitionally the indigenous were becoming what Janet Gordon, speaking for those (including many indigenous First Nation peoples) downwind of the Nevada atomic bomb tests, calls "uninhabitants" (Solnit 2000, 154), for all colonial intents and purposes not there. This ostensibly legal recategorization of environments, which today extends to the high seas and outer space, brings the environment in question into the realm of the economy, but the specific form taken by these enclosed commons, as they move from everyone's to someone's property, is that of economic externalities. As we will see, externality is the economic synonym for environment.

The old commons, now redefined as externalities, are also the key sites for dumping waste: the high seas and inner space crowded with dumped toxins, trash islands, and space junk; old mine workings filled with radioactive waste from power plants; hazardous waste dumping in the Global South. Overproduction can either be consumed (through the expansion of debt in particular) or wasted. Both of these modes of destruction, because they are subsequent to purchase, the last economic action, no longer figure in accounts. The corporation has no means of accounting for what Parikka (2015) calls the geology of the media: the geological origins or the equally geological destination of energy and materials.

While factories tend to be protected against misuse and sabotage, the desolation of Detroit and other postindustrial landscapes indicates the degree to which machinery can be sacrificed on the altar of profit. The accounting principle of writing down and writing off machinery, the annual depreciation of the book value of the technologies it uses in manufacture, enshrines waste in the heart of industrial capital, at the same time allowing it to shed, as external, any responsibility for the human or environmental outcome. Unemployment, for example, still figures as a political issue, but does not appear in a corporation's books as anything but a saving. Technological advances in automation are aimed at reducing the living labor required to produce goods, and the falling rate of profit drives it to surprising levels of invention, driving down employment. However, even invention has costs, so when offshore manufacture and assembly provide cheaper labor, fewer taxes, and weaker health, safety, and environmental protection laws than in the Global North, the only reserved elements of industrialization to remain human dependent are marketing and design. Today both tasks are becoming increasingly automated in their turn, using unpaid buzz and feedback loops from the vast data sets of consumer response.

The writing off of machinery and of whole manufacturing regions like the U.S. Rust Belt or North West of England is an accounting trick that removes them from the ledger. It is also clear that the people involved in these industries can equally be treated as externalities: those dropped from employment; those who, like the artisan miners of northern Nigeria, pick up work dropped by corporations; and those like their children who suffer the uncosted and uncontrolled externality of lead dust and mercury. Rivers, forest and floodplains, wildlife and air are equally unaccounted for in a system that recognizes only the flow of money. Financialization intensifies this process, and its crisis intensifies the exclusion of growing areas of social life from account. These expulsions, as Sassen (2014) calls them, are legal fictions like the corporation-as-person, allowing the increasingly entrenched ruling class, benefiting from fire-sale prices at the height of the recession, to use massaged figures to demonstrate, against common sense and the evidence of everyday life, that the crisis is ended with a trade expansion of some fraction of a percent. Human and nonhuman now share in this externalization. An alliance between them is essential if we are to create avenues out of the slough.

Manufacture

The Commission's hope for the future is conditional on decisive
political action now to begin managing environmental resources to
ensure both sustainable human progress and human survival.
—Brundtland Report, 1987

To the extent that our dominant technical media bear the stamp of the political-economic regime that gave them birth, they can sustain themselves only as long as capital can sustain itself. The top 1 percent of the world's population owns over half of its wealth (Credit Suisse 2013): This is not a sustainable ratio. The ongoing financial crisis that began in 2008 was declared technically over in 2014 because gross domestic product (GDP) in the core metropolitan countries is once again showing growth, albeit at a reduced level compared to precrisis figures. However, GDP is a crude yardstick that notoriously ignores internal difference within nations, and the vast and increasing if occasionally controversial evidence (see the storm over Piketty's [2014] attempt to use economic accountancy's own tools against it) that that difference has accelerated as a result of the crisis, even compared to the growing gulf between rich and poor that preceded it. Austerity measures of the kind once reserved for developing nations by the International Monetary Fund (IMF) are now employed by European Union and North American polities to ensure the effects of crisis are felt most by those least able to bear them.

Three large-scale mechanisms serve this process. As we have seen, financialization, whose essential characteristic is the trade in risk, was intended to reduce the intrinsic insecurity of investment by trading in future values. This trade in futures, itself dependent on computers and network communications, both closes down options for change and simultaneously creates conditions of debt peonage, while increasing the rate of transfer of wealth from poor to rich (Esposito 2011; Lazzarato 2012). Rosa Luxemburg ([1913] 1951) may have been the first to recognize the second mechanism. She saw that accumulation not only named the brutal expropriation of common land at the origin of modern capitalism in Europe ("primitive accumulation") but continued in the equally brutal dispossession of colonized peoples. Accumulation by dispossession, in Harvey's (2003) usage, is the continuing employment of enclosure, through seizures by capital of common goods such as land and the geology beneath it, seabeds, water and air, and public goods such as health, welfare, and security. The third mechanism is the application of extended reproduction whose theory Marx propounded in *Capital*, volume 2: the devotion of economic resources to growth rather than to satisfying fundamental needs. For many analysts, this feature underpins the other two mechanisms. The obsession with growth in this account causes not only crises of overproduction, analyzed earlier in this chapter, but also crises of overaccumulation, when wealth accrues to a diminishing proportion of the population, and they can no longer find sufficiently profitable enterprises to invest in. There are then two types of crisis, produced by excessive or failed growth, crises of overproduction or overaccumulation. It is extended reproduction, growth itself, the engine of capital, that drives both.

Growth in the twenty-first century has been characterized as cognitive or immaterial by writers as diverse as Boutang (2012) and Gorz (2010). Accounts of semiocapital, information capitalism, and cognate analyses concentrate on the exchange of symbols (intellectual property, electronic cash flow, brands) but omit or diminish the continuing role of material production and distribution on which this new development rests. Without the infrastructure of processors, memory, and outputs, and the network of cables, routers, cellular networks, and satellite communications, there would be no cognitive capitalism, which would lack the means to create its products and services and get them to market. Engineering and design, software and content, are the high-value industries of the twenty-first century but their realization depends upon the existence of this infrastructure. Their capacity for innovation, driven by spiraling synergistic demands—new hardware designs demanding new forms of content, new content demanding new forms of software, new software demanding new hardware designs—promises the level of growth that neoliberalism demands. In this sense, the immaterial sector of the economy is as committed to growth, and as unsustainable, as the material.

SEMICONDUCTORS AND SUBASSEMBLY: OUTSOURCED AND OFFSHORE

Indeed, separating infrastructure from content is only an analytical exercise: Empirically they act entirely in consort. As we have already seen in terms of energy and minerals, the electronic infrastructure and its perpetual innovations incur immense environmental costs in terms of materials and energy use. These environmental costs of digital media are also human costs, on the ecological principle that human societies are entirely integrated into their environments. This section concentrates on manufacture: the material production of goods and the labor required to produce them, along with the extraeconomic consequences of manufacture. Products like semiconductors and fiber optics have been the objects of intense investment from which they emerge as intellectual capital in the form of patents. They also require physical production in factories (semiconductor plants prefer the term *fabrication* to *manufacture*: Facilities for their production are known in the industry as fabs). As a consequence of the mechanisms of accumulation, financialization, and extended reproduction, these fabs have migrated in two intertwined but distinguishable forms, outsourcing and offshoring. Outsourcing refers to the practice of subcontracting elements of manufacture to smaller companies, often outside the contracting company's home country; offshoring in this context refers to building fab plants and other facilities beyond the home country's borders where wages, health and safety costs, environmental controls, and the tax burden required to educate workers are far lower than those won by working-class movements in the contracting party's country of origin. Implicit in both outsourcing and offshoring are the environmental costs of transporting semifinished goods or subassemblies to centralized final assembly plants, a topic addressed at the end of the section.

Also integral to offshoring and especially outsourcing is the policing of intellectual property when subassembly is entrusted to subcontractors (Ernest and Young 2012, 34). Because the labor of producing semiconductors is divided between high-value design (cognitive labor) and low-value manufacture and assembly (physical labor), the policing of patents operates on the same principle as that ascribed to al-Qaeda cells: each subcontractor operates in ignorance of the central planning within which alone their separate activities make sense. As a result, labor in subassembly plants and component manufacture is kept in as great a state of ignorance as is compatible with the efficient production of the units involved. This ignorance is not a native state but one that must be constantly produced, since any passage of the cognitive capital involved to the workers would arm them with the capacity to seize control of the means of production.

It is also important to note that many factory workers, even in sweatshops, prefer the wage labor of factory employment to the even more precarious and brutal conditions of a demeaned agricultural sector that offers the only alternative for displaced populations such as those of Indonesia, India, and China (Harvey 2003, 164; Husain and Dutta 2014). With bitter irony, many seek to distinguish themselves from "natives," a colonialist word positioning indigenous people as part of nature. For the colonists, the natives demonstrated their naturalness by failing to subject land to property relations: Only economic motivations—wage labor and property rights—counted as fully human. In the alienation of nature as environment, enclosures and colonization diminished human nature as much as they did the green world. This cultural formation, deeply internalized, has immense disciplinary power. That it is a false, historical outcome of oppression does not alter its persuasiveness. Whenever we argue against the subcontractual regimes of outsourcing and offshoring, we need to remember that the alternatives to sweatshop labor need to be better culturally as well as financially than the existing state of affairs, not only from our perspective but from that of the workers themselves. The challenge of sustainability requires us to face this ethical problem, should we determine to promote the well-being of the environment over the well-being, real or imagined, of the sweatshop labor force.

By no means can all fabs or assembly plants be treated as sweatshops. Many electronics companies have been forced by consumer boycotts and campaigns to ameliorate working conditions in the computer industry as they have in at least some cases in the garment trade. Similarly, even in head offices, there can be deep inequalities between classes of employees. Dell Computer, for example, agreed in a $9 million class action settlement in 2009 that it had failed to offer women employees equal access to training, equal pay, or promotions, establishing a Global Diversity Council to monitor its policies thereafter, extending them down its international supply chain. Such companies are to be applauded for their change, but not for the decades of oppression that preceded it, or the lives their previous policies stunted. In a similar vein, while many companies have attempted to clean up their atmospheric emissions, waste material dumping, and water pollution policies in the last five to ten years, the legacy of their previous actions is not thereby cleansed. Some perfluorinated chemicals (PFCs), gas emissions from chemical vapor deposition and plasma etching procedures in fabrication plants, persist in the atmosphere for thousands if not tens of thousands of years, and have up to twenty thousand times more impact per part than carbon dioxide on the greenhouse effect (EPA 2008). Other mineral and solid waste, much of it composed of known carcinogens and other compounds whose long-term effects are unknown, will persist in the vicinity of the plants for equally lengthy periods of time. For the many women employees who are liable to bear children, those effects last long after they might terminate their employment, and affect babies with otherwise no connection to the plants, present or past. The sustainability of the computer industry concerns its geography, including the connectedness of by-products to aquifers and atmospheric circulation that connects distant places with the source of pollution (Drange and Rust 2014; Lin et al. 2014). Sustainability also points us toward the future, in which the legacies of long-abandoned factories connect to far future effects.

In a 2011 overview of the semiconductor industry's environmental and health hazards, Corky Chew notes that PFCs are less frequently used in fabrication than previously, but that remaining dangerous chemicals include heavy metals, rare earths, solvents, epoxy, corrosives and caustics, fluorides, ammonia, and lead. Process redesign focuses on treatment of solid, liquid, and gas wastes, which themselves use acids and caustics to neutralize pH levels in wastewater, and include incineration and landfill. Some of the energy required comes from flammable by-products, but even with this saving, the energy budget of sequestering waste is at least as large as the cost of recycling. The IFC/World Bank Guidelines use a discourse peppered with expressions like "amelioration," "abatement," "improvement," "optimization," and "minimizing," in the context of a detailed set of recommendations for improving the environmental performance of the industry. The guidelines admit their applicability is greater in new facilities than in retroengineered existing plants, and note that their application is always subject to "site specific targets and an appropriate timetable for achieving them," adding that site-specific variables include such factors as "host country context, assimilative capacity of the environment and other project factors" (IFC/World Bank 2007, 1). While asserting that the industry should, in case of conflicting guidance, apply the more stringent of the options, these final notes on host countries, their relative weakness in enforcing environmental regulation, and their environmental capacity to somehow digest waste are distressing in their gesture toward a rule that can be bent. They exemplify what John Urry (2014, 10) refers to as "a kind of regime-shopping [that] preclude[s] the slowing down of the rate of growth of CO_2 emissions, which presupposes shared and open global agreements between responsible states, corporations and publics." The IFC guidelines clearly aspire to that kind of transparency, while at the same time indicating how it can be ignored.

The sad truth is that the increasing imbrication of the Internet in the quotidian operation of daily life from trade to traffic signals, the explosion in mobile media use, and the prospects for an increasingly embedded Internet of things, all suggest that we are stepped in so far, returning were tedious as go o'er. The Semiconductor Industry Association (Rosso 2014) reports "that worldwide semiconductor sales for 2013 reached $305.6 billion." It seems impossible to convert that figure into an estimate of the numbers of chips produced, given the mix of mass and specialist products involved: A unique and secure device created for the military will be priced differently than the one in a cheap watch, an RFID tag, or a credit card. The numbers, however, are growing, even as the prices have tended to drop in line with Moore's Law, and this despite the years of downturn since the global financial crisis and the increasing costs of key minerals like indium, gold, and the lanthanides. A 2002 report suggested that 200 billion discrete components (diodes, transistors, rectifiers, etc.) were produced annually, with about another billion units of optoelectronics (LEDs, laser diodes, CCD chips), memory, logic, microprocessing and other devices (Turley 2002). Today we could expect that annual production is at least tenfold. Each chip is tiny, but the collective weight of the metals and chemicals required to make them is great.

This is especially true of the water needed to build chips. According to Global Water Intelligence, "creating an integrated circuit on a 300mm wafer requires approximately 2,200 gallons of water in total, of which 1,500 gallons is ultrapure water" (Cope 2009). Ultrapure water (UPW), which typically requires 1,400 gallons of ordinary water to produce 1,000 gallons of UPW, is so pure it is considered an industrial solvent. It not only provides washing and lubrication for the polishing processes required between steps in manufacture, but unlike normal water does not carry any dissolved minerals that might interfere with nanometer-scale electronics. However, this requires the safe removal of those impurities from the source water, while also demanding the removal of the by-products of the polishing processes. Some of the mineral effluent is valuable and occurs in large enough quantities to be worth rescuing through flocculation, coagulation, centrifuges, and, for the nanoscale molecules, hollow-fiber membranes, all of which can only be built and run using appreciable amounts of energy. U.S. plants use a series of these processes, plus various chemical reagents to neutralize acids and caustics, but even so, much of what is captured is defined in federal and state legislation, notably that of California, as toxic waste. In other jurisdictions, wastewater ponds are built to allow dangerous materials to sink, but these are vulnerable to flooding and seismic activity and are illegal in the United States and European Union. Illegality, however, is no guard against illegal behavior, which becomes increasingly attractive as top-end consumers of semiconductors in the computer, phone, and games markets pressure their suppliers to cut costs. In fact, KPMG (2013, 27) reports that "losing share to lower cost producers" is perceived as posing the single greatest threat to their business models by global semiconductor manufacturers (their second greatest fear is "political/regulatory uncertainty," a likely reference to environmental regulation).

On December 9, 2013, Taiwanese company Advanced Semiconductor Engineering (ASE) of Kaohsiung City, a municipality of approaching 3 million people, was fined the maximum amount of NT$600,000 (just over US$20,000) for dumping wastewater containing acids and metals into the main river used for irrigation in the area. In June 2014, the Taiwanese Environmental Protection Agency upped the maximum fine to NT$20 million for future infringements. In the same month, ASE announced that despite the partial closure of the plant, it was planning to increase production in the third quarter of the year, and would be raising up to NT$15 billion to support the expansion (Chung and Huang 2014). Although water, including reuse and recycling, can account for up to 1.5 percent of operating costs, it is clear that given the scale of operations, fines are routinely written off as part of that cost. It was reported that ASE paid seven fines for ongoing pollution dumps between July 2011 and October 2013. The same report quotes activist assertions that the company had enjoyed tax exemptions of NT$3 billion (Chiu 2013). Both the strategic importance of the industry—ASE is the world's largest supplier of semiconductors and testing services—and its association with the technocratic dogma in development policy tend to ensure that violations of the law are treated leniently, leading to the assumption that the IFC/World Bank recommendations to conform to host country standards is an opportunity to cut costs in the interests of increasing sales to end users, in this case manufacturers of consumer electronics. (ASE blamed a one-time employee error and promised an internal investigation.)

The water issue is strategic since it involves a common good. In Taiwan as in other countries, companies pay for metered water use, but as in other countries there appears to be more relaxed metering of outflows from semiconductor fabs. In China this is particularly worrying. Fabs can use up to 30–50 megawatts of peak electrical capacity. In China, this power is most likely to come from hydroelectricity. Growth in the sector, which ran at 24 percent per annum for the decade following 2001, thus competes with itself for consumable water for power or UPW. Competition with agriculture and with other industries as well as human consumption is at its highest where the greatest densities of fabs are found: in the Yangtze River delta (Shanghai and Jiangsu) and in the environs of Beijing, regions that are counted as "dry" in the standard UNEP/UNDP measure, having less than a thousand cubic meters of water per person, while Zhejiang to the south of Shanghai is reckoned at risk. In total, over 80 percent of the country's fabs are based in dry or at-risk regions. The industry is making steps toward less profligate use of the resource, including reduction, reuse, and recycling projects and migration from intensive use of UPW. According to research by NGO China Water Risk (2013) into the Chinese government's Institute of Public and Environmental Affairs' records, there were "over 10,000 environmental violations for key semiconductor companies," the major effluents including arsenic, antimony, hydrogen peroxide, and hydrofluoric acid. Of these, arsenic is a major carcinogen in humans and animals (Chen 2006); high levels of antimony are especially toxic to aquatic life (Mengchang et al. 2012); and hydrogen peroxide, despite being used extensively in wastewater treatment, is classified as corrosive and in concentrated or aerosol form has a variety of ill effects on humans and animals (ATSDR 2014), while hydrofluoric acid is corrosive and toxic for humans, animals, and plants.

Chip fabrication employs a range of technologies besides the chemical. Chip burning is a test process subjecting semiconductors to high levels of heat and voltage; ion implantation is used in doping; and X-rays are used to check quality. It is unclear whether these processes contributed to a spate of cancers among workers in Samsung fabs in South Korea in the 2010s (Grossman 2011). Volatile organics like benzene, trichloroethylene, and methylene chloride are also common in clean rooms where chips are handled by human operators. Some three years after Grossman reported on this for *Yale Environment*, noting that the Semiconductor Industry Alliance protested that studies of links between fabs and cancer clusters were "scientifically flawed," Samsung apologized and promised compensation to a group of ex-employees who have suffered from cancer, without however accepting a link between chemical or physical processes and their illnesses (Associated Press 2014). Samsung may face environmental regulation at home: it has, however, the option on less tightly regulated regimes in neighboring Asian countries where it currently outsources much of its production (Asian Labour Update 2014). Liability for domestic workers may in any case lie with the South Korean government, to whom companies pay a levy from which claims for industrial injury are paid.

These three stories from Taiwan, China, and Korea are in some sense typical of the kinds of tale that we discover in any environmental analysis of industries of all kinds. Even the division of high-risk, low-paid labor in manufacture (see, for example, China Labor Watch 2011) from low-risk, high-paid labor in research and development parallels similar structures in the garment sector where design is highly paid and respected, unlike the work of sweatshop laborers. The same is true of automotive, aerospace, and other transport manufacture. These all comprise, in their various ways, aspects of communications; indeed, transport was typically included in the sociology of communications through the 1970s. The case of semiconductors is, however, rather different in that the consumption of the end product, by consumers and businesses, is also a source of high-value innovation, especially when a proportion of that innovation is, from the standpoint of the corporation, undertaken by unpaid consumers who pay for their own equipment in order to provide content for corporations like Facebook. However, while both are productive of revenues, only R&D and design are paid. The exchange with unpaid content producers is for a service: the platform itself. A problem this shares with chip design is the increasing standardization of the interface of the former and the design choices in the latter. The trend to innovation within standards as opposed to invention beyond them, and the differential use of paid or unpaid creativity are ultimately linked, and equally relevant to the challenge of greening the media.

The developing salience of the "produser" (Bruns 2008), the dual role of producing while using consumer goods, has become a core feature of consumption in the twenty-first century, offering not merely new ways to innovate (Benkler's "commons-based peer production" [2006, 60]) but the possibility of a wholesale reinvention of the principles of political economy (Bauwens 2005). Produsage blurs the distinction between users and producers in value chains: Production is always incomplete, as in the case of computers delivered without software installed, so that the end user has to participate in the production process. The opportunities for a cashless commons of shared benefits based on principles familiar from open-source software, Wikipedia, and open-participation science projects are immense. In the field of semiconductors, however, the entry costs are far higher than those for producing content or code. Contemporary integrated circuit (IC) design faces key challenges in accelerating the performance of processors (now approaching the scale where quantum effects hinder logic design [Waldrop 2016]), in improving performance-energy ratios, and ameliorating battery and display designs to reduce power and increase performance. These challenges mean that new chips require US$30–40 million to produce, figures that to date the peer-to-peer community cannot match. They are even challenging for venture capital-seeking start-ups, while large corporations, paradoxically, are reducing their in-house R&D in favor of acquiring start-ups once they have passed a threshold of risk, or licensing the intellectual property they require, since those are economically safer bets (Ernest and Young 2012, 6), a sure route toward standardization. Venture capital, since the global financial crisis, has been hard put to find investors interested in risk, and as a result has become increasingly risk averse itself. The end product of this has been a diminution of invention, a shift toward investing in applications, which have a better risk-to-profit ratio, and, even more perversely, a shift in the number of patents being secured away from the United States, traditionally the home of innovation in IC design, toward East Asia, where major corporations are increasingly becoming "fabless," like their U.S. counterparts (Macher, Mowrey, and Di Minin 2007). A fabless corporation typically takes on the lucrative design work, then subcontracts the fabrication of its chips. Keshavarzi and Nicol (2014) cite Nicky Lu, CEO of Etron, to the effect that China is investing US$14.2 billion in fabless design companies.

The concentration and mobility of intellectual capital has always been characteristic of capital, but this shift to East Asia is a prime indicator of the hypothesis advanced by Arrighi (Arrighi et al. 1999) and others that China is in the process of leading a new era of capital centered in East Asia. The newly diversifying concentrations of R&D and IC design on either side of the Pacific are built on the equally mobile but far more precarious labor in fabs, which are increasingly migrated further offshore, especially into Southeast Asia, Indonesia, and the Philippines. The maquiladoras, sprawling subcontracting factories along the U.S.-Mexican border, have become major economic zones since the introduction of the North American Free Trade Agreement (NAFTA), something the nineteenth-century Cuban revolutionary José Martí (2009, 309) foretold when he wrote in 1891, "He who speaks of economic union speaks of political union. The nation that buys commands, and the nation that sells serves," a lesson currently being learned in the north-south split in the Eurozone. The maquiladoras have been extensively documented for their poor workplace health and safety, exploitation of women, and environmental impacts. Summarizing much of the literature, Schatan and Castilleja (2005) argue that lax environmental regulation and enforcement, while giving a cost advantage, ultimately imprisons Mexico in the low-value end of the market, excluding it from the high-value, "clean" product of the fabs north of the border. What they do not note is that this depression of the potential of Mexican fabs is typical of NAFTA's one-sidedness. High-value fabrication remains the preserve of the dominant economy in the partnership; while it suits the U.S.-based corporations that low-value and dirty production, from which they also benefit (albeit at a far lower profit per unit), be kept discrete. In the same way, the employment of young and often uneducated rural women makes competition for (or even theft of) intellectual property unlikely, while militating against workplace organization.

Ironically, the export of poverty-level employment and environmental recklessness as a result of NAFTA has had the foreseeable result that pollution is now crossing the border northward. According to the U.S. Environmental Protection Agency (EPA 2013), deforestation has increased runoff in the watershed of the Tijuana River, whose estuary lies in San Diego County, California. Runoff from storms carries with it fertilizers, pesticides, metals, and PCBs from the maquiladoras, as well as sewage from the unplanned expansion of slum housing along the river. Two major sewage spills in April 2012 totaling 4 million gallons emphasized the lack of adequate infrastructure for the massive population growth in the factory zones and for the poverty experienced by their inhabitants. The local San Diego paper (Lee 2012) reports that one result has been concentrations of drug-resistant genes in bacteria in the estuarine wetlands, which give onto a popular surf beach, genetic material that is traceable to human waste flowing down the river. Meanwhile in the twin cities of Ciudad Juarez and El Paso, on either side of the Chihuahua-Texas border, and in Nogales, which straddles the Sonora-Arizona border, air pollution travels without regard to boundaries, carrying ozone and particulate matter less than 10 μm ("PM 10"; even finer PM 2.5 dust is also included), dust so fine it penetrates deep into the lungs of air-breathing creatures (EPA 2007; Kelly 2012). On the one hand, this has allowed Nogales to claim exemption from federal air quality controls because the dust originates in Mexico, in the tradition of blaming the poor for pollution; while on the other promoting in both cities consumer-oriented campaigns to reduce domestic and automotive emissions while continuing to turn a blind eye to industrial pollution, especially that sourced from U.S.-owned or contracted plants. By no means does all of this water-borne or air pollution derive from the electronics industry, but it certainly contributes, and its workers are constrained to drink, wash in, cook with, and breathe the results.

Even without tracing the sources of minerals and energy used in fabrication, the processes employed are clearly already deeply embroiled not only in human but in nonhuman atmospheric and aquatic cycles, local and regional. The responsibility for the ecological fallout from these processes has frequently fallen on citizens and consumers, whose boycotts of sweatshop and environmentally dangerous goods and campaigns against industrial practices have been significant. It is clear, however, that corporations resist taking responsibility, spending vast sums on legal actions blocking charges against them, and on public relations campaigns (including the expensive scientists whose reports they commission). World Bank and IMF structural readjustment has historically been a tool for exporting capital from countries afflicted by it. Along with inward investment, GDP is the key measurement of performance that keeps a country free of this invasive procedure. Governments from Mexico to Taiwan and South Korea recognize the importance of their electronics industry to these measures. The blind eye turned to environmental and employment infringements is part of a strategy to defend their populations from even worse. To the extent that taking responsibility is a human action, we must infer that the refusal to recognize and take responsibility is not. While, with Latour (2005), it is important to acknowledge the involvement of the nonhuman in the networks of labor, manufacture, and waste involved in semiconductor fabrication, it is equally important to acknowledge the role of inhuman actors, primarily corporations, and beside them the political elites who, from incompetence, corruption, or Hobson's choice, abjure involvement, and ease the operation of corporate irresponsibility.

According to an industry journal, "optical fiber production should increase from 147 million kilometers of fiber in 2011 to 204 million in 2017" (Chaffee 2011): enough to go around the Earth almost sixteen thousand times. One reason the planet does not look like an immense ball of twine is that optic cables can carry many fibers, each the diameter of a human hair. The two component technologies of fiber optics are lasers, coherent light whose waves can be used to carry signals, and glass designed to make the most of the phenomenon of internal reflection, whereby the light waves bounce from the outer walls of the fiber without losing coherence or leaking out. In the mid-twentieth century, Corning Glass patented a method for depositing doped silica ash with a lower refractive index inside a tube of pure silica to control the light, and a system for extruding the result into thin fibers flexible enough to thread through utility ducts without either snapping or disrupting the flow of data.

Industrial production in the quantities currently being shipped is not an easy matter. The largest proportion of the glass is synthetic quartz crystals grown in autoclaves, specialized boilers combining high pressure and temperature imitating the geological conditions giving rise to natural quartz, but permitting control of crystallization in the correct structure for light transport. The process also requires very pure forms of silicon tetrachloride and germanium tetrachloride and highly purified oxygen, nitrogen, helium, chlorine, and sulfur hexafluoride, each of which requires significant amounts of energy to produce while, in the various purification processes, removing impurities that have then to be recycled. The quartz is formed into a tube and dried using chlorine before fine layers of the dioxides of silicon and germanium are deposited inside, each layer fused to glass with burners operating at 1,700 degrees Celsius. The richest layer of germanium oxide glass forms the operating core of the fiber. The tube is collapsed by heating again, then sleeved with another layer of quartz of a slightly different refractive index, ensuring the internal reflection is close to total, and heated once more to fuse the components into a single column known as the preform. Finally the preform is loaded into a furnace operating at 2,100 degrees Celsius and extruded to a diameter in the region of 125 microns, cooled in a helium tank, and coated with a protective acrylic plastic cured with ultraviolet light, at which point it is ready to use.

As the EU's *Best Available Techniques* document for the whole glass industry notes, "In general, the raw materials for glass making are readily available, relatively harmless, natural or man-made substances," while at the same time, "glass making is a high temperature, energy intensive activity, resulting in the emissions of products from combustion and the high-temperature oxidation of atmospheric nitrogen; i.e. sulphur dioxide, carbon dioxide, and oxides of nitrogen. Furnace emissions also contain dust arising mainly from the volatilisation and subsequent condensation of volatile batch materials" (Scalet et al. 2013, 2–3). They note in particular that the high temperatures involved, both in creating the preform and in extruding the fiber, release impurities in the raw materials, especially those derived from recycled glass, giving off hydrogen fluoride and hydrogen chloride as gases that can be scrubbed from the furnace chimneys before release, but which have to be kept apart from the extremely pure glass required for fiber optics to work over distance (Scalet et al. 2013, 276–77). Thus the Tri-Mer Corporation, promoting their Cloud Chamber Scrubber (CCS), notes, "The emissions from fiber optics manufacturing are a very serious challenge for conventional technology. The combination of submicron glass particles mixed with chlorine and hydrochloric gases creates a number of issues. The CCS removed both PM and gases at over 99% efficiency" (Tri-Mer 2014), leaving, however, the question of how the scrubbed waste particulate matter (PM) and gases are themselves handled after removal from the flues.

The majority of externally laid fibers (as opposed to those within buildings, which need less protection from ultraviolet and water) use polyamide plastics as the preferred jacket material insulating the fibers from one another and protecting them from the outside environment. This is the family of organic molecules, derived from oil, of which the most familiar is nylon. Fletcher (2008, 13) notes, "While details of the production sequence for nylon fibres are well known, information or analysis of its environmental impacts is not in the public domain," adding both that the derivation from oil places it in the nexus of fossil fuel politics discussed in chapter 1, and that production requires the use of complex chemicals, each of which requires separate processing, and large amounts of energy (each kilogram takes 150 megajoules) and water for lubrication and cleansing. Unsurprisingly, there is widespread concern over emissions from combustion to provide the energy, especially greenhouse gas NO_2, and potentially other chemical by-products, notably hydrogen chloride. Fletcher mentions that a single UK plant was thought to be responsible for 3 percent of the country's greenhouse gas emissions during the 1990s.

Though it is now being phased out, through the mid-2000s PVC was the cladding of choice for optical cables. Concerns over chlorides in plastics, especially PVC, led to information about it being more freely available. An important document in these debates was Baitz, Kreißig, and Byrne's (2004) life cycle analysis of PVC and alternative materials for a range of uses including cables. They point to six key moments of environmental risk: source extraction, transport, energy supply, production, use, and end of life. In production, raw PVC is brittle and breaks down under light and temperature. It therefore requires a number of additives to soften and stabilize it. These include phthalate plasticizers, lead, tin, zinc, barium, a number of organic antioxidants including organotins (organic compounds containing tin) and costabilizers, and (before 2001) cadmium. The basic materials are petroleum and salt, both of which need concentrated energy levels for chemical cracking to produce ethylene and electrolysis to produce chlorine. The former can release ethylene and propylene emissions to air, and methanol and propane/butane emissions to water; the latter risks both chlorine gas and hydrogen emissions and in some processes workplace exposure to chlorine, mercury, and asbestos, while the energy required for electrolysis is identified as a major source of CO_2 and SO_2 emissions (Baitz, Kreißig, and Byrne 2004, 51, 52). Dioxins, highly toxic organic compounds, are a by-product of manufacture, but today very carefully controlled and recycled into the process. The authors cite figures to suggest that over the previous fifteen years 3,000 tons of cadmium and some 100,000 tons of lead have been incorporated into PVC products in Europe. Because the plastic has a relatively long life in use and breaks down only gradually, the release of those metals back into the environment is hard to predict or control. Much PVC is landfill; much is incinerated, which can be a safe process but requires a lot of energy, even though the released heat can be used to power the plants where new PVC is manufactured; and much will be left in the ground or underwater. The report is exhaustive and, for the lay reader, exhausting, but indicates how much energy and what risks are associated with every phase of the manufacture of a common plastic, as well as the effects of plastic after use in the environment (for which see chapter 3). The details vary between PVC, polyamides, and polyethylene, the second most commonly used jacketing material for optical cable, but similar risks seem to be involved, from plasticizers leaking into the environment to the effects on workers and the environment of cleaning machinery, including chemical scrubbers.

Polyethylene is one of the plastics currently being manufactured not from petroleum but from sugarcane, corn, wheat, and sugar beet. This step has the virtue of reducing dependence on irreplaceable fossil geology, but like biofuels has the drawback of competing with food production for both land

and water. A life cycle assessment study of biopolymers (Tabone et al. 2010) associated their raw materials with fertilizer runoff and eutrophication (the stifling of life in lakes and rivers through the effects of fertilizers), and a significant contribution to ozone depletion, acidification, carcinogens, and other ecotoxicity measures as well as respiratory effects and smog. Though this compares poorly with oil-derived plastics, it is true that growing crops act as carbon sinks, and that in use these bioplastics have less effect on the environment and are more easily biodegradable (though another challenge rises from the difficulty of sorting bioplastics from other kinds in recycling plants). In an influential report for the World Bank in 2008, Donald Mitchell argued that the most significant contribution to rising food prices was EU and U.S. demand for biofuels, to which bioplastics might now be added. Competition for wheat, corn, and other foodstuffs drives up prices, increases the use of energy required to fertilize and harvest the crops in sufficient quantities to satisfy demand for fuels, and makes the impact of droughts and famines more severe than they would otherwise be. The drive to nonoil plastics is a result as much of geopolitical concerns about the insecurity of oil supplies (and the internal politics of promoting fears about energy security) as it is to do with environmental impulses. These challenges to the technical solutions offered by capital to the crises it has produced for itself suggest that there may be no technological solution that does not require energy, land, water, or other finite resources. Sustaining consumption of goods and energy may not be compatible with sustaining life.

We return to recycling in the next section, but one aspect of the postuse life of cable needs to be addressed here. It is largely because of the inevitable breakdown of plastics that the life expectancy of optic fiber cable is between fifteen and forty years. The difference can be explained by the different placing of cables: undersea, underground, or slung between poles, especially in countries like Japan and South Korea where fiber-to-the-home (FTH, the fabled "last mile") is widely installed. The effects of these environments, including exposure to ultraviolet in sunlight, contribute to the loss of flexibility and breakup of the polymers. Long-distance cables, such as those across the Atlantic and Pacific, require repeaters to boost the signal, which in turn require power sources. The combination of magnetic and thermal effects on aquatic life, on migration patterns for example, are unknown, and the impacts on the seafloor itself when cables are laid is little understood, although reports indicate that electromagnetic noise was causing sharks to attack deep-sea cables (Gibbs 2014). Similarly, according to OSPAR, the Oslo-Paris Convention for the Protection of the Marine Environment of the North-East

Atlantic, there is little research on the impacts of the noise of cable-laying vessels, the visual impact on sea life and bottom-feeding creatures like seals, the disturbance of previously deposited layers of contaminants, and the release of new ones as the cables age (Merck 2009).

The cost of laying a major network like the Southern Cross Cable Network linking the South Pacific, Australia, and New Zealand to the Internet can be over a billon dollars (Starosielski 2011). Negotiating landing rights can also raise both environmental and social frictions (Starosielski 2012), while licenses to dig trenches or tunnels to carry cable safely across land can be almost as expensive as the physical task of laying it (recalling that exposed fiber on poles will age more swiftly and therefore does not provide a cheaper option for trunk lines though it might be viable for short FTH runs). The temptation must be to overprovide capacity to allow for future growth without having to lay more fiber. But as the carrying capacity of new cable designs increases, following the Jevons paradox, demand follows it, creating the need for more fiber. Meanwhile as existing cables begin to break down under environmental pressures and release their freight of chemicals into the underground and undersea environments, we are unlikely to witness any grand cable reclamation schemes, likely to be at least as expensive as laying it in the first place. Undersea cables in particular will lie on the seabed for generations, with unknown consequences, as other cables are laid over them.

According to Harvey (2005, 157–58), "By 2000, IT accounted for about 45% of all investment, while the relative shares of investment in production and infrastructure declined," representing "an unfortunate bias in the path of technological change away from production and infrastructure formation into lines required by the market-driven financialization that was the hallmark of neoliberalization." While it is just about conceivable that consumers might be able to discover enough about the manufacture of a specific chip to make informed decisions about which kind of computer, phone, or game console to purchase, it is far less likely that they will be able to act on the kinds of optical cable their Internet service provider uses to connect to the global infrastructure of network communications. The decline in the use of PVC is largely due to the pressure of activists, concerned scientists, and those government officials who, despite being attacked as bureaucrats, have defended the environment against the worst predations of corporate capital. Even where there are adequate avenues for consumer pressure, and despite the enormous growth of Internet use among consumers, by far the largest proportion of Internet traffic is military and business-to-business, and of that the largest proportion, as Harvey adumbrates, is the finance sector. Elena Esposito (2011, 104) adds that the functioning of markets, and perhaps especially of derivatives, depends on the mutual observation of financial operators: a process that today demands a massively redundant self-surveilling network system. Given the absolute priority ascribed to the economy in the sociopolitical administration of global society, this situation leads to the downgrading of other claims to importance. Among them, the effects of these all-too-material networks on the environment are among the least prioritized.

A report commissioned as part of the UK government's Foresight project, largely inspired by the "Flash Crash" of May 6, 2010 (when the U.S. equity market dropped in the region of US$800 billion in a matter of minutes), noted of the new algo-trading:

> The novel aspects of the dynamics of markets with significant proportions of computer based high frequency traders include: (a) that interactions are taking place at a pace where human intervention could not prevent them—an important speed limit has been breached; (b) that, given this, computer based (and therefore mechanical) trading is almost obligatory, with all of the system-wide uncertainties that this gives rise to; (c) that information asymmetries then become more acute (and indeed different in nature) than in the past; and (d) that the source of liquidity provision has changed, to computer based and high-frequency trading, which has implications for its robustness under stress. (Foresight 2011, 8–9)

Under such conditions, estimates that anywhere from 50 to 80 percent of financial trading is now automated give a clue to the scale of traffic that fiber optics now carry, the requirement that any serious trader should employ these tools, and the strategic importance that traders, corporations, and governments attach to increasing the amount of fiber available for increasing volumes and speed of trading. Since at least 2007, before the current crisis, firms providing information for the finance industry have been employing computers to track data flows concerning price and trading trends, news that in turn is largely read not by the famed rational and informed subjects of economic theory but by other computers, converted into trades, and recycled again as news. The absence of human agency in these cycles is another indicator of the "too fast to control, too networked to fail" principle driving the potentially irresponsible expansion of environmentally unsound infrastructures in semiconductors and optic fiber.

It is equally clear that the strategy of empowering consumer choice to green the media industries is not applicable to fiber and chips, the largest and the smallest elements of the digital infrastructure. The myth of consumer choice as the driver of markets likewise has no place in the eco-critical analysis of workplace media and their infrastructures, even when these infrastructures are also integral to creative industries as well as their financiers. On the contrary, as we will see, consumer discipline, rather than choice, is a key element of the system, and it is this discipline that consistently degrades human and organic environments.

TRANSPORT

We have mentioned at several points already the significance of transport costs to digital media: The delivery of fiber optic cable to seabeds and underground conduits is only one of these. Raw materials have to be shipped to processing plants; processed minerals, fuel, and organic chemicals have to be freighted to factories and electricity generation plants; chips and subassemblies from offshore fabs have to travel to finishing plants; and finished goods have to be transported to wholesalers, retailers, and customers. One of the upshots of these transportation networks is that people too have had to migrate, away from destroyed homelands, or toward the centers where jobs are being created, with a smaller number of expensive cosmopolitan elites traveling to and fro between design, manufacture, and sales centers. As we have learned, digital equipment now uses at least as much energy as the airline industry, but the airline industry is also integrated into the digital production cycle, while road, rail, and especially maritime transport also form essential logistical parts of the making of a digital culture. We have already mentioned oil tankers, trains, and pipelines, and will raise the international maritime trade in waste electronic goods: Here we need to consider the significance of freight in the production chain and in delivery of finished goods to customers.

The global maritime container freight business handles up to 3 percent of global GDP at any given time. Because of the low-grade diesel fuel typically used on freighters, emissions from vessels in the global fleet contribute between 3 and 4 percent of global carbon dioxide emissions, significant amounts of sulfur (shipping fuel is allowed to contain up to 3.5 percent: U.S. long-haul trucks are restricted to 0.015 percent), and, of increasing concern, emissions of particulate matter in the form of black carbon (Pruzan-Jorgensen and Farrag 2010, 6). Oceana, an NGO devoted to protecting the marine environment, reported in 2010 that the simplest measures would reduce these emissions drastically: 35 percent cuts could be gained from a combination of slower steaming and propeller maintenance, for example.

Other proposals, several under consideration by the International Maritime Organization (IMO), which regulates open-ocean transport, focus on new kinds of fuel or using sail and kite as additional propulsion methods, new hull coatings, and waste heat recovery. These, however, can only be applied to newly designed and built ships, not to the existing global fleet: 58,900 cargo vessels in 2012, including over 6,000 liner vessels, huge container ships capable of carrying several warehouses' worth of stock. Without calculating for the effects of engine noise and turbulence on marine life, or spills of fuel and the occasional loss of a vessel, the sheer bulk of international maritime trade militates against any easy solutions. The IMO has been hard pressed to secure intergovernmental agreement on regulating black carbon emissions. In April 2016, even in the wake of the much-heralded Paris Agreement on the UN's Framework Convention on Climate Change, decisions were still pending in an argument at least six years old, with sticking points including the definition of black carbon and measuring methods, partly because, as an agreement between nations, international waters fall outside the terms of the Agreement. Efforts to stem emissions have clearly taken a back seat, as in the submarine cable business, to the urgent task of delivering the world's freight.

This urgency is compounded by the offshoring of manufacture. The fractured supply chain that brings semiprocessed raw materials to distant processing plants, delivers the primary material to manufacturers, takes components to subassembly plants and subassemblies to finishing, and thence to wholesalers and retailers and finally customers requires a vast network of road, rail, and seaborne transport, and a logistical system to match. That system is dependent on computers, and in certain respects feeds directly into the design of both computers and their application to labor (Neilson and Rossiter 2010). It also directs us toward the complex regulation of trade between the different priorities of traders, nations, and their component elements. Containerization itself was adopted as a way of minimizing both pilfering in dockyards and the power of dockworkers, whose numbers and political muscle plummeted after the old methods of hauling goods were abandoned. The adoption of RFID tagging in the container freight industry made the logistical management of goods far easier (Hayles 2009) and helped control smuggling. For at least a decade now, however, many governments have been as much if not more concerned with terrorism: with potential attacks on ports, or the use of enclosed containers to smuggle weapons and possibly combatants into their territory (Willis and Ortiz 2004). The rival priorities of trade and territorial integrity only increase the pressure on swifter transport times to make up for delays at borders, increasing fuel use, and air pollution. At the same time, they increase the pressure on logistics to smooth the path of trade goods through customs and security.

As the container industry modifies its practices to match emerging security regimes, one solution has been to identify those ports with direct shipments to the United States, and to insist that they install the same security as applied in the United States. This kind of standardization is feasible because there exists a set of at least partly agreed goals among key bodies like the IMO, various U.S. government agencies, the World Shipping Council, the UN Council on Trade and Development (UNCTAD), and the port authorities themselves. Yet it is equally clear that no such agreement is available for environmental protections. The added security at ports has a second function: It increases the surveillance opportunities for the management of dockworkers. While increasing the transparency of freight to customs and security, the new logistics increase their opacity to dockers in the same movement that makes them harder for smugglers and political opponents to access. At the same time, the logic of outsourcing and offshoring that drives the increase in maritime trade is also being applied to that trade itself, with increasing competition to provide deep-water ports and shore labor at the lowest competitive rates. This now includes dividing dockworkers between those in permanent employment and contract workers, with the latter frequently excluded from union membership and associated benefits (see Panimbang [2011] for an example of these practices and struggles against them in Indonesia). This breakdown of organizing power is the obverse of increasing logistical organization in the management of supply chains, in which human operatives are increasingly reduced to functions—governed by mechanically applied key performance indicators—of a regime that now bridges biopolitical management of resources, including human resources, with discipline, and both with the protocol logic of a system in which humans are treated as components, and their capacity for individual or collective action circumscribed as tightly as possible by the logic of the system (Galloway 2004).

Port cities are known for their migratory populations. Cities like Hamburg, Marseilles, San Francisco, and Liverpool have always been hubs for migrating populations, inbound and outbound, as well as for goods. Many have fostered slums, and most have nurtured intensive industries situated to take advantage of water transport. One effect of these population concentrations is persistent organic pollutants (POPs), especially polyaromatic hydrocarbons associated with sewage works and incomplete burning of fossil fuels like diesel, and with riverside industries including docks, boat dismantlers, oil refineries, and power stations. Especially in larger molecules, POPs are persistent because they are not water soluble and mix more easily with oily substances, and so tend to aggregate in sediment. Many are as old as the Industrial Revolution that powered the growth of the great ports, and are especially vulnerable to the kind of dredging often employed to open older ports to the deep-hulled liner ships now used for bulk transport. In many ports, especially in poorer regions (and port cities have often been the centers of poor regions), rivers are also a source of drinking water and fish. A particularly unpleasant characteristic of polyaromatic hydrocarbons is their association with mental health disorders in childhood, in addition to damage to DNA (Tang et al. 2012). Estuarine sediments are far easier to study than seabeds, and undoubtedly have higher concentrations of POPs than the open seas. But the principles are the same.

Maritime trade has always made use of the commons of the open water. It has a long tradition of throwing human and animal waste overboard and casting unwanted materials into the sea in emergencies. Human- and wind-powered vessels were relatively few and relatively low impact. The advent of steam, the development of mercantile empires, and the intensification of diesel-powered globalization increased the amount of traffic, the number of wrecks, and the levels of pollution in this commons. Lying, however, beyond national boundaries and the reach of most policing bodies, the open seas have ceased to be home to Foucault's (1986) ideal heterotopia of the ship, and have become, under regimes of competitive capital, accelerated modernity, and logistical protocols, victims of the true tragedy of the commons that follows on privatization.

The few protections that had been in place for shipboard labor were increasingly eroded in the 1970s' shift toward flags of convenience promising lower taxes, fewer rights for workers, and more lax environmental regulation (DeSombre 2006). When the ship ceased to be a piratical heterotopia, at least in imagination, and modified its historic, quasi-feudal, quasi-military organization of labor to become a floating extension of the factory conveyor belt, it entered into systems of control of planetary scale, from GPS to software designed for scheduling business events, allowing synchronization of travel times with available berths and land-based systems to coordinate expected arrivals at factory gates or retail stores. This global infrastructure and its miscellany of conflicting governance regimes shares its organizational diagram with the Internet itself, which it feeds with material supplies, and on which increasingly it depends for its activities. Like the cable infrastructure, it has risen from the operation of open markets to produce highly centralized industrial norms and concentrations of capital investment, in both ships and the systems (such as satellites and port facilities) required to monitor their movement, intense enough to exclude new entrants to the industry, or alternative means of transport sufficient for current levels of trade.

Maritime transport systems are also integrated into the tail end of the life cycle of digital media. The European Environment Agency "estimates between 250,000 tonnes and 1.3m tonnes of used electrical products are shipped out of the EU every year, mostly to west Africa and Asia," with Interpol stating that one in three inspected containers leaving European ports contained illegal e-waste (Vidal 2013). Legally, most countries now insist on domestic recycling of waste computers and mobile phones, and the same is true of waste materials from manufacture. Here land transport is key. Rust and Drange (2014), for example, show the migration of various toxic wastes from Californian Superfund sites—dumps recognized as especially dangerous by the EPA—to a variety of intermediary processing plants before, in at least some cases, making their way back to Californian landfills. They include a map for an important greening technology, carbon filters used to scrub particulate matter and noxious gases from fabs, noting the energy expended in treatment and transport, the expense, the low targets nonetheless unmet, and the production of new waste compounds from treatment of incoming waste materials.

This suggests, once again, that technological solutions for technological problems may not be any more sustainable than the problems they set out to solve. It is worth reiterating that the major function of container fleets and land transport is not business-to-consumer but business-to-business delivery, including legal and illegal shipments to legal and illegal recycling zones, and consequently that consumer power has little chance of impacting industry practice. Likewise, while open networks, software, and hardware initiatives can moderate the environmental impacts of digital media, these very large infrastructures have evolved to exclude competition from alternative modes of supply. Two strategies therefore propose themselves. First, the much-maligned role of states is critical in running ports, including the majority that have been taken out of public ownership and handed to private capital. Ironically, the demand for security, replacing older tax collection regimes minimized in neoliberal free trade treaties, reaffirms the state's role in port inspections, the only places where regulation of environmental infringements can realistically be enforced. Second, while it is unlikely that transoceanic trade, in data or goods, can be curtailed, the carriage of subassembled parts that constitutes such a large proportion of trade, along with the bulk carriers of mineral ores, could be minimized by a logistics that concerned itself with reducing the distances between raw materials, subassembly, and end users. Driven by exclusively economic efficiencies, the idea of environmental efficiency does not figure in contemporary logistical software and practice. Where corporations have punished workforces for raising wages and living standards by exporting their jobs to low-wage and low-protection regimes, they have increased the amount of traffic required to move goods and part goods around the world, an inefficiency that would be resolved by onshoring those old employments.

There are problems with each of these solutions. The state has, since the later 1970s, become increasingly vulnerable to corporate power, and more constrained by treaty obligations framed in the neoliberal polity that has reigned since the 1980s. Corruption, as noted above, is rife precisely where austerity measures have lowered the numbers and pay of government employees. Reterritorializing manufacture would create crises of unemployment not only in relatively wealthy countries like Taiwan, South Korea, and China, but in Southeast Asia, the Philippines, and Mexico. Huge numbers of rural migrants have arrived, often illegally, in new manufacturing districts—250 million rural migrants have moved to the cities in China alone ("The Great Transition" 2014), the largest migration in human history. Shifts in global trade impact heavily on migrant workers who suddenly find themselves without livelihoods when firms close, or sectors move production elsewhere (Harvey 2005, 148–49). In such a closely integrated system, simple solutions are as unsatisfactory as technical solutions are in the example examined above concerning bioplastics.

This is not to argue that we should cease campaigning for state regulation and enforcement of environmental standards, or that social as well as economic values should not be included in any calculus of benefit from changes in the digital media supply chain. Least of all is it to argue against new forms of social organization. The individualist model of consumer choice has limited effects: Social organization, such as that undertaken by global networks of dockworkers, is alone of a scale needed to operate in these terrains. Prior to the major assaults on it in the later 1970s and 1980s, organized labor had become tainted by protectionism, sexism, and racism to the point that it began to lose its legitimacy, but this is no reason not to both reform trade unions, a process that has been advancing for thirty years, and devise new forms of social action. The grounds of social action are always the existing conditions of society. To understand what forms such social action might take, we need first to understand more about what is often said to be the greatest obstacle it faces: contemporary consumerism.

Workers in the north suffer from the export of jobs to offshore and out-sourced subcontractors. They envy the industrial employment of their circum-Pacific neighbors. On the other hand, typically in the dark about racism in the EU and the segregation of U.S. society, with its vast African American, Hispanic, indigenous, and migrant underclass, workers in off-shore fabs envy the levels of consumption available to their North American and European opposite numbers. The geography of this new division of labor is complex but can be expressed as the increasing spatial divorce of produc-tive and consumptive work. Consumption becomes work when, under con-ditions of produsage, it is undertaken not for the fulfillment of needs or the realization of aspirations, but as a disciplined function required by capital to remove the excess product manufactured in the pursuit of expanded ac-cumulation and growth. For capital to continue to grow, the working class of the wealthy nations now has as its chief function not mass production but the mass consumption of excess product, in cycles such as that leading from overconsumption of junk food to overconsumption of pharmaceuti-cals, exercise, and diet products to counter its effects.

Parallel to the transformation of factory discipline into consumer dis-cipline in the Global North lies the restructuring of consumerism. Under classical conditions, consumption came after the economic cycle. After pur-chase, commodities lost their relevance to exchange, becoming once again pure use values. Today, and since Keynes, consumption itself has been drawn back into the economic. Given recurrent crises of overproduction, consumer discipline is oriented toward training the consumptive class in what they are supposed to consume, a process in which the mutual instruction of consum-ers by consumers, for example through social media, is an intrinsic part. As in the factory, there is a strict hierarchy of these compulsory enjoyments, marked for example by the taste hierarchies of newspapers, magazines, radio stations, and TV broadcasting. The phenomenon Bourdieu (1986) analyzed as cultural capital has become, through the personal targeting encouraged by online advertising and marketing tools, a way of breaking down the soli-darity of cultural collectives by instructing individuals in what they are sup-posed to desire. The sheer repetitiveness of particular tropes of sexualized imagery is an indicator of the lack of trust corporations place in their con-sumers, finding it necessary to remind them over and over, in case they for-get, how to be desiring machines responding reliably to symbolic triggers. Consumer discipline, unlike factory discipline, instructs us not how to operate socially but how to operate antisocially: from mode of production to mode of destruction. The industrial mode of production after automation increases beyond reason the amount of stuff to be used up. The consumerist mode of destruction takes this stuff out of the economic cycle, leaving nothing in its wake but debt and externalities. Thus responsibility for accidental spillages, toxic waste, and carbon footprints passes to the productive (the attribution of this or that disaster to human error) and consumptive workers (the attribution of environmental damage to consumer choice).

A constant of the division of production from consumption is the migration of aesthetic labor and enjoyment to the elites, and a parallel anesthesia—deprivation of the senses and eradication of aesthetic pleasures—of the workers. In the productive realm, this is easy to see in the degradation of working and living environments and of the surrounding country; among consumers it is grounded in the depreciation of skills associated with living well, such as home cooking, homemade clothes, handcrafted furniture, and vernacular architecture. In their place, value-added manufacture provides standardized products with customized additions (T-shirt emblems, a differently colored front door), while comedians vie with one another to deride amateur music or home-knitted garments. This is not to suggest that popular culture has not produced works of great depth and beauty, but that the industrial structure of their production and dissemination scrapes away their intimacy, devalues their capacity for permanence, and through celebrity cultures and intellectual property regimes diminishes the possibility of communities taking ownership of the cultural events on offer. For the producers and consumers of streaming audio services, the object of consumption is not individual works but music in general. In this sense, consumption moves to occupy itself no longer purely with use values but with exchange values. Marx distinguished between living labor, the production of use values, and objectified labor, its abstract form, which produces not things but exchange value, "undifferentiated, *socially necessary general labour*, utterly indifferent to any particular content" (Marx 1976, 993, original emphasis). What he could not predict was that this indifference to particular content would become a characteristic not only of factory labor but of disciplined consumption.

Bifo notes of informational labor that "it means the distribution of value-producing time regardless of its quality, with no relation to the specific and concrete utility that the produced objects might have" (Berardi 2009b, 75). The meanings and pleasures of cultural forms, he implies, have been lost in the semiocapitalism that reduces shared symbols to exchange values. It follows that the consumption of symbols has, like labor, lost its materiality, its specific and concrete utility. Its place is taken by payment for the consumed goods and services and the value generated by paying attention to the advertising embedded in the flow of media. Thus the division of labor between those forced to work and those forced to consume, while unjust and divisive, is at least equitable in divorcing both productive and consumptive working classes from meaning and pleasure. In production for exchange, the concrete, intimate reality of use turns into the abstraction of the commodity. In parallel, the warmly sensual pleasures of the aesthetic turn into methodical consumption, the opposite of aesthetic: anesthetic. It is then not consumerism as such but the division of production from consumption that minimizes the possibility of comprehending the system in its entirety, and therefore the possibility of a common revolt against abstraction and anesthesia.

This anesthesia extends to the loss of truth to materials in media, specifically truth about the foundation of media technologies in the material environment. Metaphorically, it might be feasible to speak of certain forms of media message as toxic (pornography, race hatred), but discursive violence should be distinguished from actual toxicity. In this instance, the metaphor hides the truth of toxic media, the toxicity of production processes integral to the integrated circuit. The same is true of the digital sweatshop, those call centers and data-processing centers where the semiotic labor of shifting symbols or converting human conversations into data are undertaken in states of high abstraction. Digital labor, the work of translating into symbols and manipulating those symbols, already has a high degree of abstraction in terms of the relation between workers and content, in much the same way that the division of labor in the subassembly supply chain deprives workers of a relationship to any finished product. But that abstraction is driven to a higher level by the mock-Hegelian logic that Bifo identifies: "Absolute Knowledge is materialized in the universe of intelligent machines. Totality is not History but the virtual assemblage of the interconnections preprogrammed and predetermined by the universe of intelligent machines. Hegelian logic has thus been made true by computers, since today nothing is true if it is not registered by the universe of intelligent machines. . . . When History becomes the development of Absolute Computerized Knowledge difference is not vanquished: it becomes residual, ineffectual, unrecognizable" (Berardi 2009b, 73).

Bifo comically overstates the universality of these machines that capture and codify the wisdom and skills of previous generations: Their claim to universality only appears so from within the universe of intelligent machines. Similarly, the market presents itself as universal, but only so long as we are within the market. In fact, everything the market excludes as externality nonetheless retains its reality. The environment, whose exteriority to the market is a perpetual and nagging contradiction of its claim to universality, is real all the same. Similarly, from the standpoint of the market, human labor, in production or consumption, is given, like the environment, in that capital does not pay for its reproduction or education. Human populations remain real, even though they are external in the sense that waste product, or indeed junk product, is regularly dumped into them as into reservoirs, with no account taken of potentially lethal effects. In the cyborg logic of the corporation, human difference is now an externality: a source of creativity to be exploited, and a sump for disciplined consumption of excess production.

The falling rate of profit that drove the 1970s crisis resulted in a new biopolitics, displacing the body at work to a broader activity of reproduction (the service sector boom of the 1980s) and distributed manufacture analyzed above, guided by statistical models of risk first developed to manage the balance of bad debts against disciplined repayments. But Théorie Communiste (2011) are wrong to argue that the working class is no longer working and therefore has no identity, no economic purpose, and thus no politics. First, production carries on under other conditions and away from the heartlands of capital. Second, the old working class, now precarious, migrant, and casualized, has the job of taking on the debts produced by the constant crises arising from borrowing from future projections to pay for past crises in the capitalist system. Third, equipped with computers and credit cards, their unpaid creative labor in street fashion, music, and social media is the lifeblood of an increasingly standardized capitalism decreasingly capable of creativity. And fourth, the old working class has become the affectless, disenchanted class of consumers whose work is to consume the devalued goods produced by overproduction's attempt to escape the falling rate of profit. Their new task is to provide the disciplined labor required to destroy that overproduction in pursuit of the very growth that otherwise generates crisis. The precariat—the class of workers who have only short-term contracts, often migrants with few social benefits—generated by offshoring, the end of welfare, and the destruction of working-class organization in the 1980s still has two final functions: to borrow, and to use its loans to consume. This purposeless cycle, whose misery was performed by rioters for the surveillance cameras of London in August 2011, belongs to the metropolitan precariat's disciplined mode of destruction. The carnival of destructive riot is only a breakdown of discipline and debt repayment, an instinctively brutal reaction to debt peonage in the same way that sabotage was a refusal of factory discipline. As factory sabotage fails to confront the mode of production, consumer riots fail to challenge the mode of destruction.

Semiocapitalism divides its derivation of wealth from handling symbols into two sectors. One sector operates through international regimes of patents, copyrights, trademarks, and designs, the other through finance and computerized algorithmic ('algo') trading. Those who are not privileged to sit at the center of intellectual and finance capital produce a diminishing amount of the exchange value in each commodity. Those who can, or are forced to, work. Too often such workers are treated like the victims of the Bangladeshi factory collapse of April 2013: supernumerary, unregarded, a repressed that returns only momentarily as news item. Those who cannot are abandoned to civil war, famine, and disease, conditions that, in the case of the Congolese war, have persisted for over a decade as the unconscious of metropolitan consumption (United Nations 2002). Meanwhile, metropolitan lumpen proletariat populations superfluous to both intellectual work and offshore industry, with diminishing health, education, and social resources, prey to drugs and guns, are pushed further into ghettos that increasingly resemble the reservations set aside for indigenous peoples in the genocidal heyday of settler expansion. With the abdication of vision common to parliamentary parties of the industrialized and in many instances the industrializing world, the only organic intellectuals left are the gangs, building alternative economies and confronting the police in an ethnoclass war to secure human status (Wynter 2003). Between civil war and gang war, the trajectory of the mode of destruction instigated by consumerism would appear to lead to the autodestruction of the consumer class. That this course—punitive debt conditions risking the terminal desuetude of the populations it relies on to make and to consume—is suicidal does not register in the ethos of the cyborg for which profit alone is calculable, and all other effects are simply left out of account.

Bifo concludes that "difference is not vanquished: it becomes residual, ineffectual, unrecognizable" (Berardi 2009b, 73). The indifference of capital is twofold: the indifference of commodities when anything can be exchanged indifferently for anything else that diminishes cultural difference, Bifo's argument, but also indifference to externalities, both human and ecological. This second indifference is premised on the universality of neoliberalism, which is however already premised on its externalities and incapable of functioning without them. To the extent that both workers and environment are now external to capital, they are thrust out of the universe of neoliberalism. At the same time, the IFC/World Bank (2007) note on "the assimilative capacity of the environment" places a demand on ecological systems to provide the unpaid work of dealing with the fallout of semiconductor production, a demand equally borne by fab workers, while at the same time requiring individual workers and consumers to shoulder responsibility. To the extent that produsers and workers undertake that responsibility, they typically either collapse into inaction before the scale of the task, or move toward a kind of bitter indifference. When the ideological weight placed on the family became unsustainable in the 1950s and 1960s, there was a rush to divorce; when the weight of ideological individualism is crushing, the individual falls apart. This implosion of the self can appear in mental illness, a frequent accompaniment to sweatshop labor made frighteningly public in the Foxconn suicides (Moscaritolo 2013; Taffel 2012). Alternatively, realizing that the self is no longer the source of action can lead to participation in group formation and political activism and a turn toward a new politics of nature. Moving beyond finite media will demand not only a sustainable community of workers but equally a sustainable commons embracing workers and consumers, and beyond that a communion of workers, consumers, and environment.

Marx observed that in the commodity, "the relation of the producers to the sum total of their own labour is presented to them as a social relation, existing not between themselves, but between the products of their labour" (1976, 164). Eco-critique adds: In the commodity form, the relationship between producers, produsers, consumers, and the externalized environment appears in disguise, hiding the true involvement of all four under the sign of exchange value. At the same time, the reverse of Marx's formulation is also true: Today, relations between things (commodities) appear to us in the fantastical guise of a relationship between people. Most obviously in social media, we believe we are experiencing interpersonal and even genuinely social relationships, whereas in fact what we are experiencing is a relationship between proprietary sequences of code on proprietary platforms in which ostensible actors are in fact playing the part of commodities ("Brand Me"). Once again, however, we should be attuned to the fact that among the things that are thus disavowed in this new fetishization of social media relations are both real relations between people and real relations between people and their nonhuman environments. Any commons on which sustainable media might be built involves a migration from the bogus universality of capital to the active integration of the undifferentiated human and nonhuman, declaring their mutual incompletion and need for support, and producing a politics in which the question "How are we to live?" might at the very least be posed, and without which it cannot be answered.

Governance

The Earth is one but the world is not.
—Brundtland Report, 1987, 1A, 1

INTEGRAL WASTE

The four great challenges of contemporary political life are global trade, the Internet, human migration, and safeguarding the environment. Of the four, global trade has achieved a kind of conflicted peace. Finance is free to move. Although financial crises and competition between economic sectors, institutions, and governments create exceptions, sleights of hand like corporate bankruptcy allow amazing fluidity. Data, which as we have seen are integral to the movement of finance, are likewise almost entirely unrestricted. However, data are subject to far more regulation. Crime, terrorism, pornography, spam, identity theft, intellectual property, and the security of online trade are among the themes addressed in the major international forums where Internet governance is addressed. The Internet functions despite being at the center of what commentators refer to variously as a "battle" or "war" (deNardis 2014; battleforthenet.com). Many governments impose significant political as well as moral censorship on Internet services. Silos of encrypted or payment- and password-protected data are common. In the hactivist slogan attributed to Stewart Brand, "Information wants to be free," but data are everywhere in chains. On the other hand, falling costs of information transfer, the seemingly inevitable vulnerability of all communications to leaks and attacks, and the overwhelming demand of capital for instant and total mobility are constant pressures to reduce restrictions to the barest minimum. Media governance is shaped by the argument between the freedom of information to move and the restriction of data to authorized users.

Freedom of human movement, meanwhile, is subject to increasingly virulent restrictions, not only in Australia, the EU, and the United States but in civil wars like that between the state of Israel and its Palestinian citizens, and in insurgencies like those of the Islamic State and Boko Haram. Restricted immigration confronts forced emigration, often by ethnic cleansing pioneered in colonial clearances and the reservation system in settler colonies. Other migrations are driven by flexible accumulation, the new organization of capital emerging after the crash of 1973 that David Harvey (1989, 147) describes as "flexibility with respect to labour processes, labour markets, products and patterns of consumption," involving increasingly precarious employment, offshoring, and outsourcing, increasingly rapid product cycles, and an internationally mobile labor force. The economic migrants so often decried by metropolitan politicians are mobile not because they want to leave home but because their economic survival demands it. Thus while money can move at will and data within limited constraints, people are both restricted and compelled to move or to stay. Movements of money are relatively unsupervised, so much so that money laundering has begun to worry even the world's financial centers. The Internet includes enclaves of intense security and others of untrammelled exchange. Meanwhile, the movements of people are highly managed. Cosmopolitan elites are by and large free to go where they will, but all others are governed by complex sets of international agreements and surveillance operations like the EU/NATO Mare Nostrum, intended to survey and quell Mediterranean migrations from Africa in Europe (Heller and Pezzani 2014).

The environment shares features with all three. It is subject to what the current jargon calls multistakeholder governance, involving not only nation-states but markets, expert bodies, and civil society organizations, which, however, in the case of environmental action have not produced shared policies, institutional forms, or convincing instruments to effect change. Like trade and the Internet, the environment continues to function but is surrounded by threats. Like migrants, it is subject to regimes of exclusion, especially from political debate, where it is spoken for and spoken about but has no voice of its own.

The term *governance* describes a regime outside government (which properly speaking is the exclusive domain of the state). Governance comprises a mixture of state policies, legal instruments, and norms of behavior modeled on systems used in corporate management. This section begins with the politics of waste as a problem of governance. It looks at the physical detritus from the orgy of consumption that has powered both the unchallenged accumulation of wealth and the political stability of wealthy countries in order to understand both its scale and why there have been so few attempts to raise it as a political issue, or to create political solutions for its management. This analysis leads to an analysis of another global system, the Internet, in which instruments for governance, fragile and subject to attack from both markets and nation-states, have evolved in the last forty years robustly enough to maintain a surprisingly accessible and democratic communication space. Internet governance analysts rarely turn to environmental issues, seeing them as not exclusive to the Internet (being shared with other communication media and thus beyond the remit of Internet-specific policy bodies). Yet in a number of instances, including Green MPEG, analyzed below, environmentalist discourse is echoed in the language, if not the practice, of governance. By analyzing the current forms of governance through which decisive policies are formulated and implemented, we can examine what options are open for the management of waste and of other issues in digital media's environmental impacts, and determine whether we have inherited a polity capable of taking action to ameliorate the condition of the global environment.

Contemporary accumulation continues colonialism in the Global South (exocolonialism), and internally in the Global North (endocolonialism). This section argues that colonial governance also provides the model for managing the waste products of neoliberalism in a process that turns both natural world and parts of the human population into environments, in this case dumping grounds for excess products. We will also see how the principles of waste and its management and the process of environmentalization are conducted at the microscopic level of Internet technologies, feeding back into the evacuation of meaning and affect from environments as they were previously from the economy.

Waste is not an unfortunate by-product of consumerism. Without waste, there can be no consumer capital. Waste takes the form not only of garbage or of waste electrical and electronic equipment (WEEE in EU parlance) but also of populations excluded from the centers of capital. The undoubted catastrophe of WEEE and the consistently colonial structure of the recycling industry can no longer be seen as curable aberrations: We live in the age of integral waste. This is not only the waste produced by the built-in obsolescence required to generate new debt for new sales of new equipment to disciplined consumers in the new mode of destruction, but the endemic structural waste produced by typical neoliberal industries such as electricity generation and transmission. Even prior to the privatization of national energy grids, energy industries were built in order to waste power. The process goes as far back as the enclosures of common land in the period of primitive accumulation, from the late medieval period to the early Industrial Revolution.

Primitive accumulation refers to the beginnings of capitalism in the mass expropriation of common lands and the displacement of their populations, who thereby became the free laborers on which industrial capital depended. The history of primitive accumulation is indistinguishable from the histories of both the environment and of colonialism. The word *colonizing* describes the process of taking over a territory while at the same time excluding it from participation in the colonizing power. Thus if we say that capitalism has colonized the production of energy for heat and light, the term is partly metaphorical but also indicates a historical continuity. Capital has always colonized new areas because it is compelled to expand by the law of the falling rate of profit: There are close parallels between exocolonialism—territorial expansion—on the one hand and endo- (inward) colonization of energy and other public goods on the other. The first great enclosure effected by nascent capital in the era of primitive accumulation was the enclosure of common land. For millennia, the poor had supplemented their crops and husbandry with grazing, hunting, gathering plants and fruits, and collecting fuel in commonly held woods and waters. The European enclosures of the early modern period seized what had been common land and alienated the peasants from it, increasing their dependence on landowners and later on urban landlords and employers. The newly privatized commons divided land between legally protected domain and lawless wilderness. The etymology of the word *wilderness* reveals significant ambiguities: In Anglo-Saxon, where the word first appeared, it signified an area set aside for wild deer, a domain protected from peasants and poachers (those still acting as if the wild belonged to everyone) to ensure the nobles the best hunting. In the colonial era, wilderness still meant an area conserved, either for privileged colonial hunters or, later and equally controversially, for Western scientists and the tourists who followed them. More recently, such conservative conservation has been increasingly allied with neoliberal development policy. In its exclusion from these enclosed hunting reserves, and consequent combination with even wilder landscapes left out of the enclosures like mountains and open seas, the remainder, which came to be called nature and later environment, was associated with the most dangerous places, and the ones most inimical to human habitation. On one hand, these provided artists, and thinkers like Kant and Burke, with models of the sublime, an inhuman other as gateway to the Spirit. On the other, it presented an estranged nature defined by being beyond human (Williams 1973, 127–41). This process of splitting the world between human and nonhuman is the basic form of environmentalization. In enclosures, nature ceases to be the common inheritance of all and instead becomes either alienated property or the savage site of threat. The more humans defined themselves over against nature, the more they defined nature over against themselves, in this way formalizing and enforcing the split between the natural environment and humanity, which in the process became a nonnatural, religious, or rational quality.

With peasants forbidden to collect firewood from the old commons, a division of labor between suppliers and consumers of energy emerged, which later structured the development of coal mining, and later still huge electricity-generating and distribution projects, which had the added benefit of becoming too big to allow competitors to enter the market. Without being too romantic about the past, proximity to nature in the commons meant that renewable fuel could be cheaply gathered, and used with minimal waste. The inbuilt waste inherent in a centralized electricity-generating system, on the contrary, guarantees that corporations are paid for energy that cannot be consumed, while the environmental impact is dissipated even beyond the reach of carbon trading, since the waste heat is released not at the point of production but over the network as a whole.

This integral waste functions environmentally in both senses: It is dispersed into the remains of the commons—air and water in particular—and it can be treated as an economic externality. This concerns not only climate change but the reduction of superfluous populations to externalities condemned, as in the case of recycling villages of Africa, India, and China, to bear the brunt of the waste inherent in resolving crises of overproduction. The same is true of the extraction of precious metals, clustered in regions previously thought desolate enough to be turned into reservations for the unwanted indigenous populations of settler colonialism: the Keystone XL pipeline, catastrophic oil pollution in the headwaters of the Amazon, the removal of Suomi from their traditional reindeer-herding territories in favor of oil drilling in the now-thawing Arctic, or the repeated protests of Koara and other traditional peoples against displacement, sickness, and permanent damage to country from uranium mines in Western and South Australia. Sassen argues that populations no longer deemed economically useful in the metropolitan centers as well as in the developing world are similarly being expelled from the calculations of the economic. Unemployed people are increasingly written out of the statistical account of GDP, while welfare cuts reduce the count of those who are deemed to participate in what remains of society. This process parallels the exclusion of indigenous peoples and the sub-subcontracted waste pickers of the digital dumps of the Global South. This waste of people points then to the thesis, explored in the final part of this section, that whole sectors of the world population are themselves becoming externalities. In chapter 3 we will see how they also become environmental.

GOVERNING WASTE

Rust belts have become a commonplace of neoliberal geography. Concentrated in these waste landscapes are the effluvia that are no longer of account to the bankrupt companies that have abandoned them. Waste is a way of destroying the fruits of overproduction without incurring costs that need to be charged to the overproducers. As economic externality, waste is not an unfortunate by-product of the pursuit of wealth: Under current conditions, waste is integral to industrial and finance capital's equation of environments with externalities. Integral waste is at the core of the neoliberal mode of destruction and its redirection of wealth away from both populations and environments toward ever-smaller elites. The function once served by conspicuous consumption is now served by conspicuous and inconspicuous waste. Those who make their livings in the vast waste dumps of the Global South know and experience waste in their senses and their cells, but from the point of view of the economy, it is mere externality, a necessary corollary of growth, but not therefore accounted as a cost against growth. On the contrary, the cost-free externality of the natural environment means that dumping has no economic cost and is therefore excluded from the calculation of benefits and losses. This is how waste becomes integral.

The scale of the problem is by now widely acknowledged, and some aspects associated with resource extraction and manufacture have already been covered in this book. The Basel Action Network's (2002, 2005) influential reports opened many activists' eyes to the illegal global trade in waste electrical and electronic equipment, a theme that has continued to be addressed in social and United Nations forums. Grossman (2007) and Gabrys (2010) have devoted whole books to electronic waste, and Maxwell and Miller (2012) devote considerable space in theirs to the issue. Perhaps no symbol, other than the polar bear on an ice floe, encapsulates the trashing of the planet so precisely as the Great Pacific Garbage Patch (Moore and Phillips 2011), but we might as easily point to Werner Herzog's stunning documentary *Lessons of Darkness* (1992) with its portrait of the burning Kuwaiti oil fields, or Sebastião Salgado's apocalyptic photography of the goldmines of the Serra Pelada in the 1980s. To recite once again the litany of metals, plastics, and chemicals would serve little purpose. We already noted the preponderance of increasingly rare minerals like indium in waste sites; Li-ion batteries contain small but significant amounts of nickel and cobalt, two very valuable minerals that might pay for their extraction. But because valuable metals are wrapped in plastics or hidden inside larger assemblages like screens or motherboards, getting at them is uneconomically time-consuming unless the underpaid workers in recycling villages burn off the worthless plastics, releasing their freight of organic molecules into the air and water. Some recent technologies like modern plasma screens, which bombard phosphors with liberated ions for a hundred thousand hours before end of life, have yet to enter the waste cycle: No one knows what their chemistry will produce. The labor of recycling is dirty, dangerous, and bitterly underpaid; the places where it is conducted are polluted beyond belief, and require a transport and logistics operation of global span. Yet this is a more economic system than retaining the waste at home and dealing with it mechanically. Waste is a matter of waste people and waste places as well as waste materials. It is for this reason that those zero-waste activists who argue that waste should be referred to as a "resource" (Palmer 2005) are incorrect. Even though there is every reason not to cast materials aside and to recognize the value that remains in waste, the word *resource* suggests that waste can be resolved inside an economic system whose treatment of environments as resource has already proved disastrous. The argument presented here is that waste extends well beyond unwanted materials to include a founding principle of contemporary capital: material, human, and environmental waste is essential to meet growth targets.

Digital media are responsible globally for seven kilos of waste per person per year, totaling 50 million tons in 2012: Huabo et al. (2013, 24) estimate 177 million used mobile phones were dumped in 2010, encouraged by the planned obsolescence of the technology. Like old TVs, computers, and games consoles, the majority of this waste equipment goes to landfill at home, or is exported in defiance of international law as enshrined in the Basel Convention on the Control of Transboundary Movements of Hazardous Wastes and Their Disposal, a treaty ratified by every nation in the world bar two: Haiti and the United States of America, who both signed without ratifying. Export is open to the risks of transport by road, rail, and sea noted in earlier chapters. The waste products of energy, manufacture, and end-of-life disposal include radioactive minerals with half-lives measured in tens of thousands of years, and minerals like titanium, upheld by the industry as a low-energy alternative to aluminum (Allwood and Cullen 2011, 46, 141) and a major feature in casings for laptops and mobiles, which does not decompose for thousands of years. The handling of waste in recycling villages in West Africa, India, and China is notorious for its association with high rates of childhood cancers and shortened life expectancy, without mentioning the toxification of the local ecology. Those that go to landfill leach their component elements and compounds more slowly but with equally deadly effect.

The 4RS approach—reduce, reuse, recycle, and recover—adopted by many environmental agencies is certainly one way to lower the number of devices thrown away, but it places an ethical obligation on end users, including institutions like universities, hospitals, and small entrepreneurs, rather than on the design of devices or the economics of disposal. Parallel efforts toward sustainable design are undoubtedly sincere but also require alternative materials and the energy needed to turn them into workable products that, moreover, have to compete with the glossy and often cheaper products of more wasteful competitors. While ethical and individual work on disciplined consumption along with ethical design may contribute to lessening the problem, its scale and global reach require a political rather than an ethical response. This in turn raises the risk of green fascism, sacrificing democratic process to what it is hard not to paint as demands for emergency political remedies. There is, equally, risk associated with engaging the market as the solution for the problems that the market has produced. This is the problem with emissions trading, through which rich countries and corporations can shift the burden of their polluting to poor countries and populations, without resolving the initiating problem. Politically imposed concepts of environmentalism and market solutions based on them both feature in the discourse of sustainable development adopted by the World Bank, which makes them conditions of its partnerships with social movements and NGOs as well as government departments in developing nations, many of which it has had a hand in establishing. Assessing these developments, Goldman argues that "the environmental states emerging around the world today are marked by the specific needs of transnational capital, which are shaping the form of legality and eco-rationality that have prevailed in Southern countries. Green-neoliberal pressures have fragmented, stratified, and unevenly transnationalized Southern states, state actors, and state power in ways that defy simple definitions of modernization" (2005, 183).

Goldman argues that the green policies adopted by agencies like the World Bank are in fact deeply political in that they encourage care for the environment (and for other people) only in forms that serve the interests of the specific form of economic rationality they have adopted as an item of faith, neoliberalism. The discourse of sustainable economies combines neocolonial conservationism with neoliberal adherence to market values, rezoning whole areas of the country under imported environmental designations in the interests not of nationalizing but transnationalizing territorial resources: building sustainable dams, for example, in the interests of entering the global trade in energy, rather than nurturing local culture, agriculture, or pisciculture. In Goldman's critique, powerful development agencies like the World Bank shape policy and legal structures in their client governments to produce a new kind of neoliberal colony, the "environmental state." Traditionally, national governments had the task of protecting their populations and land against foreign incursion. These environmental states, Goldman argues, have been brought into a specific kind of environmental rationalism that serves the interests, no longer of foreign states, but of economic globalization. Neoliberal environmentalism—sustainable development—is one of the phenomena that underpins the fractured nature of global, local, and municipal waste management. It is also a good example of the diffusion of responsibilities between international treaty bodies, corporate interests, and national and local government, a diffusion that makes it hard to discern which agencies have responsibility for waste.

Zero-waste activists have usefully emphasized the hierarchies existing within waste. One such hierarchy concerns those materials that are easily identified and recovered from domestic and workplace refuse: aluminum cans, glass, and paper are relatively easily sorted and relatively valuable. Complex artifacts of the kind forming digital waste, and complex materials like many forms of plastic, are less easily sorted and recycled. Swiftly biodegradable waste is relatively easily handled and relatively valuable, more persistent forms of waste less so. Materials at the lower end of these hierarchies—those that are both persistent and complex—are the ones that tend to enter the equally complex flows of waste between territories. Municipal and national governments can come to serious conflict over the siting of recycling plants, landfills, and incinerators, but are likely to agree on the need to manage persistent complex waste away from population centers, setting in train the transport cycle.

At the same time, waste also appears in less immediately physical and remediable forms, especially in air and water pollution, neither of which is easily restricted to a particular location. Often directly caused by waste processing, atmospheric and water pollution each have their own guardians: national and international bodies, UN agencies, expert groups, advocacy-based NGOs, and social movements working to resolve their production and mitigation. Biermann and colleagues (2009, 18) estimate that "in global environmental politics more than 700 multilateral agreements are in force. Most have evolved independently, cover different geographic and substantial scopes, and are marked by different patterns of codification, institutionalization, and cohesion." Though Biermann's team is guardedly supportive of this fragmentation, we have seen in recent years how ineffective these interconnecting organizations have been in climate change forums despite immense public interest. Moreover, NGOs are often fronts for corporate interests (for example, the Business Software Alliance funded by Microsoft: Benner and Witte [2004, 40] refer to NGOs organized by government, business, and powerful donors as "gongos, bongos and dongos"). Lobbying from corporations, industry representative associations, and NGOs established to argue for corporate interests has been at least as powerful as democratic action, and few major political parties have attempted to make climate change policy a significant electoral issue. This immobilized polity gives us a clue to the complexity and stasis equally observable in the far less publicized governance of waste.

Zero-waste activists also highlight the vested interests operating in the waste system. Since the waste industry earns its income from managing and storing waste, it has little incentive to increase levels of recycling. Yet the recycling industry is largely dominated by waste management operations. Like the privatized prisons analyzed by Sassen that earn their revenues by keeping people in jail, with therefore no reason to rehabilitate them, the contradiction between waste storage and recycling fails to produce a public good: the reduction of waste through maximal reuse of materials. Other limitations obtrude: Most plastics can only be recycled a handful of times before they begin to lose the qualities that make them useful, becoming brittle and porous, and losing their transparency or ability to hold dyes. After reaching this point, they move typically from recycling to waste, so that the absolute removal of disposal from recycling is not possible, without the expenditure of large amounts of energy to reconstitute them into usable form.

A central truth of the waste cycle is that it does not deal in things, of the kind tracked in studies of ordinary commodities (Appadurai 1986). Instead, waste deals in disassembled matter: in pieces, elements, and decomposition. Parts can be hacked from what were once coherent objects to become something else, and the raw components of refined metals and expensive compounds can find their way back into the commodity cycle. All of these practices are, however, fraught with risk. The tin that we observed in chapter 2 being extracted from the Andes, for example, returns as a component of organic molecules. Organotin compounds are a favored stabilizer for PVC plastics, such as those used for weatherproofing and insulating fiber-optic cable. Organotin was outlawed as a pesticide by the European Union in 2003 due to its extreme toxicity, and especially its effects on marine mammals that concentrate the compound as it flows out into open water. In global recycling villages of West Africa, India, and southern China, burning off the PVC casing to get at the valuable metals inside releases the organotins. Although the form used in PVC is not highly toxic, when burned along with other chemicals, there is a strong risk of conversion to triorganotin, a virulent phytotoxin. Thus not only are we not dealing with objects, even the materials they are made of are subject to chemical and biological transformations.

The current approach, legal and illegal but especially the latter, is dominated by the market. As Gregson and his colleagues put it, "the places in the world where the arts of transience are most vividly articulated are precisely those places where materials and 'wastes' are lightly regulated or unregulated and those where end-of-life goods inexorably find their way to as a result" (2010, 823). Light or avoidable regulation of the kind ignored in the illegal transborder transport of waste is a policy goal of neoliberal governance, which takes it as dogma that the market delivers best when least constrained by rules. This is true only to the extent that the wealthy can afford to purchase freedom from the unpleasant or harmful effects of waste, while the poor, faced with the primary task of survival, are condemned to dwell in it. There is thus no incentive for the wealthy to cease transporting waste away from their own dwellings, or to curtail their profligacy, and thus no reason or evidence that this lightly regulated market in waste is capable of delivering solutions to the scale and danger of the problem. This is especially visible in illegal dumping at sea, a practice that seems to extend from the U.S. military dumping radioactive waste (Karl 2001) to widespread dumping of oil ("USA: German Shipping Companies" 2012). Although there are strict rules, maritime dumping can fall between many stools: if in inshore waters, national jurisdiction prevails, but there may be a split between investigators (the U.S. Coast Guard, for example) and prosecutors (in "USA: German Shipping Companies" [2012], the Environmental Crimes Section of the Justice Department's Environment and Natural Resources Division). In international waters, the major agency is the IMO, but without a fleet of its own, with millions of square miles of ocean to police, and very little data on dumping sites, enforcement is exceptionally difficult. In addition, evidence can take years to surface, as in the case of radioactive waste washed up on the Somali coast by the 2004 Indian Ocean tsunami, said to have been dumped by operators taking advantage of the collapse of the Somali government (BBC 2005). In the twentieth century, after Russia the UK was the largest offender in ocean disposal of radioactive waste, much of it in its own territorial waters (IAEA 1999). There is thus the additional problem of ambiguity as to the siting of dumps, in or outside international waters, and therefore of its legality or otherwise, based on territorial claims to inshore waters and therefore to national rather than international jurisdiction, not the movement and impact of the radiation.

New smart materials and technologies, including those developed for their low-carbon efficiency like wind turbines, will in the nature of things be damaged, corrode, or be superseded and enter the waste cycle, in some cases without planned end-of-life policies. The new environmentalist discipline of life cycle analysis addresses the biography of objects, like mobile phones, from raw material to disposal. But as Anna Davies (2012, 194) notes, policy and academic attention to life cycle analysis of nanotechnologies and renewables like photovoltaics is not only embryonic but dissociated from discussions about governance and regulation. This disassociation is also noted in Khoo and Rao's (2009) comparative analysis of resistance to waste sites in Malaysia and East Germany. Despite great differences, both countries share some important features. First, transport occurs not only between but within nations; second, poor nations also generate waste, while promises of economic growth premised on monetizing the waste chain only generate yet more waste; third, waste management policies within nations reflect internal economic, social, and often ethnic differences between regions; and finally, even on the national scale, separating waste production from waste management causes political frictions (Khoo and Rao 2009, 966–67). Differential mobilities and immobilities arise as polluting waste gravitates to the least regulated and poorest regions, nationally and globally. The value of immobile wastes reflects not their intrinsic worth but the cost of extracting them from the complex assemblies that they have been assimilated into. Small quantities of valuable materials embedded in large quantities of less valuable ones, like the grains of rare earths used to dope chips, tend to accumulate in these poorest, least governed regions, although the toxins associated with them may well, sometimes in only a few years, enter geological and aquatic cycles and enter the biosphere, unsettled by the action of waste pickers or the digging of wells nearby. Immobility is only a slower form of mobility.

These tendential patterns of waste reflect the investment of local and global players in both regulating and enforcing regulations. The regulations themselves come in a variety of forms, from guidance and standards to laws, and from a surprisingly large number of players. Not only are these regulatory forces often mutually incompatible; each is often shaped by clashes between ideals and realities, and by compromises and conflicts, that can make the rules or guidelines themselves internally contradictory or challenging to decipher and implement. Even the definitions and trajectories of waste are open to interpretation and critique. This book was largely inspired by reports from the Basel Action Network (2002, 2005) and Greenpeace International (2005), yet their argument that electronic waste export is a North-South trade is contested by Lepawsky (2014), who emphasizes evidence for trade flows in waste between developing countries of the Global South, for example from China to Bangladesh, or from various countries in Southeast Asia and the Middle East to Indonesia. Lepawsky notes two limits to his statistical analysis. First, the UN Commission for Trade and Development figures he uses often characterize relatively wealthy nations as "developing" (Hong Kong, Saudi Arabia) because of their regional geography. Second, he is forced to use figures for battery recycling because UNCTAD's COMTRADE database has no category for e-waste. While defending his use of these figures, even in making a controversial case, Lepawsky points to a major problem. Given that much of the transborder trade in e-waste is illegal and some of it is conducted under conditions of military secrecy, and given the absence of a COMTRADE code covering e-waste, there is no common basis for agreement on the scale of the problem. Without that, governance is reduced by the common test of evidence-based policy. That the lack of evidence is itself evidence of the problem is not a solution to this absence.

Global governance scholars point to a different problem in the UN system. There is a clear hierarchy of organizations under the UN. For example, UNEP, the UN Environmental Program, like UNDP responsible for development, is a program. Programs are lower on the hierarchy than organizations, such as WTO (trade), WHO (health), ILO (labor), and FAO (food and agriculture). Clearly, environmental issues touch on all four of these neighboring bodies, and according to some advocates should be promoted to organization status to bring a coordinating role in matters recognized as key policy domains like climate change and sustainable development. Commenting on this state of affairs, Oran R. Young criticizes the idea of reformed UN governance, which would be actively resisted, in any case time-consuming, and inevitably incomplete given the entrenchment of particular political interests at various points in the system. Instead he proposes "to focus on substantive initiatives rather than on organizational reform and to launch programs that can attract the participation of many separate entities" (Young 2011, 3). While his judgment of the UN system's capacity for reform is undoubtedly justified, his solution runs straight into the problems outlined in Goldman's (2005) critique of the World Bank, where pragmatism has been tainted by dogma, especially neoliberal dogma, and, far from ameliorating conditions, has typically made them worse.

The second critique of Young's program is that in effect this is how the challenge of global trades in e-waste is currently being handled, with no effect on the end results. Unlike the WTO, which has powerful sanctions it can apply to member states failing to comply with its rulings, no UN body has sanctions to apply to e-waste exporters. The IMO has jurisdiction over maritime transport but, as we have seen, no means to enforce rules. National governments and their agencies act to catch what they can, but this depends on the strength of civil service branches like the Coast Guard and Customs

and Excise, which, as we have seen, have been weakened by austerity policies stemming from agencies like the World Bank and the IMF, and from the
global banking industry. Port authorities do the best they can under similar
constraints, but they are now almost universally privatized, and therefore
constrained to produce profit rather than surveillance of waste exports, especially as they are already bound to deliver loss-making security objectives
for the state. National governments and treaty organizations can only deliver legislation that they believe will be acted on, in this instance by three
distinct industries, waste management, transport and recycling, each with
different goals than those espoused by legislators. These compromised legal
instruments must then somehow be enforced. Self-regulation may work for
major firms with trusted brands to protect, but these three industries include
hundreds, even thousands, of smaller firms, many of them quasi-fictional,
fly-by-night outfits who, even if caught, are able to dissolve their legal status
in hours and reopen under another trading name in another territory. The
trade in illegal e-waste exports is a prime example of market anarchy leading
to deep social and environmental harm.

The opening paragraphs of this chapter argued that waste is integral to
free market capital, especially to the demand for growth placed on it by the
falling rate of profit, and the consequently regular arrival of crises of overproduction. The arguments established in this section demonstrate that the market is incapable of self-regulating for environmental good. Unfortunately the
political instruments we have to hand, even when disposed to address e-waste
as a priority, are severely limited in their capacity to enforce their regulatory
regimes. Nonetheless there are regulatory regimes, like the Basel Convention, that should do more than give us a benchmark for outrage. In fact they
do provide a significant service, one which though it seems at first merely
discursive, like much discourse operates as the principle of institutions, and
impacts directly on the political economy of waste. This governance regulates
the passage of matter between the economy and the environment.

Waste is not dirt in Douglas's (1966, 35) classic definition: It is not matter in the wrong place, not something intrinsically or culturally out of place.
Rather, waste has to become waste and does so by being displaced. Two
events are typical. An object becomes waste by being disconnected from the
other parts that make it work: a mouse or a monitor severed from the CPU;
batteries removed from a device; anything disconnected from its electricity supply or network. Alternatively, and more radically, something becomes
waste once it is removed from the commodity cycle. From the point of view
of the economy, matter is void the moment it ceases to function as a bearer

of economic value: From the moment it is bought, it loses its exchange value. Becoming useful in the act of being consumed, it loses its connection with the economic cycle. The longer its working life after purchase, the more wasteful it becomes economically speaking, because it inhibits the consumer from purchasing a replacement. Once consumers decide they have had enough of it and throw it away, that act of wasting places matter back in the commodity chain. Waste becomes, as Palmer (2005) implies, a resource to be plundered. Delivered free of charge to the recycling industry (and often enough with payment for its removal by increasingly privatized waste removal companies) waste matter reenters the economy through recycling—another instance of the neoliberal environmentalism noted by Goldman. It is only once it has passed through recycling that whatever cannot be recovered becomes void again, in the sense that it becomes an economic externality, no longer of value. Inert economically during its working life as use value, the ex-commodity then reenters the economy as raw material for further extraction of surplus value, but once that has been expended, it again becomes inert. In this final phase, waste is environmentalized. When it becomes externality, it also becomes environment. As resource it can be plundered; as pollution it can be excluded. During its commodity phases, matter is governed by the market.

It is only during its noneconomic phases, in use and as environmental, that governance passes to the political sphere. Even here, however, where governance has been instituted at state levels, its implementation is fraught with problems. In the United States, the absence of any federal legislation (related perhaps to the failure to ratify the Basel accords) has led many states to create their own laws and implementation bodies, often at odds with one another. One instructive example is the circular traffic of Californian toxic waste mentioned above, where used scrubbing filters and other detritus is freighted from plant to plant across the continental United States, each process generating new, often more concentrated toxic waste, and in some cases even increasing the quantity—from Silicon Valley to the Calgon plant in Kentucky, whose own wastes are trucked to Michigan to a plant that sends its waste to Wisconsin, some of whose wastes end up back in Superfund sites in California after significant expenditures of energy and a substantial transport carbon footprint (Rust and Drange 2014). The business of cleaning up hazardous waste creates more hazards—more clogged filters, more contaminated protective gear—but generates sufficient profits for its absurd merry-go-round to continue unquestioned.

The European Union has instituted two major directives, but fines vary by a factor of one hundred between member states, and implementation falls to the European Union Network for the Implementation and Enforcement of Environmental Law, which in turn relies on customs and excise officers, police forces, tax inspectorates, and other civil service institutions, many of them facing austerity-related cuts. In recipient countries like Ghana, both legislation and enforcement are hamstrung by debates over whether these are indeed toxic wastes or instead valuable economic resources (Bisschop 2014), while their civil functionaries are even fewer, worse paid, and thus more vulnerable to corruption than their European counterparts. Faced with growing public concern, schemes to provide certification for ethical recycling began to appear, among them e-Stewards, established by the NGO Basel Action Network, and Responsible Recycling (R2), with participation from the scrap industry. In his analysis of their operation, Graham Pickren (2014) notes the overwhelmingly northern discourse defining the elements of the recycling trade, bundling together moments in the cycle when waste becomes commodity with those when it is valueless, the easily recoverable with the more challenging (and, we might add, focusing on the materials rather than the energy used to extract them), while excluding the recycling workers of the Global South from the process of defining terms or setting the criteria for labeling. Indeed, the power to label has been handed to self-appointed labeling institutes, together with the right to use or sell the information contained therein as they choose. In little, we see here the major failing of waste governance: that even when discarded materials pass out of the economic cycle, the model for political action is economic. Agency too often belongs with commercially motivated quasi-NGOs. Even when it is supposed to rest with disciplined consumers, their rational choices are misshaped by commercial labeling. When purchasing behaviors do threaten change, they are as vulnerable to intervention as voting, which, as we saw in Greece in 2015, is always reversible by economic muscle.

INTERNET GOVERNANCE AND CONSTITUENT POWER

Modern universal intercourse can be controlled by individuals,
therefore, only when controlled by all.
Marx, *The German Ideology*, I.d.10

As Douglas Kahn announces in the opening lines of his work on communication arts, "radio was heard before it was invented" (2013, 1). The radio spectrum is a critical resource for the information environment as infrastructure of broadcast, cellular network, satellite, and microwave components of the information environment. Since the first Radiotelegraph Service

Regulations, signed in Berlin in 1906, particular wave bands within the spectrum have been allocated to nation-states, overlapping wavelengths being handled by international treaty. In Europe and its colonies, the newly discovered radio spectrum was treated as res nullius and deemed to form a public good. States therefore for the most part took over the whole spectrum for national purposes, including military, emergency services, and state or public service broadcasting. In 1912, the United States opted to reserve one area of spectrum for state use, and to sell licenses for the remainder to commercial interests. Both approaches rapidly killed off citizen radio enthusiasts and their stations along with activist and common-interest activities (Douglas 1987), and for most of the twentieth century the use of the spectrum for two-way communication was the monopoly of the military, state services, and commercial interests. The radio regulations now in force fall under the International Telecommunications Union (ITU), founded as an intergovernmental body but which has increasingly extended membership to corporations (McLean 2003).

At the same time, and in common with many other international treaties, while recognizing the status of corporations as legal persons, radio regulation does not recognize the claims of nonnational groups, especially indigenous peoples. The nature of the radio spectrum as commons was brought to international attention by a claim made by Rangiaho Everton to the Waitangi Tribunal, the body set up by the New Zealand government to adjudicate claims under the Waitangi Treaty, which established the terms of settlement between Maori and colonizers at the close of the Maori Wars in 1840 (Belich 1986; King 2004, 151–67). The tribunal report notes:

> The claimant says that the Radiocommunications Act 1989 fails to acknowledge Maori rangatiratanga over the radio spectrum and that, in assuming for itself the exclusive authority to manage the spectrum, the Crown is ignoring the Treaty principle of partnership and failing to establish, in consultation with Maori, adequate principles, policies, and legislative framework for Maori partnership in spectrum management. The claimant alleges that the Crown is continuing to develop and pursue spectrum management policy without Maori participation, and is creating a property right, and selling that right, without consultation with, or the agreement of, Maori. (Waitangi Tribunal 1999)

The word *rangatiritanga* derives from the term for a chief, and means both the kudos and power of chieftainship and the land belonging to it: It is often translated as "sovereignty," although that term had no translation in Reo Maori at the time of the treaty. The terms of the treaty give Maori rangatiritanga over all forms of commons that preexisted the European arrival in Aotearoa, New Zealand, including the right to contest colonial laws declaring a resource open to property rights. Settlements under the treaty include return of fisheries, lakes, and forests to Maori, and such cultural victories as the renaming of Mount Cook as Aoraki and its return to Ngai Tahu, who in turn gifted it to the people of Aotearoa, New Zealand. Reviewing the radio spectrum claim, the tribunal recognized among its key findings that

(i) nothing in the terms of the Treaty of Waitangi allows or foreshadows any authority on the part of the Crown to determine, define or limit the properties of the universe which may be used by Maori in the exercise of their rangatiratanga over tikanga Maori [right ways of doing];

(ii) where any property or part of the universe has, or may have, value as an economic asset, the Crown has no authority under the Treaty to possess, alienate, or otherwise treat it as its own property without recognising the prior claim of Maori rangatiratanga. (Waitangi Tribunal 1999)

The significance of this case is that Maori understanding of the position of the spectrum is poles apart from its commodification under European property laws, even when the economic significance of the thing is allowed: neither res nullius nor saleable property. Broadcast wavelengths belong to the commons.

The issue is not merely historical. Radio spectrum is vital to the system of geostationary orbital satellites linked into the Internet, to cellular telecommunications nets for mobile media, and to Wi-Fi and Bluetooth local communications. Brecht may have been the first to argue that "radio should be converted from a distribution system to a communications system" (1979, 25). Enzensberger (1970) made the same argument for television in an essay hugely influential on the early community video movement. To some extent, mass access to the Internet has realized those dreams, but as Kathryn Milun (2011, 93) points out, "the legal organization of frequencies remains a centralized infrastructure licensing their use." The allocation of spectrum to nations by the ITU was initially based on resolving rivalrous use of wave bands: Today multiple use of narrow bands is an everyday occurrence, and the rationale for national sovereignty accordingly diminishes; and yet increasingly nation-states are turning to auctions in which spectrum is not only licensed but sold to corporations. This extreme privatization of the commons underpins several key arguments in Internet governance addressed below, such as net neutrality, the principle that all information should be treated equally.

The space created by the construction of wired telecommunications networks differs from the radio spectrum in that it is a human construct. The Internet is the most tangible form of a new kind of environment, one built by humans from the outset. Like the natural environment and the radio spectrum more particularly, it began as and retains features of a commons. Established as a protocol—a system of rules for hardware and software allowing digital machines to communicate regardless of their operating systems— connecting a small number of computers used by U.S. defense contractors, the Internet spread slowly enough for its management to be undertaken as a public service by a few engineers throughout its early years. The mass expansion following the release of the Mosaic browser in 1993 led to newly complex relations between these self-regulating scientists and established national and international telecommunications organizations (Froomkin 2003).

The Internet environment is older than the World Wide Web's http protocol. Older protocols for basic connection, e-mail, and file transfer were established through the informal network of engineers responsible for the early experiments. Many of the functions they undertook became small, and later much larger, organizations, among them the Internet Engineering Task Force and the Internet Corporation for Assigned Names and Numbers (ICANN), the latter governing one of the few limited resources in network communications, the numerical (IP) address of connected devices and the human-readable names (.edu, .uk, .org) associated with them. Several UN institutions also had a major part to play. Surprisingly, one that was largely missing, especially in the 1980s, the period when contemporary standards were being set, was the ITU. The ITU is one of the oldest treaty organizations, established to facilitate international telegraph communications, and looking after both technical standards for cross-border communications and the economics of charging for sending, transmitting, and receiving messages between national systems. Because the years of Internet standardization corresponded to the period of rapid deregulation in telephony, the ITU's members, largely national telecommunications providers, were in no position to intrude on what appeared at the time a marginal activity. Others, however, like the International Standards Organization (ISO) and the Institute of Electrical and Electronics Engineers, a professional association whose technical councils provide important forums for discussion, were able to gain strategic positions in the ITU's absence. Other organizations involved include the IMO, which we saw earlier overseeing transoceanic cables, the United Nations Office for Outer Space Affairs overseeing communication satellites, and content-oriented institutions like the WTO and the World Intellectual Property Organization. National governments had, by the time of the UN World Summit on the Information Society meeting, recognized the importance of the Internet for trade, security, citizenship, and cultural activity. Many others have a stake or a claim to participation, demonstrated in the 205-page "Final List of Participants" at the 2005 Tunis summit released by the ITU, ranging from disability and youth groups to environmentalist, development, and religious NGOs.

Beyond the technical administration of the Internet lie complex relations with other bodies. Social media platforms like Twitter and Facebook and search engines like Google, not to mention online retailers like iTunes and Amazon, are also important intermediaries, technically and historically capable of controlling the use of their networks by suspending accounts or supplying personal data to other commercial or governmental interests. Regional Internet Registries, responsible under ICANN for administering the allocation of addresses within geographical areas, have the capability to deny or suspend connections. Internet Exchange Points (IXPs), key crossroads connecting subnetworks to one another, ordinarily require potential members be incorporated or otherwise legally recognizable, hold an assigned network identity from a Regional Internet Registry, and, though IXPs are typically nonprofit, pay an annual fee substantial enough to deter smaller or poorer groups, such as indigenous organizations (deNardis 2009, 2014).

Motivations across and within these multiple players are as varied as the organizations they represent: ideologies of engineering efficiency, free markets, open access, social justice, religious beliefs, pro- and antihacking, pro- and antipiracy, legal, commercial, and governmental concerns, and few that can easily be accommodated in a single regime without radical contradiction. It is a miracle that, under these conflicting pressures, the Internet continues to function. For some, the miracle is the result of grassroots self-organization; for others evidence that U.S. models of free enterprise have triumphed; and for others still that the Internet is a dangerous haven for terrorists, fraudsters, pornographers, and anarchically irresponsible computer hooligans. Unsurprisingly, Internet governance is angrily fought over at global, regional, and national levels, even as the system continues, despite that, to operate. Given the rhetoric of immateriality (which these very problems disprove), it is equally unsurprising that environmental impacts of the Internet are rarely if ever a focus for discussion.

This unstable governance configuration reemerged as a topic of international significance when the UN devoted its annual summit conference to the topic of Internet governance in 2005. While there were important debates on technical issues, at the core of disagreement was the claim by a number of nations, led by China, that Internet governance, on the model of spectrum allocation a century earlier and of telephony despite its privatization, was a matter for states and international treaties, not for self-regulation and commerce, by then the major force in Internet content (Mueller 2010, 55–80). This trajectory only seems to be contradicted by government-organized spectrum auctions passing control of wave bands from states to corporations: National governments' control over who is allowed to enter auctions is one of the ways that states operationalize their role as handmaidens to capital while ensuring the exclusion of alternative voices. The usual *argumentum ad absurdam* raised at this point is that it is only right to exclude terrorists and pedophiles; in practice it is indigenous and environmental activists, among others, who are excluded, leaving them to negotiate as best they can for scraps of airtime from the corporations favored by the auction system.

One alternative to this cascade from the ITU to nations to corporations is Benkler's judgment that "there is no such 'thing' as 'spectrum'" (1998, 2): that spectrum is an artificial construct designed to marry with existing legal concepts of property which require that there be a thing to be owned. Benkler argues that this proprietary model, whether state administered or marketized, is only a means to obstruct people wanting to set up their own antennae, so that spectrum owners can conduct a monopoly. Against such state- and market-dominated initiatives, the self-regulation model defended by Internet activists like Mueller (2004) can nonetheless be criticized. There is an implicit elitism in the principle that anyone may join debates on engineering specifications, when only the highly trained will be recognized by their peers, thus quietly marginalizing the claims of indigenous, colonized, and ex-colonized participants. This exclusion is not at all as powerful as it has proved in other international arenas, and far less so than in global governance structures like the WTO and the IMF where corporate interests hold sway. Nonetheless, the absence of marginalized peoples from decision making is a critical weakness in the existing nexus of governance, and in the Internet Governance Forum established in the wake of the 2005 Tunis summit and the wider networks providing governance.

Constructing the Internet as environment involved not only restricting governance but enclosing this common space inside property laws. The principle of net neutrality is the de facto agreement that the Internet carries materials regardless of the status of the message. This is contested by telcos who argue that having invested in the infrastructure, they are entitled to privilege their own paying customers over messages derived from rival corporations

(Wu 2003). Where net neutrality is not observed, activities without the support of corporate players are disadvantaged: delayed and subject to data loss. Perhaps more significantly, in order for such a market-driven prioritization to work, the fundamentals of network communication would have to be re-engineered. This foundation is the suite of software rules known as TCP/IP (transfer control protocol/Internet protocol). This in turn rests on a basic tool, packet switching. A message or a web page, a file or a video stream, is converted into small units, each of which is enclosed in a packet containing code for the sender and addressee, and instructions on how to recombine each packet with its fellows at the receiving end. Each packet finds its own way through the network, jumping from node to node, and from network to network—for example, from a university server to a transatlantic cable provider to a local Internet service provider to a Google account. Two principles make this work smoothly and efficiently. First, the multitude of networks composing the Internet, with some exceptions, agree to "peer," that is, to transport one another's packets so that they can find the quickest route at any given moment, and make maximally efficient use of the available pathways. Second, none of these networks opens the envelope to check what is in it.

The second principle bears consideration. If networks "know" what is in a given packet, they are responsible for it. The argument goes that senders and receivers should be responsible, by analogy with the postal service, which carries everything perfectly legally because only senders and receivers commit criminal acts by communicating illegal material. There is a second reason: Opening every packet to see what it contains expends time and energy. Discriminating between paid and unpaid and therefore prioritized packets would require either additional code added to each and every packet, or additional protocols for identifying their content. As currently implemented, this end-to-end process is as simple as its makers could achieve. It is designed to carry anything from text to video, spreadsheets to advertising, without differentiation. Equally, it was built according to the pioneering ethos of the early Internet, and for many its guiding principle still, that all the protocols required to make the net work should be free, both in the sense that there would be no charge for them and in that they would remain open to development. The attack on net neutrality thus intervenes at a number of levels into the TCP/IP suite. It introduces proprietary code into the transport layer; it uses it to complicate the underlying architecture; it ends the anonymity that protects network operators from legal obligations; it undoes the peering arrangements that ensure swift transport of data; it ends the principle of openly agreed protocols; and it forecloses the free movement of information in order to create a property value in the speed of transmission. The contrast is between a loose, mutually interdependent, and evolving environment and a highly regulated, enclosed colony of corporate property rights.

The net neutrality debate has been conducted, like much Internet governance, largely behind closed doors. This is especially the case since the regulation of service providers generally falls within national jurisdictions, where such issues, being largely disconnected from electoral politics, can be presented as technical matters of communication management rather than issues of public concern. To the extent that the Internet is the public sphere of the twenty-first century, this is disingenuous. To the extent that governments have, under the influence of neoliberalism, increasingly devoted themselves to implementing regulation proposed by commercial operations, the rules tend to be those that most fit the market. However, in the case of net neutrality, the conflict is as much between, for example, content providers like Google and Yahoo and network providers like British Telecom and Verizon, or between fixed-line and mobile providers, as it is between proponents of free expression and proponents of the nominally free but actually highly regulated market. An example is the regulation of neutrality in IXPs and peering arrangements, which are entirely private relations that also have impacts on the preferential treatment of network traffic of particular forms or from particular networks. The absence of IXPs, especially in developing countries, effectively demotes their traffic by delaying it and increasing the expense and vulnerability of developing nation networks (deNardis 2014, 127). The consequent deep inequality of influence is the result, in Castells's analysis, of "relentless pressure from two essential sources of domination that still loom over our existence: capital and the state" (2009, 116) that, in Lessig's account, "produce not no regulation at all, but regulation by the most powerful of special interests" (2006, 337–38). Citing both of these, Des Freedman sums up: "Despite different inflections in different countries, the internet is implicated in a fundamental neo-liberal transformation of the power relations inside the regulatory process" (2012, 97). Net neutrality matters not only because it excludes indigenous and other colonized and marginalized constituencies, nor exclusively because capital, in its competing forms, threatens to overwhelm the processes of information exchange, but because the process of redesigning the fundamental principles of Internet communication forecloses its evolution as a media ecology, while preserving it as an environment, that is, as something external to human affairs.

This is particularly significant for developing nations, many of which cannot afford the membership fees demanded by regulatory bodies and can only implement standards but not help design them. This developing global class system applies to both telecommunications and the radio spectrum. In both instances, the historical legacy of colonialism meets the new conditions of the information economy to form an infrastructure, now increasingly mingling the two. Spectrum auctions for direct broadcast by satellite, digital terrestrial television, and 4G mobile wave bands are undertaken as exercises in political economy from which the population is excluded, and only states and corporations have agency. The design and application of universal standards like the TCP/IP suite, the HTML language, and the MPEG codec occur without participation from end users, and exclusively from the standpoint of a northern, masculine, scientistic, and instrumentalist point of view. These qualities are, through their technical standardization and universality, increasing their embedded role in contemporary communication and cultural life. They are the principles shaping the information environment.

Though we drew a distinction between Internet and trade governance on the one hand and environmental and migration governance on the other earlier in this chapter, a common feature links Internet and environmental governance emerging from the above analyses. The crisis of Internet governance appears as a conflict between on the one hand a compromised regime of privatized and national actors—the latter, however, taken qua sovereign state rather than as collective public decision making—and on the other the emergent governance of all of us, represented, however, by volunteers who make it their business to establish and protect the Internet, to provide for its users, and to speak on their behalf. A parallel situation exists in environmental governance: an uneasy alliance between capital and states with the latter trying to balance the short-termism of the former by protecting what remains of nature, often in the name of future generations of exploitation (cynically put, this is the meaning of the phrase "sustainable development"). Against this unholy alliance, in which predation is merely slowed by regulation, are ranged a raft of local initiatives and global civil society actors struggling to speak on behalf of nature. Both regimes suffer from the same deficit. Neither Internet nor environmental governance are based on what Negri calls "constituent power."

Power as constituted is concretized in institutions like the state and the law. According to Negri, constituted power stands over against constituent power, which is its origin but which constituted power strives to subordinate to itself. Constituent power is strength (*potenza*), the capacity for action, "a force that bursts apart, breaks, interrupts, unhinges any preexisting equilibrium and any possible continuity. Constituent power is tied to the notion of democracy as absolute power" (Negri 1999, 11). It is "the radical apparatus of something that does not yet exist, and whose conditions of existence imply that the creative act does not lose its characteristics in the act of creating" (Negri 1999, 22). Very different historical acts like the American, French, and Russian revolutions are explosions of constituent power which ground and legitimate the states that come after them, even though "sovereignty presents itself as a fixing of constituent power, and therefore as its termination" (Negri 1999, 22). Constituent power is, on the contrary, an explosion of communal will whose "active elements are . . . resistance and desire, an ethical impulse and a constructive passion, an articulation of the sense of the insufficiency of existence and a deeply vigorous reaction to an unbearable absence of being" (Negri 1999, 23). For all the criticism leveled at it in these pages, global trade can claim to have been born from just such resistance (ethical demand for freedom from the insufficiency of feudally regulated life) and just such desire (to construct networks of trade in pursuit of satisfying an infinite demand for more). But such cannot be said of either the Internet or the environment. Instead, both are subjects not of constituent power but only of a constituted one. Both are the objects of governance systems, ad hoc and crisis prone as they may be, which were not brought into existence by mass movements who claim ownership of them or demand to participate in their constitutions. Thus they share the same deficit, but for different reasons.

The Internet was built to be inclusive of the homogenous group of white, male engineers who built it. Its expansion, especially in the 1990s, placed this expert club as protectors of a wondrous resource, rather like benevolent park rangers protecting the reserve against tourists. Its historical roots in U.S. military research and its rapid commercialization after 2000, however, meant that the club found itself hemmed in by both state and commercial agencies increasingly interested in what they were protecting, and increasingly integrated into increasingly formal governance structures. In this way, a well-meaning group of enthusiasts found themselves constituted, rather precisely, as expert functionaries of a constituted power. The environment emerged as a political issue in the 1960s, and is to that extent able to claim a genealogy in which constituent power played a role. But as with the club of engineers, early environmental activists saw themselves as speaking on behalf of an environment that, however, was unable to speak for itself. The institutionalization that rapidly ensued tended to exclude those early activists from the governance system, unless they accepted the mode of governance by exclusion. Where some visionaries did seek ways for nature to speak on its own behalf, as object of governance the environment was defined by its exclusion from the process of governing. Thus both Internet and natural environments share a radical structure of exclusion, in which they are constructed as objects of rule. For actor-network theory, assemblages like the Internet and the environment are complex networks of human and nonhuman elements, in which agency is not exclusively a human attribute: things also act, contributing to the management and evolution of the system as much as human agents do (Latour 2004, 2005). The somewhat apolitical ambitions of Latour's actor-network theory, however, rarely specify the hierarchies and conflicts of actors in these elaborate networks of interaction. In the case of global trade, both commodities and money have agency, and the market, the cyborg of cyborgs in the same way that the Internet is a network of networks, has immense political power, while individually and even collectively humans have very little. In the current cases, neither the technological elements of the Internet nor the natural elements of the environment have agency, being governed with no part in their own governance. Rather than being founded in an inclusive upwelling of desire and demand, both Internet and environmental governance were formed in the act of exclusion: Both are governed on the principle that the materials that constitute them are objects of rule constitutively excluded from governing.

On this basis, we should recognize in both the historically ancient form of sovereignty. While superseded in the metropolitan centers by discipline and biopolitics, sovereignty remained intrinsic in the colonizing gesture that first seized and enclosed the green world and that later enfolded the radio spectrum. That same colonial sovereignty is maintained, as Mbembe (2001, 29) argues, in the ongoing work of *commandement*—a term describing the suspension of one law common to all in favor of privatized rights belonging to specified individuals and companies—and, we should add, of the continuing accumulation of capital by dispossession revealed by Luxemburg (1951) and Harvey (2003). Sovereignty's practice of excluding the objects, human or otherwise, of governance from governance brings to fine focus the exclusion of human populations other than those operating on behalf of power and wealth, or those power and wealth can suborn to act as technical functionaries, from the governance of Internet and environment alike. They raise important questions about the capacity of politics as currently constituted to deal with environmental crisis or the communicative ecology that would allow for full public participation in its resolution.

It is in the interests of those who control technological governance to encourage the perception that these are arcane, uninteresting, and unimport-
ant matters. Looking into the development of particular technological standards shows why and how they matter: what these processes mean for the
operation of media technologies, and how they combine to shape the way we
perceive information and communications. Indeed, governance shapes how
we perceive at all, especially, in the case at hand, the granular level at which
technical and natural difference are excluded from perception and how particular software applications feed on and reproduce the closed system of environmentalization. In the storms of innovation characterizing the planned
obsolescence economy of digital media, the atmosphere of intense competition over price and new product lines belies the deep standardization of
core tools like semiconductors, constrained to work with now entrenched
protocols like TCP/IP, firmly embedded infrastructures like IXPs, and shared
standards like MPEG, tools that shape the possibilities for any future participation in global networks and local communicative politics.

At its January 2013 meeting, the Motion Picture Expert Group, which
gives the MPEG standard its name, discussed two major initiatives associated with MPEG-M, the latest version of the most widely used compression-
decompression (codec) tool for the transmission and display of audiovisual
materials. One of them was the draft requirements of the MPEG-UD (user description), which had already been slated for inclusion in MPEG-M; the other
was Green MPEG. These adaptations of the MPEG codec hook into existing
technologies including broadcast equipment, TCP/IP and other basic network
protocols, and production and display technologies from cameras to TV sets.
Every video and games device on the planet depends on codecs: MPEG occu-
pies the dominant position in moving-image coding. It allows cameras and
displays to interoperate in the two standards for scanning, interlaced and
progressive, which share the fundamental architecture of images, the bitmap
or raster. Scanning isolates the picture elements (pixels), refreshing them at
twenty-five frames per second, with individual pixels illuminating and fad-
ing between scans. The goal is to fox the eye into seeing continuity. The scale
and speed of raster scans are below the threshold of human perception. As
Siegert argues, "Real-time processing is defined precisely as the evasion of
the senses" (1999, 12). This is also true of hardware processes like scanning.

To maximize the efficient delivery of audiovisual signals, MPEG shares
with most other codecs a series of interlocking techniques. Like the embed-

ded audio compression it is paired with, video compression uses a bundle of techniques derived from experiments in human perception, for example, how one sound masks another, the high or low frequencies machines record but humans do not perceive, and persistent or random effects we have trained ourselves to ignore. Video compression uses three main techniques: key frames, blocks, and vector prediction. The aim is to reduce the amount of information being sent, while maintaining sufficient resolution and color differentiation at the display end to satisfy the typical viewer or standard observer. Transmissions are divided into segments marked off by key frames, as in animation. Beginning and end key frames are determined by abrupt changes across the whole frame, typically at a cut but often cued by pans or other major changes in the frame. The division into key frames happens very quickly, microseconds ahead of the segment's delivery in live broadcasts. The beginning and end key frames are compared, and major differences within the otherwise more or less similar series of frames marked: areas of greatest action, in particular.

The sequence between key frames is then parsed in larger aggregations of pixels: blocks (4 × 4 pixels), macroblocks (16 × 16 pixels) and Group of Blocks (GoBs; 64 × 64 pixels or more). The principle is to send the smallest amount of data necessary. Therefore large areas that stay more or less the same between key frames, like sports fields, are treated as GoBs. Smaller areas that stay the same, like the shirts of the players, will be treated as macroblocks. Smaller blocks and individual pixel information are reserved for areas of the image with the greatest number of changes, such as faces. Blocks are programmable as slices of irregular shape (though still based on the square pixel). In a close-up of a refereeing decision, for example, the greatest detail will be focused on faces and gestures, while backgrounds will be transmitted with much less detailed information (Cubitt 2014b).

The MPEG codec manages color for displays with a limited gamut, typically 40 percent of what the normal human eye can distinguish. Color is coded numerically and is thus freed from any semantic base, democratized (every color code is equal), and commodified (any color can be exchanged for any other). Color displays are calibrated against an ideal standard observer. Three qualities derive from these histories: abstraction in the service of commodification, standardization in the service of resource and human management, and efficiency expressed as speed and scale (Cubitt 2014a, 111–51). Efficient color transmission demands reduction of small gradations to whole numbers (MPEG offers temporal dithering, a technology for flickering between whole-number colors to produce the optical effect of a color midway between them). Efficiency, central to engineering, in this instance coincides with both management and commodification at the heart of the governance procedure that produces electronic standards like MPEG. Visual culture is colonized in the biopolitical economy in the form of the micro-management of commodified perception.

A raw bitmap has at least eight bits of information for every pixel, often far more. Sending all that information is energy intensive, so MPEG uses vectors, algorithmic expressions that describe movement (including color change) as a formula. In our sports broadcast example, instead of listing every pixel and its data, codecs send a description of the arc described by the ball, while leaving the background motionless—on the principle that we aren't interested in every blade of grass, only in the sport being played. Vector prediction is based on the first and last key frames, tracking the likely movement across the area of the screen. All these calculations, including key framing and segmenting, are performed by subprograms within MPEG on the fly. The narrower the bandwidth of a connection, as on a Skype call, the more lossy the display. All codecs are lossy, even the so-called lossless ones. Efficiency here means exclusion of the contingent colors and movements of grass: exclusion of natural processes as mere background noise.

The principle of maximum efficiency has to take account of the variety of platforms that a given content will be supplied to, from mobiles working on cellular networks to professional monitors attached to HD cameras. Content providers want to be able to deliver efficiently from a single file, for example, through cloud distribution services, to HDTV, laptops, and handhelds. Rather than multiply file types—with the consequent costs as well as the loss of primary data that conversion implies—they seek a way to use a single content bank to deliver to all platforms. This is the goal of MPEG-M. One of the services they require from the codec is therefore information about the end-user platform: There is no point sending HD signals to low-fi devices. This is the basic feedback loop of the user-description layer, MPEG-UD, within the MPEG-M specification. Any given implementation of MPEG standards can elect which components (also known as layers) they want to use. Free-to-air digital terrestrial broadcasters might be happy without the user description layer; online services like Netflix are far more likely to use it. The current MPEG-4 codec includes a layer for digital rights management (DRM): MPEG-UD is envisaged as including DRM in the UD layer.

The "Draft Requirements on MPEG User Description" issued in January 2013 specify an architecture in which three components (User, Context, and Service Descriptions) feed a Customized User Description engine for specified transmissions. The Motion Picture Experts Group is clearly aware of the privacy issues, especially when they envisage health information being handled remotely via MPEG systems. Users will have access to their descriptions, and will be able to alter or delete data, and decide what data can be released to which service provider. But, recalling Siegert (1999) on media operating below the threshold of perception, and observing the tendency of the majority of users to leave default settings in place, then it is not only surveillance and the enforcement of copyright at the code level (included in the Intellectual Property Management and Protection layer) that should worry us. The feedback loop sends back invaluable data about the consumption and cultural patterns of end users, converting their attention to media into a new form of commodity, and promoting the advance of a new mode of standardization, ostensibly personalized but actually the material form of consumer discipline.

The attendance for the last meeting of 2011 lists over three hundred delegates. Among them are the major corporations involved in audiovisual media transport: hardware and component manufacturers and network corporations including RIM, Cisco, Huawei, Mstar, Panasonic, Technicolor, Nokia, Dolby, Thomson, Orange and many other telcos, Canon, Ericsson, NHK, NEC, NTT, Fujitsu, JVC, Sharp, Samsung, LG, Phillips, Google, Skype, Apple, Microsoft, Qualcomm, and NVIDIA. Also represented were large teams from several universities including Tsinghua, Poznan, the Universidades Politecnicas of Madrid and Catalunya, and the Fraunhofer Institute, whose board of trustees is a who's who of German electronics industries. Attendance does not give us data on which subgroups each delegate attended over the five days of the meeting, whether this was a typical turnout, or which divisions of a particular firm were represented (Disney was the only content provider present, and they were represented by their Zurich technical research group). Although this was a meeting of engineers employed by corporations, their task was to grapple with solutions for the problems of efficient delivery. We can perhaps imagine the old Internet Engineering Task Force slogan echoing among their discussions: "We don't believe in presidents, kings or voting; we believe in rough consensus and running code."

Nonetheless there is an agenda, or rather a specification of problems that the engineers are invited to address. This agenda setting is an outgrowth of a significant aspect of MPEG governance: patents. Formats for MPEG carry an ISO/IEC number. This refers to two standards bodies, the International Electrotechnical Commission, an NGO composed of national representatives (and affiliate nations from the developing world with limited access to resources). It is headquartered in Geneva, also home of the ITU, along-side sister organization and source of the ISO abbreviation, the International Organization for Standardization, known in French as the Organisation internationale de normalisation. Membership in these organizations increasingly reflects the power of corporations to set global standards and norms, to create the standard conditions of normal perception, in particular standards that are no longer cost free and open to rewriting by any user. Martin Bryan (2007), convenor of one of the major ISO/IEC committees, remarked on his resignation, "The days of open standards development are fast disappearing. Instead we are getting 'standardization by corporation.'" A similar opinion was voiced by Mark Shuttleworth of Ubuntu during the storm over OPENXML, Microsoft's proprietary version of an open standard for marking up documents: "'It's sad that the ISO was not willing to admit that its process was failing horribly,' he said, noting that Microsoft intensely lobbied many countries that traditionally have not participated in ISO and stacked technical committees with Microsoft employees, solution providers and resellers sympathetic to OOXML" (Rooney 2008).

While MPEG is not the property of a single corporation, it is represented by one, MPEG-LA, a patent pool or one-stop shop where manufacturers and service providers can go to license MPEG products. The MPEG-LA boasts of the efficiency of its "many-to-many licensing model," which draws together twenty-nine holders of the multiple patents built into MPEG processing. Its website provides a link to a letter from Joel L. Klein of the U.S. Department of Justice Anti-Trust Division assuring potential clients that this is not a monopoly in the letter of U.S. law. The list of patent holders is impressive. It includes some once-bitter rivals like Microsoft and Apple, or JVC and Sony. Compared to the immense thicket of lawsuits that has bedeviled mobile technology in the smartphone patent wars of the last decade (O'Donnell 2014), we are right to be surprised at this Edenic agreement. Smartphones are still heirs of the "walled garden" approach, by which telecommunications service providers tried to keep customers inside a controlled zone of the network that they either owned or licensed. Global audiovisual industries, by contrast, thrive on exporting product across broadcasting and network systems, and therefore have a far higher stake in standardization.

The list of patent holders is impressive in including not one human being. Patent law, originally contrived to support inventors, is now with only rare exceptions the domain of corporate entities. The membership of MPEG-LA is, strictly speaking, inhuman. This observation should illuminate the terms *standard* and *normal* in the various translations of the ISO's name, and the term *universal* that MPEG-LA has adopted for its public relations. The website mentions "averting legal costs and concerns" as one virtue of one-stop shopping for licenses. A small company trying to license a DVD-printing outfit could be stuck licensing one patent after another, and would live in fear of missing one. Of course there is a slight ambiguity in the phrasing: potential clients wishing to avoid future legal costs and concerns would be well advised to get their licenses from MPEG-LA. The ISO has been criticized for charging too much to license standards to developing nations. The MPEG-LA has been criticized for its bitter dispute with Mozilla and Google, both of whom have been pressing for the use of open-source codecs like Ogg Theora and VP8 that, MPEG-LA contends, infringe pool partners' patents. In its submission to the Justice Department, MPEG-LA declared that it would never refuse a license. Technically, it is not in breech of that pledge. Its claim that this position is "allowing for investment in product and reinvestment in innovation" is perhaps less certain. The history of electronic engineering governance is littered with preemptive patents (applied for before any working prototype has been demonstrated) and spoiler lawsuits designed to ward off competition, either by acquiring not-quite-spurious patents for not-quite-off-the-drawing-board ideas, or by threatening legal proceedings that market entrants cannot possibly afford. This passes for innovation only where we bear in mind Stiegler's (1998, 34–37) distinction between innovation as normal science and invention as radical breakthrough. True invention becomes less and less likely, the more materially and financially entrenched protocols like the MPEG codecs become.

According to the major document laying out the requirements for Green MPEG,

> The main objectives of Green MPEG are:
> Efficient multimedia processing and transport: The standard will enable building interoperable solutions for energy-efficient consumption of media in this context.
> Enable efficient media encoding based on the energy resources of the encoder or the feedback from the receiver.
> Enable efficient media decoding and presentation.
> (ISO/IEC JTC1/SC29/WG11 N13468, April 2013)

In their background statement, the authors note that both ultrahigh-definition video transport and supply to mobile devices pose significant problems, the former threatening existing network fiber capacity, the latter the restricted bandwidth of cellular networks. The second bullet point directs attention toward another new challenge: the bandwidth required to return user data via MPEG-UD to the source of the signal. This will be an asymmetrical relation—download will far exceed upload—but will add significantly to the loading of signal. The "energy resources of the encoder" also come into play. Since MPEG-M is a dynamic system, it will be able to respond to fluctuations in the power available to the sender, whether that be someone initiating a VoIP call from Dhaka, or a broadcaster coping with power outages in Lagos. The new developments will result in new patents and new licenses to use them. As Laura deNardis (2009, 204) puts it, "Standards with embedded intellectual property rights, in the form of patents . . . raise the prices of these broadband technologies. Emerging markets without an installed base of existing products disproportionately bear the cost increases engendered by this escalation of embedded intellectual property rights."

The Internet that we know was birthed in the United States; the major language of its engineering documents and debates is English; and the major Internet corporations have a strategic influence on U.S. state policy in an era when the U.S. economy depends increasingly on entertainment and computing sectors (along with pharmaceuticals and weapons, also critically involved in the patent system and electronic communications) for its exports. Other states, as we saw above in the case of OOXML, can be bought off or bullied by corporate interests. As the first entrant, the United States and U.S. corporations have a powerful position; countries or regions without highly trained engineers, an advanced university sector, or the commercial and political clout of the BRIC countries (Brazil, Russia, India, and China) stand to lose not only economically but in terms of steering policy toward their interests, for example, toward open-source codecs, which promise to be far less expensive for developing nations. Green MPEG then drags us into an odd terrain where the aesthetics of data loss in encoding-decoding meets with new commercial surveillance technologies and laws governing digital rights management and patents, all in a policy framework where the dynamics of neoliberal governance overwhelm claims for emergent nations to participate in systems design, or civil society organizations struggling to maintain an independent voice. Is Green MPEG then merely another example of greenwashing, stealing the terminology of environmentalism in the interests of corporate profit?

Batteries did not get more efficient because the majority of the world's population do not have access to regular electricity supplies but because the increasingly nomadic and rhizomatic management style of corporations required both CEOs and the digital precariat to be able to work on the move. Green MPEG is likewise designed for the uses of highly disciplined network consumerism, rather than the interests of developing economies. Television, perhaps a luxury in the industrial world, is vital to democratic process in regions with low literacy rates. Encoding and decoding licenses add only a small percentage to the costs of manufacturing thousand-dollar computers, but a far greater proportion to the technologies of the poor. The principle of ownership over a normal, standard, and universal means of communication goes against all principles of justice, from Rawls (1971) to Sen (2009). Though MPEG-LA pledges never to refuse a license, it still has the legal right to withhold one from anyone unwilling or unable to pay, and the right to set the level of payment (as seen in long-running disputes over continuing charges for MPEG-2 patents after they had reached their term; Swanson 2013).

The principle of integral waste extends to the design of patents. Engineers are brought in to solve problems generated by neoliberal marketization of public goods, the resulting monopolistic behaviors supported by governments, and the drive to obsolescence powered by perpetual innovation at the level of protocols like MPEG. Increasing the number of pixels and the brilliance of backlights is not the same as increasing resolution: We are already close to the limits of human visual acutance (the ability to descry the clarity of edges) with a 1080 screen a couple of meters from the viewer, but we are instructed as disciplined consumers to hanker for bigger screens with higher 4-K and 6-K resolution, and the bandwidth and codecs necessary to support them. Also, MPEG-M further consolidates the monopoly tendency, concentrating control in the hands of profit-driven corporations, and including in it data from passive viewing in the same way as it harvests data from online activity. The sheer scale of the data involved beggars description: It also beggars those who have to pay for the machinery and energy required to gather and store it. Ironically, the engineering principle of efficiency integrates with the principle of economic waste.

A second result of efficient standardization is a decay of cultural control over perception in favor of commercial control. Just as lenses construe the world according to a very specific notion of how the visual should be constructed, so the bitmap armature of MPEG structures the mode of perception in the twenty-first century, schooling us to see in restricted color ranges, to unperceive the actual fog of a decompressed image, mentally reconstructing its original. Most of all, it teaches us to ignore the untidy randomness of the wind in the grass: MPEG teaches us to fail to see. Posing this managed perception as at once universal standard and private property is both a contradiction in terms and a dialectical condition that, alongside the fundamental incompleteness of the scanned image, offers us one form of hope. The wild years of network invention are largely over: Consolidation and the perpetual minor modifications of planned obsolescence have replaced them. The export of this technical, legal, and perceptual apparatus to populations that have no control over them is morally, politically, environmentally, and in the medium term even economically wrong. Standardization locks down the creative potential of technology even as it excludes nature by defining it as noise. As Mary Douglas argues, order gives the world meaning by giving it structure: "As we know it, dirt is essentially disorder. There is no such thing as absolute dirt: it exists in the eye of the beholder. . . . Dirt offends against order. Eliminating it is not a negative movement, but a positive effort to organise the environment" (Douglas 1966, 2).

It is our passion for order that creates the terms not only for language as our fundamental taxonomic tool, but for all communication, an ordering that distinguishes this from that, foreground from background, message from noise, the community of speakers from the world of others who do not share (our) language. Most of all, by reducing the nonhuman mediations of light and color, MPEG coding excludes natural process as noise. The elimination of dirt, as Douglas goes on to argue, is a deeply cultural act of constructing order. Eliminating natural process as visual noise belongs to a very specific and potentially inhuman mode of order.

Not only does MPEG encoding write in little the grand design of biopolitics and commodification: It makes it less and less possible to see beyond the prison house of pixels. Internet governance has become a ground for scholarly and political activism over the last ten years. That activist stance rarely extends to the codecs governing audiovisual culture with the same virulence and vitality, despite (or perhaps because of) the subperceptual levels at which the management of populations is currently conducted through them.

As the increasingly universal currency of exchange in visual culture, MPEG design engages an extremely fine mesh of norms governing the mediation of contemporary intercultural relations. Indigenous knowledge is especially vulnerable to such imposed universals, as for example in the attempt to patent traditional medical use of turmeric (Shiva 1997). Linda Tuhiwai Smith makes the case that the divorce of indigenous knowledge from the people to whom it is proper (but not property) is not only an abuse of power but undertaken, with whatever well-meaning motives, in the frame of a globalization of Western economic values:

The people and their culture, the material and the spiritual, the exotic and the fantastic, became not just the stuff of dreams and imagination, or stereotypes and eroticism, but of the first truly global commercial enterprise: *trading the Other*. . . . It is concerned more with ideas, languages, knowledge, images, beliefs and fantasies than any other industry. Trading the Other deeply, intimately, defines Western thinking and identity. As a trade, it has no concern for the peoples who originally produced the ideas or images. . . . Trading the Other is big business. For indigenous peoples trading ourselves is not on the agenda. (Smith 2012, 92–93)

Tracing this trade back to pre-Enlightenment accounts of imperial voyages, Smith points toward the origins of semiocapitalism (and we might add, the very idea of abstraction) in the theft of knowledge, now deracinated and tradable, from indigenous peoples whose originating meanings and pleasures, being of no concern, are reduced to mere background noise in the transmission of semiotic goods. The heart of this trade is the erroneous re-imagining of knowledge as data, as tradable commodity. The specific manner in which this is accomplished in the twenty-first century is the translation of the audiovisual experience of lives, cultures, and knowledges into the universal frame of the MPEG codec. Among the problems this raises are (1) the translation from culturally specific to universal format; (2) the organization of control over design of this format; and (3) the exclusion of environments as noise and of technical effects other than those designed in, since almost all visual technology works to the same standard. The model of the standard observer equally eradicates from concern any differences, biological or cultural, in modes of perception, excluding everything that does not conform to its standard as universal. In Tuhiwai Smith's perspective, these exclusions are premised on the exclusion of first peoples, first from their own cultural goods, and today from the design process shaping audiovisual transmission of their heritage. For indigenous peoples this is an insidious, silent perpetuation of settler colonialism that, according to Patrick Wolfe's definition, is marked by the fact that "the colonizers come to stay—invasion is a structure not an event" (1999, 2). The MPEG codec as universal means for communicating perception remodels both exocolonization of indigenous peoples and the endocolonization of metropolitan populations at the quantum level, its efficiencies excluding as noise what elsewhere we have seen excluded as environment and externality.

Abstraction arrived in Western art, no doubt, the art historians tell us, because of the autonomous logic of art itself: a move from depiction to a concern with the tools of painting and sculpture. One important document points us in another direction, however. In 1914 a leading light of the Bloomsbury group of English aesthetes, Clive Bell, published his book *Art*, which argues, in its first chapter, for the existence of an aesthetic sensibility apart and distinguished from the mere enjoyment of a good likeness. This early defense of abstraction hinges instead on the appreciation of "significant form," a thesis Bell defines through recourse to the idea of primitivism: "In primitive art you will find no accurate representation; you will find only significant form. Yet no other art moves us so profoundly. Whether we consider Sumerian sculpture or pre-dynastic Egyptian art . . . or, turning far afield, we consider that mysterious and majestic art that flourished in Central and South America before the coming of the white men, in every case we observe three common characteristics—absence of representation, absence of technical swagger, sublimely impressive form" (1914, n.p.).

The trade in the Other is then not only an orientalizing or eroticizing expropriation: The obverse of affective appropriation is the abstraction of a work from the culture in which it had meaning. Wrenching colonial artifacts from their cultural roots allows them to be seen as pure, meaning-free expressions unburdened by thought. If we take meaning to be the semantic coincidence of reason and emotion, what Bell articulates for his class is the rational side of orientalism. Similarly, the trade in the Other enshrined in the universal transmission standard MPEG is the direct heir of a longer history in which the act of colonial expropriation is the very type and origin of the process of absenting semantics from form, of abstracting, which lies at the heart of MPEG's algorithms. The rationalization of messy human perception, with its ragbag of religious and political connotations and its unpredictable ability to see the same thing twice in very different ways, was one of the first achievements of that scientific psychology which undergirds the automation of emotional response in MPEG-UD, with its hierarchy of what signifies and what is noise. This too is a legacy of the abstraction of "primitive" art from the local knowledge of materials and from the cultural significance that informed their first makers and users. The simple disconnection of collected items from their origins prepared them for enumeration, reordering, and commodification. This disconnection, effected by the geopolitical expansion of Europe, forms the technical infrastructure of the contemporary aesthetic and its exclusions of nature, technology, and specific, nonuniversal cultures. The governance of digital media is in this sense too a continuation of coloniality by other means.

CHAPTER 3

ECO-POLITICAL AESTHETICS

Such is the aestheticizing of politics as practiced
by fascism. Communism replies by politicizing art.
—**Walter Benjamin**, "The Work of Art in the Age of
Its Technological Reproducibility"

So how are we going to get out of this mess? The usual levers we pull are
not going to work. Economic, technological, and social responses to environmental crisis cannot resolve the challenges, and politics can work only
if there is a radical change in how we conceive of and pursue politics. This
change hinges on the very media whose environmental impacts have been
the subject of this book. Politics is already an (an)aesthetic practice. Only a
politics rebuilt on aesthetic principles, that is, by remaking communications,
offers the possibility of changing the conduct of relations between human
beings and nature, and between both of them and the technologies that so
profoundly and multifariously mediate between them.

Concluding his final version of the famous essay on technology and the
work of art, Benjamin reads war as the outcome of "the discrepancy between
the enormous means of production and their inadequate use in the process
of production." As a result, he declares, "Imperialist war is an uprising on
the part of technology, which demands repayment in 'human material' for
the natural material society has denied it" (Benjamin 2003b, 270). War is the
most extreme form of waste, of equipment and ammunition, buildings, lives,
and land. For Benjamin, the task fascism set itself was to make people re-

gard technological warfare as an artistic event. Thus politics had become an apology for the vicious reaction of technology to its subordination to profit. Overaccumulation demanded the explosive expenditure of war; fascist politics provided the brass bands and regalia. It is the contention of the current chapter that it may be necessary now to reverse Benjamin's judgment. The politics associated with neoliberalism have become anesthetic. The politics of ad hoc and fragmented neoliberal governance analyzed in chapter 2 is inadequate to the aesthetic and political challenge of environmentalism, and to the new suppression of technical evolution by the politics and economics of standardization.

The Poverty of Economics

The anonymization that capital learned by stealing "primitive" artifacts and developing a purely aesthetic relation to them is symptomatic of capital accumulation. It is an advanced form of a historically normative means of accumulation. Colonial enclosures not only demonstrated the relation of armed force to accumulation; enclosure has been a response to capital crises dating back centuries in Europe (Neeson 1993; Thirsk 1958; Thompson 1963) and in European colonialism (Corr 1999; Crosby 2013). Enclosure, this chapter argues, created the modern distinction between population and environment. The same rationale drove the Industrial Revolution to enclose the commons of everyday skills and to ossify them as the dead labor of the factory, which became the alien environment of the new working class. In our times, knowledge has been enclosed, alienated, and converted into an environment of databases and databanks from which we, the population, are excluded and which confronts us as an alien power. Capital persists through the ongoing privatization of the commons. Common wealth becomes private debt.

Denuded ecologies, once common lands but now external to accounts, are so because they have become environments. The anonymization of the workers whose skills are now embedded in factories, and the anonymous ancestors whose knowledge is now traded as patents, belong to the same regime of anonymity that accompanied colonial rule and slavery. This process now affects knowledge. Just as color was stripped of its semantic roots, so knowledge has been stripped of its intimate relation to the knower, in order to become tradable information. The abstraction of indigenous knowledge was the first historical model for this becoming-environmental of data. This process, in which MPEG shares, is the latest form of that "trading in the Other" that Smith sees not only as a blight on indigenous people but as the very root of Western alienation from populations and lands. If there is to be a genuine public intimacy other than that contained by the formal protocols of semiocapital, if there is to be an end therefore to anonymization, abstraction, and alienation in twenty-first-century media, then it will have to start at the level of a new commons. While some contemporary thinkers (e.g., Badiou 2012; Dean 2012; Žižek 2010) believe that this commons will be communist, this chapter argues that it will be communicative.

One source of the problem, the artificial separation of politics from economics, is critiqued in Marx's own works where, as Ellen Meiksins Wood (1981, 67–68) writes, "His critique of political economy was, among other things, intended to reveal the political face of the economy which had been obscured by bourgeois political economists." The idea that the economy had an existence apart from politics (or psychology or ethics or any other social science) was not raised by the discipline's founders, Adam Smith, John Stuart Mill, and Karl Marx. It had to be invented, through a long, complex, and as yet incomplete project (Milonakis and Fine 2009), which, if Harvey (2010) is correct, has resulted in the economic becoming the mask of an actually political project of reinstating the old class division between the impossibly rich and the unrelieved poor. The economy is to that extent a real abstraction: The faith placed in it gives it the power to make real changes in the world. Criticizing economics for being premised on an abstract concept only proves that the economy is inadequate as an explanation for our current crisis, and that its ascendancy is instead a symptom. The problem then is that given its role as agent in the world, it has no desire to do anything other than reproduce the conditions of its own existence, that is, the absolute separation of the economy from the rest of human activity, a separation that derives directly from the separation of human from natural worlds, and stands in causal relation to the separation of the human from technology.

The task of the economy is to reduce everything to exchange, a process in which the particularity of things and actions is dismissed in favor of their exchange value. Marx (1976, 131–35) makes the distinction between "useful labour," which is always a specific undertaking like tailoring or weaving, and "simple average labour," the general form of labor, fragmented by the division of labor, that ignores the specificity and difference of useful labor. In the production of commodities, the material specificity of craft is abstracted into its general form as simple labor. At the same time, the specific geology of place and the ecologies of flora, fauna, and indigenous people are fragmented and converted into anonymous things so they can enter the circuits of exchange as commodities, or be expelled. This controlled simplification and abstraction of people, places, and processes in the interests of exchange value is why the market cannot be the engine of an ecologically open future. Refusing to accept the economic as the driver of history opens the way to recognizing difference, rather than interchangeable, indifferent objects, as the basis of a new politics. For Negri, "*the common is that which distinguishes*" (2008, 162, original emphasis). Contra the idea of a global commons that belongs to all, Negri's formulation allows us to recognize claims to differential access: indigenous claims to specific places, events that belong exclusively to women, or territories out of bounds to humans. It promotes difference as meaningful and useful, against the indifferent regime of exchange value. Negri continues, "Language and cooperation have to contain within them *a break at the level of practice*" (2008, 162, original emphasis): The media of the commons are not smoothly integrated like the imagined integration of the universal free market, but marked by radical difference. If we understand his premise to apply also to nonhuman mediations, then the common, necessarily including the natural and technological, can no longer be abstracted as environment and externality from the human polis. On the contrary, nature and technology must be recognized as having their own claims to act, to offer that idiosyncratic, useful labor that produces the common and the differences within it. In this spirit, eco-politics can only come into being when we distinguish between what we have now—the administration of the public in the polity—and the potential of politics as the operation of constituent power. Chapter 1 distinguished communication between divided termini and mediation as the open interconnected ecology of everything. Communication of and through difference is the means and mediation of the goal of an ecological aesthetics and politics.

The Enclosure of Technology

The only historian capable of fanning the spark of hope in the past is
the one who is firmly convinced that even the dead will not be safe
from the enemy if he is victorious.
—Benjamin, "On the Concept of History"

The absence of human beings among MPEG patent owners is utterly alien to indigenous peoples, for whom the ancestors who invented a way of working are known by name and addressed in working with their inventions. In Maori culture, where dialogue with the ancestors is central to both aesthetic practice and community decision making, the names of ancestors are familiar. In the West, where, as the hallmark of modernity, technology replaced tradition, the names of our ancestors are all but forgotten. We ignore the numberless anonymous artisans whose skill with the needle bred the sewing machine, whose eccentric motion in turn was the vital principle in moving pictures. We turn into patents the common heritage of sleights of hand, the foundation of continuous-motion illusions. A thousand perceptual and mechanical ideas generated over millennia are concentrated into the MPEG-LA patent pool, while their origins are erased in favor of property rights. Selectively forgetting ancestral wisdom about handling waste, while equally selectively picking out those chemical and land management techniques that can be turned to property and profit, denies and disguises the ancestral presence and the common heritage. The difference between traditional cultures and modern is as small as this: the anonymity that comes from treating the dead as exploitable resources rather than partners in dialogue. Benjamin's analysis of war as revolt of the machines cited above describes, in this perspective, the revenge of dead labor on the living. The dead have become externalities in the unholy construction of capital.

In the section of *Grundrisse* devoted to machines, Marx advances the theory that machines produce value by embodying previous labor: "The accumulation of knowledge and skill of the productive forces of the social brain, is thus absorbed into capital" (1973, 694). Technologies are, in a sense that many indigenous worldviews would endorse, the concentrated form of the skills, knowledge, and creativity of the past. Their concentration and concretization in machines constitutes a second enclosure. Capital mobilizes the commons in the form of the shared stock of wisdom, knowledge, and skills Marx calls "general intellect," in order to expropriate it and place it over against the factory worker, turning it from common possession to a machine for domination, discipline, and the extraction of labor. Dead labor congeals to form the technologies of production comprising factories and machines that Marx defined as fixed capital, as opposed to the liquidity of money and workers. The historical gift of previous generations whose expertise, knowledge, and creativity was taken from the commons lies embedded and embodied in today's machines. Anonymous and ignored, our ancestors inhabit our technologies.

Kant (1952, §65) and Hegel (1969, §1543) agree that machines are distinguishable from living creatures because a living creature is its own teleology, but a machine's teleology is always external to it. Living is its own goal; the goal of a machine is whatever it has been designed to do, something beyond and apart from itself. Marx's reference to the virtuosity of the worker, "his understanding of nature and his mastery over it by virtue of his presence as a social body" (1973, 705), expressed in his handling of a tool, suggests that this distinction is one that is distinctively capitalist, and indeed Marx emphasizes the continuity between worker and tool, rather than the absolute distinction between them inherited from the German Idealist tradition of Hegel and Kant. In his later writings, Heidegger distinguished archaic tools like axes and earthenware that, in his mystic phenomenology, possess Being, from dams, trains, and televisions that do not. So Heidegger suggests that Kant and Hegel's teleological distinction remains in force, but now referring only to modern technologies while hand tools refer back to an idealized past. For all three, the distinguishing feature of technologies is that they are given as parts whose assembly into an organized unit, whose very reason for existing, is oriented outside them. The corollary is that organic beings are intrinsically whole and inwardly oriented, a presumption of individual integrity and self-identity. The intense sociality of human beings and the ecological interdependency of animals, insects, plants, water, geology, even subatomic events, disproves the Idealist thesis of self-sufficient teleology. Similarly, the thesis is incorrect that machines are incapable of serving purposes for which they were not designed, or of evolving in ways that are not subservient to external human goal setting. In the age of cybernetics, when smart machines link together in networks of self-regulating devices from thermostats to artificial life (a-life), this presumption cannot hold unanalyzed.

After the enclosures, "productive work came to be defined as money-earning work (primarily wage-labour)" while subsistence activity was held to be unproductive, so beginning the long institutional sexism of the economy (Wallerstein 1983, 24–25). Under industrialization, however, many subsistence skills were privatized in machinery and later in the service economy. Colonies likewise promoted the development of semiproletarian households. Taxation demanded money, which required some form of wage labor, while restrictions on movement hampered full engagement in the wage economy (Wallerstein 1983, 39), both depressing wages and maintaining a pool of nominally unproductive domestic and subsistence skills for future exploitation. Indigenous skills associated with ceramics, dyes, horticulture, navigation, and specialist techniques like high-altitude smelting in the Andes or the care of cochineal beetles in Mexico were looted from the commons of their originators, industrialized, and the products sold back to the colonized. The alienation of dead labor as feared alien other reached its apogee in the factory, an environment inimical to human desire and ways of living. As Benjamin intimates, this alienation is at its most concentrated in the application of technology to war, and most of all to colonial invasion and genocide. But even in the form of enforced labor in the plantations of the Caribbean, where rifle and stirrup saddle enforced discipline, the process of enclosed ancestral knowledge being used against the living ensured that technology would appear to them, and to us, for the first time as something nonhuman and antihuman: as an environment, surrounding the human but no longer part of it.

The virtual autonomy of the dead in the form of general intellect does not imply freedom from natural laws. Quite the contrary: No one is more subject to natural laws than the dead. In their actualization at the point of death, the dead alone have reconciled themselves completely with the laws of nature. It is that reconciliation which reappears in ideologies of universal law as the absolute without alternative. In instrumental technology defined by obedience to law, the dead hand of the past appears as the ideological reason why the future may not emerge. But death is more than actualization. The purpose of dying is to convert accumulated skills and knowledges into potential at the service of future generations. To understand death as purely natural or, as Heidegger seems to imply, specifically human is to miss its generative function in the general intellect embodied in technologies, and to condemn us to a politics dedicated to the permanent subjugation of its creative potential.

Machines, Marx argued, are products "of the human will over nature, or of human participation in nature . . . the power of knowledge objectified" (1973, 707). With this minor correction ("participation"), technologies do not have to be the expression of a will to mastery, but can signal human participation in natural processes (Schmidt 1971, 15), a direct result of the new social combinations brought about by the division of labor in factory systems. The actualization of the general intellect in the factory introduced by the enclosure of tools instigates a new relation with nature, grounded in what at an earlier stage had been work alongside and in conjunction with both natural processes and material resources. The utopian promise of the machine was always to relieve humanity of the necessity of work. Capital failed to convert this social intelligence into free time (Clastres 1987), instead devoting it to excess productivity in pursuit of profit, and perverting the potential locked up in ancestral technologies to the point of directing the self-annihilation of accumulated technologies and living labor all at once in its wars, one more clue to the suicidal inhumanity of the corporate cyborg.

Because our machines appear to us both as dead and as instruments, we neither attempt dialogue nor recognize autonomy among them, and treat them as objects, that is, as the end results of processes rather than their beginnings. They appear to us as actual: as things which are only capable of repeating the actions engineered into them in their past. In so doing we ascribe an identity to them, not of the ancestors but of the machines in which they have been imprisoned. But in the anonymous afterlife of technology, the skills, knowledges, organizational techniques, language games, and communicative tricks of the dead are embodied in forms that are capable of much more than the instrumental repetition decreed by external teleology. Machines and forms of organizing, once we consider them as communicative, are no longer constituted as essences and identities. The resurgence of interest in genealogy suggests that the lack of ancestors is becoming a felt absence. Deleuze and Guattari's (1985, 1–50) desiring machines likewise evidence a need to communicate, the germ of a constituent power. Just as our severance from nature reappears to us as a need to commune with it, so these symptoms point toward a need to dialogue not only through but with machines. Dialogue in turn presumes that communication is motivated by lack of whatever it is we seek in communication, and that the other's capacity to communicate indicates its autonomous desire for a missing completion too. Communicative agency is grounded in this radical instability of desire as lack, a lack in particular of a whole, complete, and desire-free self-identity. Communication implies nonidentical entities capable of becoming otherwise. As instruments of capital, the ancestors are condemned to identity. As general intellect, however, the dead, unnecessarily silenced, alien, feared after millennia of priestly ministrations, emerge *in potentia* to the living world of the virtual.

The Data Environment

Debt, the central instrument of finance capital, is the disappearance of the future into its simulation, a symptom of what might be called, following Žižek (2006, 317–18), the worldlessness of neoliberal capital, a term already floated in Arendt's (1958a) *The Human Condition*. For Arendt, to be worldly signified having a stake in a common world, specifically in the form of property, a form poisoned, however, by its privatization as wealth at the dawn of capitalism. In Žižek, the absence of a shared world is marked by the extreme subjectivity of experience, expressed for example in goalless rioting. To be worldless is to lack a sense of the proper: of one's connections to both the natural and the human world. Worldlessness is thus connected to the process of colonialism and its contemporary form, globalization, as described in the *Communist Manifesto* (Marx and Engels 1969): "In place of the old wants, satisfied by the productions of the country, we find new wants, requiring for their satisfaction the products of distant lands and climes. In place of the old local and national seclusion and self-sufficiency, we have intercourse in every direction, universal inter-dependence of nations."

Neoliberalism extends this communicative interdependence from ecological principle to the new role of the metropolitan working class, whose labor is no longer required for production but to destroy, on a planetary scale, the overproduction forced by the falling rate of profit that is also the engine that moves work away from workers. According to Žižek, the parsimonious, puritanical, production era's deferred gratification has been replaced by the consumption era's compulsory enjoyment. This destructive enjoyment of meaningless, unwanted, and all too often toxic commodities is worldless because it is separated not only from communities of meaning but from the bonds of the sacred and the particularities of place that mark participation in an ecology.

Ejected in the process of enclosure from the worlds we once inhabited, we are worldless, and generate the remaindered world as environments in reaction to the condition of worldlessness, projecting our lack onto the alienated landscapes, technologies, and data that we inhabit only as strangers. We are not posthuman, because we have not been human since the first enclosures. The formal structure of our sacrifice of humanity is the economic externality of all our environments, those inalienable parts of ourselves—place, skill, knowledge—that have been alienated from us. Land, skill, and knowledge that were not ours to sell or give were taken, alienated in order to become property. Ironically, what could never be given is now treated precisely as the given: data. To become data, land, skill, and knowledge had to be reduced to a common arithmetical form: land as map, skill as bookkeeping, knowledge as database. In the form of data, as Alex Galloway (2012, 82) notes, knowledge has no intrinsic visual form. The same might be said of labor in the enclosure of skill in the factory environment: Labor as such became invisible as it became commodity. Today in the form of data, knowledge suffers the same disappearance.

Invisibility has been central to the worldlessness of computerized knowledge since the 1960s. What was once an avant-garde refusal of the retinal announced by Duchamp (Cabanne 1971, 43) has become a core strategy of dominion. The purpose of data is neither to know nor to picture but to manage and predict. Manipulation of variables is constrained by respect for software rules, by the maxima and minima that shape their functioning, and increasingly by the sheer inertia of amassed data. Databases predict the predictable, consistently erasing as aberrant those outlying actions that cannot be reduced to behaviors. The heterogeny of time is abstracted and reduced to homogeneous space. This tendency to absolutize Cartesian space is deeply ingrained in digital hardware, logic design, and software, orchestrated into an arithmetic form that in-forms, and that we have come to see as identical with, the idea of information.

The concept of environment is then an abstraction that nonetheless acts as if it were a reality. In this it is not alone: Exchange value is abstracted from useful work and its useful products; the commodity likewise abstracts from real social relations; and as the crash of 2007–2008 demonstrated, the purest abstraction of finance capital has very tangible effects on real lives. Observing this tendency of capital to create abstractions with material effects, Marx christened them "real abstractions" (1973, 85–88). In his commentary on the *Grundrisse*'s pages on technology, Paolo Virno argues that since Marx's day, the real abstraction of money has been replaced by the real abstraction of technoscientific codes and paradigms. Post-Fordist production is so dependent on information and communication that the general intellect is no longer restricted to fixed capital but has become living labor, "the indivisible knowledges of living subjects and their linguistic cooperation," constitutive of reality, and in excess of "what can be deposited in machines" (Virno 1996, 270). Virno might then be read as arguing that the dead are not only expropriated and exploited in the form of dead labor. Their role as the makers of language is also exploited in new forms of living labor, not only organizationally but now far more deeply imbricated in symbolic networks. However, as Virno (2004) argues later in *A Grammar of the Multitude*, this innovative power to make new systems is no longer a side benefit of employing workers: It is written into our contracts. Jacques Ellul (1964) proposed a definition of technics as ensembles of machines and human actions. Virno stresses the creativity of workers in finding new ways to reduce their work, using all the unexpected affordances of the factory. In such misuse of equipment we learn to participate in technology as we participate in nature, and to that extent to enter into dialogue with the dead. However, as Virno goes on to argue, the cunning of workers' work-arounds is regularly taken from them by capital as sets of practices that can be formalized to increase the efficiency with which surpluses can be extracted from the human-machine ensemble. Factory survival strategies, including office workers' tactical misuse of their computers, are a first alliance siphoning the energy of the dead for the use of the living. Through its surveillance of workplace improvisations, capital is learning to extrapolate from even these alliances a new form of enclosure.

In his reading of the same passages in the *Grundrisse*, Negri argues that since in contemporary capitalism "production is already completely communication, then the sense of the antagonism [between labor and power] will have neither a place nor a time of foundation separate from communication itself" (1996, 160). Unlike the commons defined by differentiation, the factory produces itself as a communicative milieu in which the struggle between labor and bosses is reduced to a matter of the direction of communications. Any antagonism is abstracted as a matter of disciplined encoding and decoding of instructions. So it is that communication, now redefined as know-how, is abstracted from genuine human relationships, to become the object of a new enclosure. Such reduced communication is central to capital, undergirding everything from supply chain and factory management to financial flows, for which reason, therefore, capital endeavors to ensure that communication does not exist in any democratic or mutual form between workers and factory owners, between humans and machines, or between humans and nature. The governance issues raised in chapter 2 belong to this regime of communication control, grounded in the enclosures that divide human from natural, and human from technological, ensuring the servitude of natural and technical environments through colonization of lands, colonized peoples, and the dead. The difference between Marx's time and our own is that wherever communication protocols emerge between these phyla, capital that once tried to shut them down through discipline now works to exploit them as biopolitical resources. Today, the ongoing process of enclosure and expropriation moves to colonize the general intellect.

The third wave of enclosure, the enclosure of knowledge, also began in colonialism. Colonial science sought not only to expand its taxonomies by including the flora and fauna of its new dominions, and by building new planetary sciences like meteorology. It also began the increasingly systematic collection of native wisdom. The term *wisdom* is marked by colonialism: We speak of wisdom for the most part referring to discourses external to Western rationality, but especially discourses that have come to us as fragmentary or as lost, in many instances as a result of colonialist violence or colonial disease. Nonetheless, precisely because it carries the reminders of these histories, "wisdom" can refer to the knowledge of colonized peoples concerning ways of conducting their relations with the world and one another. Farming practices, making medicines, methods for taming, hunting, and working with animals and plants, all became targets of acquisition, at first in a naive outburst of euphoric rationalism, but very soon in the machinery of expropriation. The first stage of expropriation is to disentangle knowledge from practice, distilling it into a separate regime of facts. Once identified as an object of colonial knowledge, the fact can become an object of exchange: Objectification of practice as data is integral to the commodification of ideas.

The enclosure of knowledge is in this respect only a further stage in the colonization of skills. In the former, however, it was the knowledge of the dead that was expropriated in order to become technology. In this phase, it is living labor, and especially the general intellect—shared and common knowledge, expressed in language, culture, design, and ways of doing things—on which the transmission of skills and the invention of new activities depends. The capture of this kind of wisdom and know-how was first attempted in works like d'Alembert and Diderot's *Encyclopédie*, accomplishing only the basic task of converting common knowledge into information: It remained to convert it from the useful form of information into the exchangeable form of data. Capital overcame the democratic liberalism of the Encyclopédistes in the reaction against the French and American revolutions, instigating laws, especially for patents, to govern the conversion of ideas into properties. In digitizing this information, capital has been able to complete the enclosure by installing traditional wisdom, along with the knowledge generated by living labor in the commons of the general intellect, in databases. Already prepared for commodity circulation through intellectual property laws, knowledge converted into information was ready to become a new environment. The environmentalization of information as data sets it apart from those who once knew it: Now they confront it as strangers. We would now rather trust an online map than the directions a local gives us in the street. Alienated from our own knowledge, the human subjects of the data environment experience another way of being human. Land enclosures turned farmers into agricultural laborers; industrial enclosures turned artisans into workers. The new change is so recent we have yet to find our terminology, but we might say that it is changing knowing creatures into "prosumers" of knowledge: people who both produce and consume it in relations no longer of shared information but of data exchange, and therefore mediated by exchange value. What is clear is that today knowledge is no longer something held as common sense between people, as familiar as a hammer in the hand once was. Knowledge has become an environment confronting us as something apart: alien and inhuman, even antihuman.

The data environment has two functions. First, it encloses knowledge in the commodity form of countable and exchangeable units; and second, it extends the principles of datafication back over previous environments, searching for extractable information that can be deployed for the production of further commodities. Both processes apply to the conversion of interpersonal relationships into data, a process that extends to nonvoluntary data systems such as the use of facial recognition in public surveillance systems (Kember 2013). Such systems can be traced back to time and motion studies of the factory worker (Smith 1999), to nineteenth-century laboratory experiments in pursuit of the elimination of fatigue (Rabinbach 1990), to attempts to structure communicative environments to minimize distraction (Crary 1999), and to the early beginnings of eugenics (Wegenstein 2011), the nascent forms of biopolitics.

In recolonizing the natural world, the latest enclosures reinterpret the environment, no longer as nature but as the data of nature. The shared knowledge of the world we call science has developed advanced tools for seeing through the phenomena of the natural world (woodlands, breezes, waves breaking on beaches) to their underpinning abstractions as numbers and as exemplars of universal laws. Territories once marked as the domains of local gods are now countable constellations of facts, knowledge about which can be turned into instruments of rule and profit. As new models of factory communication reduced talk to the level of instructions, the remaking of nature as data smooths out the contradictions of enclosure and externalization. Nature is no longer outside of accounts. By accounting for the unaccounted, providing systematic models for measuring and regulating the activities of environments, the database economy draws nature into the circuits of capital. Moreover, where the boundary between human and natural once posed a threat to the integrity of the human, now the same regimen of arithmetic order can be applied to both. Where data are presented as the common form of both natural and human ecologies, they provide the perfect tool for policing the boundary between them where, Foucault argues, contemporary politics is enacted: "Biopolitics' last domain is . . . control over relations between the human race, or human beings insofar as they are a species, insofar as they are living beings, and their environment, the milieu in which they live" (2003, 244–45). The contradiction is overcome, but produces another: How now are we to distinguish human from natural? Indeed, given the digitization of knowledge and of both the production and circulation of capital, how is either to be distinguished from technology? Is it the case that in the datafication of human behavior, human populations find themselves on the wrong side of a border in which, as merely living beings, they are themselves in the process of becoming environmental?

Reversing the conditions of previous enclosures, semiotic labor—the production and manipulation of symbols in the design, media, marketing, and financial sectors among others—externalizes producers and consumers alike in the guise of data, and therefore as objects of the data environment rather than its rulers. There is some merit in beginning to understand the free market of neoliberalism as an environment: produced by everyone but accessible to none. From a certain point of view, the market is indistinguishable from the data environment. It is no longer the circulation of goods that matters but their symbolic status as brands, and their statistical presence as market shares and performance indicators. The market is more concerned with the exchange of electronic symbols—increasingly handled by machines—than with traded goods and physical money. Automated stock taking, RFID-tagged containers, geo-tagged mobiles, commercialized medical records, cookies tracing Internet behavior and loyalty, and debit cards logging purchases all create an environment in which logistical tracking is at least as important and profitable as producing goods. Under such conditions, the distinction between human population and data environment is as entrenched as the gap between worker and factory or peasant and wilderness, while biopolitical government becomes ever harder to identify in actual human beings.

While the Internet increasingly appears to be an environment, filled with opaque databases we cannot access, the market rules as at once a data environment we cannot but inhabit, and as an agency of political as well as economic power from which we are excluded. Successively deprived of land, skill, and knowledge in the enclosures of modernity, the human stands now at the brink of a fourth enclosure, that of the body. Increasingly treated as environment, both the individual body and the biomass of the human population are today seen as threatening and alien sources of disease, but also as terrains open to exploitation through bioscience, and commodification through dietary, pharmaceutical, and surgical modification. The human body can therefore now function as exchange value, not only in the form of labor, as in the industrial phase of capital, but as a cost-free environmental res nullius open to commodification, and available as externality for dumping of excess production and waste. After the first enclosures, Luther declared everything below the waist as nature, and damned. After the Industrial Revolution, Darwin declared everything from the neck down as nature. Freud heralded the new dispensation by making everything from the face back nature's instinctual domain. The residue is the rational brain, enunciated in the purposive instrumentalities of cognitivism and neuroscience, a mind whose function is either to provide unpaid creativity for, or paid functions in, corporate cyborgs. In this sense the environment has grown at the expense of the human, to the extent that the human person could today be understood as a technical performance with biological organs as its infrastructure. Anyone who does not fit this model is reduced to increasingly menial and marginalized manual labor or to the status of economic externality: population without purpose.

The inherent contradiction of enclosure and externalization is the Klein bottle of environmentalization: What is inside is equally outside; enclosure produces externality. Excluded environments become external to the populations that inhabit them, yet as ecological science has always argued, ecology is internal to the species. At the same time, unlike the natural environment, which had a previous existence as primal mediation, data come into existence as a result of previous enclosures and therefore "information is . . . embedded in a perpetual labour process that we know better as communication" (Söderberg 2008, 72). As data become environment, something new occurs: they become externality (unpaid productivity of human activity), raw material, and private property, as nature had before it, but they also become product, service, and commodity. This enclosure-exclusion binary is intrinsically contradictory, unstable, and therefore unsustainable.

The heart of this contradiction is private property, defined in law as the right to deprive others of enjoyment of the thing owned: The foundation of property is deprivation. In the 2008 mortgage crisis, private property turned out to be the property of corporations, when financialization's victims were simply and legally deprived of their homes and goods. Private property entails privation. The commons entails communication. Against the capitalist model of property as privation operated by cyborg corporations, struggles for communal sharing, from the Diggers of the English Revolution to the Movimiento al Socialismo government in Bolivia, demonstrate that the development of communication is integral to the development of communal ownership. The data environment embraces human as well as natural worlds, reducing both, but therefore also making mutual communication between them increasingly possible. The three enclosures—of land, skill, and knowledge—produce not one but three environments: nature, technology, and data. Even as it differentiates between them and their inhabitants, environmentalization establishes the conditions for communication between them. The privative model extracts on behalf of the diminishing part of the world that remains internal and environed only the commodity form of exchange value from this communication. The ever-growing external residue becomes the grounds for a different commonwealth.

The Unsociable Society

It is important to distinguish the commons from the social. The commons is by definition communicative, therefore mediated by matter and energy, and so material. Society is an abstraction. Like the economy, it has no material existence other than as a concept; one that spawns even more ideological and abstract entities like the general public and public opinion, terms that articulate the arithmeticization and datafication of humanity. As Latour argues, "The social cannot be construed as a kind of material or domain" (2005, n.p.): It is not something that can do or have done to it. Constructing the modern idea of the social required at its foundation divorcing the human world from its environing neighbors through a particular formation of instrumental, technoscientific rationality, with an associated attack on "superstitious" beliefs in the deep entanglements of human and natural affairs. Habermas (1984, 48, original emphasis) argues that "the demythologization of worldviews means the desocialization of nature and the denaturalization of society. This process . . . apparently leads to a basic conceptual *differentiation between the object domains* of nature and culture." To Habermas, the division of natural and social domains is conceptual, rather than actual. Its historical appearance was for him a symptom of secular science's demythologizing of human-natural relations. The conceptual and ultimately cultural division of the social, nature, and technology and their consequent subjugation leads directly to the tragic misrecognition of their mutual interdependence and therefore of what the social is or, more significantly, might become. Lost in the severing of the social from the physical and technical are those elements of humanity that are most technological and most natural—the virtuality of the dead and what Arendt describes as the natality of the newborn: "The new beginning inherent in birth can make itself felt in the world only because the newcomer possesses the capacity of beginning something anew, that is, of acting. In this sense of initiative, an element of action, and therefore of natality, is inherent in all human activities. Moreover, since action is the political activity par excellence, natality, and not mortality, may be the central category of political, as distinguished from metaphysical, thought" (1958a, 9).

Natality is the potentiality that is the birthright of all infants, who may do and become anything but who, as they age, become more and more actual, more and more determined by what they have done and been, until the point at which they have actualized themselves completely, the point of death. In opposition to mortality—an opposition that pitches Arendt against her teacher Heidegger's theme of "being-toward-death," a life lived in and against the expectation of its own extinction—Arendt proposes life as the unfolding of an at-first latent and undifferentiated capacity to change, to become other, and to remake the world otherwise than how the infant finds it. Contemporary constructions of the social, however, depend on the sequestration of this natality, just as they do on sequestering the virtuality of the ancestors, their capacity to bring true invention into new generations. The social, society, is under these circumstances just as much a consequence of the divorce of human, natural, and technical as, and no more a solution than, the economy.

What then of technological invention as a social resource? According to a posthumous report (testifying to both the man's status and his enduring legacy), at an 1883 meeting of the International Fisheries Exhibition, Thomas Huxley, the most lauded British scientist of his day, opined,

> I believe it may be affirmed with confidence that, in relation to our present modes of fishing, a number of the most important sea fisheries, such as the cod fishery, the herring fishery, and the mackerel fishery, are inexhaustible. And I base this conviction on two grounds. First, that the multitude of these fishes is so inconceivably great that the number we catch is relatively insignificant; and secondly, that the magnitude of the destructive agencies at work upon them is so prodigious that the destruction effected by the fishermen cannot sensibly increase the death rate. . . . I believe, then, that the cod fishery, the herring fishery, the mackerel fishery, and probably all the great sea fisheries are inexhaustible; that is to say, that nothing we do seriously affects the number of fish. And any attempt to regulate these fisheries seems, consequently, from the nature of the case, to be useless. (Huxley 1895)

With benefit of hindsight, we know that the Atlantic halibut were fished out by 1850 (Lear 1998, 61), forty-five years before Huxley's speech, and that the Atlantic cod have been driven to the edge of extinction since (Kurlansky 1997). Yet we harbor similar ideologies about the other supposedly infinite resources on which the economic dogma of endless growth depends. Against all geological evidence and common sense, energy economist Maurice Adelman (1972) argued in the year of *The Limits to Growth* that "minerals are inexhaustible and will never be depleted." Might it be the case that today's faith in inexhaustible human creativity, especially its ability to generate technological solutions to contemporary crises, masks an impending technological crisis in the near future? The more nature is accounted for in metrics and as data, the less room it has to surprise us. The more human knowledge is rendered as environment, in processes that are increasingly automated, the less the human population exceeds its measurement. The more human action is reduced to behaviors, the more it becomes its measurement, its autoarchiving in the database economy. What heterogeneous innovation there is must come from an increasingly homogeneous population, and from a technical infrastructure whose engineering solutions and organizational shape are more and more isomorphic with capital itself, that is with the very forms that it is charged with renovating. Engineering and design are increasingly defined as problem-solving disciplines, but where the problems they are to solve are set by an increasingly standardized system, the space for pure creativity in technology diminishes. Innovation comes from difference, but consumer discipline depends on the resolution of difference as one or another marketable identity.

Nor can user-generated content become a universal, popular platform for innovation so long as the infrastructure that would permit it is founded on the integral waste of finite resources. Deferring the costs of overexploitation, pollution, and environmental degradation is a short-term solution: Evading them entirely is pathological. The privilege granted to innovation of lethal and wasteful technologies like weapons and cars and in the extraction and accumulation of raw materials fritters away what invention is available. Calibrating development against the intensity of media infrastructures (measured by features such as inward investment in transport systems designed to remove anything of value) only increases exploitation and waste. Benkler's (1998) proposal for the socialization of innovation is utopian so long as it is subsumed into the technical and data environments, informed by their instrumentality and made subservient to the inhuman logic of profit. The neoliberal formation of society distances the social from its own constituents, replacing commonwealth with private property and manic accumulation. The social, to the extent that it is subsumed into instrumentalized technology while excluding the organic environment, is then not the solution but the problem.

CHAPTER 4 ECOLOGICAL COMMUNICATION AS POLITICS

Ecological communication, this closing chapter repeats, is both the means and the goal of ecological politics. Ecological communication is not a pipe dream but a historical and contemporary actuality. Coal has communicated with humans for centuries. In Tyneside, northern England, coal seams reach the coast, giving lumps of sea coal to gatherers in sheer geological generosity. By the time of Queen Elizabeth I, the worthy priors of coastal Northumberland were mining and sending coal to London, where the Company of Brewers, recognizing the communicative overspill of coal burning, offered to fire their breweries in the vicinity of Westminster palace with wood because the queen "findeth hersealfe greatly greved and annoyed with the taste and smoke of the see coles" (Galloway 1882, 24). In 1582, however, only four years later, the communication was reversed when the queen obtained a ninety-nine-year lease on the Tyneside manors of Gateshead and Whickham together with their coal pits, which became the center of the early coal industry. From 1578 London to 2015 Beijing, coal has sent messages about the consequences of burning it. SourceWatch (2015) lists twenty-seven different modes of pollution from coal. From acid rain associated with high-sulfur coals to the killer smogs of Philadelphia and London (and now China), and from fish poisoned by particulate mercury to the toxins once released from smokestacks now destined for the landfill (Freese 2003), coal communicates not only in the present but from the past to the future. From 1582 to the twenty-first century, when it provides over 40 percent of the world's electricity (Greenpeace 2008), it has been communicated as exchange value, where it retains some hint of its ability to communicate itself. In the era of greenwashing, coal is communicated without that ability. The World Coal Association (2015), for instance, announces that "continuous improvements in technology have dramatically reduced or eliminated many of the environmental impacts traditionally associated with the use of coal." David Tyfield (2014, 60, citing Tollefson 2011), however, points out that "the International Energy Agency (IEA) calculates that CCS [clean coal systems] could contribute over 15 per cent of global [greenhouse gas] emission reductions needed for the mid-century target of 450 ppm of CO_2. This would need 3200 CCS projects sequestering 150 [gigatons of] CO_2. In fact, CCS is dragging along, with virtually no progress since 2007 and not a single full-size coal-fired power plant with CCS in operation." The industry's version not only spins the truth but ignores the communication of coal itself, even as it suppresses the economic motivation for doing so. The long mediation of prehistoric sunlight on primeval forests and oceans, of geological processes and upheavals, the transport systems of Northumberland colliers, all disappear in the accelerations of burning, exchange, and financialization, to vanish entirely, with not even a puff of smoke, in the instant messaging of public relations and marketing: ironically, since spin requires the energy it disposes of so glibly. The lesson of coal is that we do not simply invent but reconstitute an ancient communication between phyla. But we must do so on the basis of the current alienated and repressed condition of environmental communication.

The Politics of No Politics

The environmentalization of information implies the informationalization of the environment, of all three environments, which thus become objects of semiotic labor and control in addition to their previous regimes. Oil, which first appeared in seeps from shallow reserves in Mesopotamia and in North America, where it was used to fuel smoky lamps, emerged as use value. Since fossil fuels for the most part were underground, they could be treated as terra nullius, the property of none and therefore prey to enclosure in the colonial manner we have witnessed throughout this book. In Mitchell's (2011) analysis, oil provided a technical ensemble whose fluid form made resistance by organized labor much more difficult. Here oil passed into the industrial environment, part of the surrounding world, no longer integral to the human. In more recent years, oil has taken on a second, financial existence, amplified by fears of Hubbert's (1956) peak oil thesis. From here on, oil was no longer simply a material. It was to be counted and assessed in terms of future re-serves. Gambling on the price curves likely to be triggered by depleting re-serves in turn feeds back into exploration and the advance of prospecting into more dangerous Arctic or contested regions, and dirtier forms like shale oil. In the era of finance capital, oil as information is as important a com-modity as oil as fuel. With such moves, the natural environment enters the information environment.

This analysis is weak to the extent that it is predominantly economic, and in its reliance on only one form of value: monetary. The persistent divorce between economics and politics deprives economics of its chance to establish alternative values to the merely fiscal. The task of imagining modes of action capable of creating an alternative to informationalization and the debate over which actions to take and why, is what we call politics.

Chantal Mouffe (2005) argues that contemporary political administra-tion is characterized by its belief in consensus, a matter, as Aristotle (1992, III, 1282 b 21) might have said, of agreement on shared values, rather than of confrontation. The practice of government by focus group and opinion poll is the natural outcome for Mouffe of the norms derived from consen-sual debate that Habermas (1984, 1989) admires but Mouffe claims ignores those who do not share them. Such would be the consensual mode of rule in self-organized groups of engineers like the IETF analyzed in chapter 3, and in other states that have tuned electoral representation to harmonious governance by bureaucracy. Just as the market depends on an infrastructure of laws and regulations provided by the state and can never be pure, so the communicative community is constantly prey to power and to ethnic, gen-der, and class distinctions and the ever-finer-grained identities that disci-plined consumers are invited to make their own. The function of contempo-rary politics in the service of an ideal consensus, Mouffe asserts, is precisely to quell disagreement.

Rancière (1999) makes the case that politics truly worthy of the name only begins when hierarchies are challenged by those who have been left out: what he calls "the part of no part." The part of no part is, for example, the party to a contract who has no part in drafting it, as is the case when we accede to Internet protocols or a social platform's terms of use. At the level of political theory, the part of no part is deemed by default to have signed up to a social contract that they have had no part in designing. Politics, Rancière argues, arises in struggles for inclusion in the work of governing. In the early Indus-trial Revolution, the factory was deemed a private enterprise distinct from the political. It was a space of unidirectional communication: Workers were asked only to understand and obey instructions. Unionization was never just a dispute over wages but about recognizing the factory as a political space, a place where workers could demand a share in designing their contracts. This demand was based on a prior condition: that workers were the equals of their bosses, in the sense that they had the right to speak and negotiate with them. It was this demand, rather than the increased wages, that shocked nineteenth- and early twentieth-century polities into sending troops in to quell strikes. Demanding to communicate not only established a new kind of political agent but changed forever the order of those polities, forced to accept the equality of those they had excluded before.

The challenge raised by the claims of marginalized human populations—indigenous, migrant, nomadic, and imprisoned—goes beyond asking to be admitted to the economic realm. Nor is it merely a matter of enfranchising into an otherwise unchanged polity. Admitting these challengers changes the meanings of central conceptual and legal tools like "citizen" and "nation." Thus, writing of alternatives to the prison culture of the United States, Angela Y. Davis writes, "Positing decarceration as our overarching strategy, we would try to envision a continuum of alternatives to imprisonment—demilitarization of schools, revitalization of education at all levels, a health system that provides free physical and mental care to all, and a justice system based on reparation and reconciliation rather than retribution and vengeance" (2003, 107). The lesson of this extension of citizenship to prisoners is that admitting a new cohort into the polity implies a radical overhaul of all the distributed benefits—education, health, and justice—that constitute the good life, the goal of politics.

The precise calibration of participation can be observed in the 2015 dispute over the Carmichael Mine, a proposed open-cast coal mine to be dug in inland Queensland, with a newly built railway to carry the coal to a new port facility that, like the uranium proposal discussed in chapter 1, gives directly onto the Great Barrier Reef. The federal government and its allies strongly supported public investment in the railway, but the state's Labour government elected in 2015 stopped that part of the plan. In August 2015, the mine was halted in a legal action on behalf of two endangered local species, the yakka skink and the ornamental snake. Federal officials described this as a "hitch," easily overcome, and dismissed the environmental activists who had brought the case. Covering the story, Michael West (2015) of the *Sydney Morning Herald* opined that "the project is likely to be jettisoned, not on environmental grounds, but because it is grossly uneconomic," while the *Australian Financial Review* (Ludlow 2015) noted plummeting coal prices and the reluctance of major investors to finance the project, perhaps as a result of doubts over the transparency of proposed mine operator, the Indian transnational Adani (Cox 2015a, 2015b). Nonetheless, in April of 2016, the mine and the railway were approved by the Queensland Government, although court cases from the Australian Conservation Federation and traditional owners remained outstanding (ABC 2016). Coal has had a massive return to favor in energy generation since the Fukushima disaster persuaded Japan, Germany, and many other countries to turn away from nuclear power. But the huge coal markets of India and China were in rapid decline since 2014, taking the price down since miners had created oversupply in the belief that no such downturn would happen. Protection of the reef and the endangered species has been successful, at least temporarily. Important for this argument, however, is that the traditional owners of the land had no part in the legal debate. In March 2015, elders of the Wangan and Jagalingou people made a formal declaration that they did not consent to the use of their land, in accordance with the UN Declaration on the Rights of Indigenous People, to which Australia is a signatory (McGrath 2015; Milman 2015). However, their claim to the land has been pending in the Native Title Tribunal since 2004. While the environmental activist Rainforest Alliance successfully lobbied U.S. banks not to fund the Abbot Point dock project on the reef (Milman 2014), and other activists succeeded in delaying the project in federal courts, it is ultimately economics that will decide, and the indigenous owners most affected are cast in the role of the part of no part, allowed to speak, but not listened to. Australia's troubled history of recognizing indigenous citizenship has parallels elsewhere. Extending full citizenship to European Roma (European Commission 2012), for example, would require an extensive reimagining of what we understand by citizenship and what we mean by Europe, a question that at this time of writing threatens to tear the European Union apart. If enfranchising indigenous Australians, prisoners, or Roma produces such change, what are the stakes for the inclusion of nonhuman participants in the global polity?

What's Wrong with Rights?

In ancient times the artisans, in modern times the landless, slaves, and last of all women were governed without the possibility of joining in the work of governing. Today immigrants and refugees are governed and policed by coercive regimes in which, however, they have no say (Abizadeh 2008). Today we speak of these achievements in terms of a legal discourse of rights. Drafted in the wake of World War II, and during the formative years of the

United Nations' Universal Declaration, Hannah Arendt's *The Origins of To-talitarianism* (first published in 1951) argued that there is an unbridgeable gap in the terminology of rights, especially in the founding document of rights-based politics, the French revolutionary Déclaration des droits de l'homme et du citoyen. The strictly secular provenance of modern rights discourse was established alongside the absolute right of nations to self-determination, including their right to oppress or purge minorities (a feature of the constitution of Israel as a Jewish state). Legal rights therefore became necessary precisely when, and because, older traditional and religiously sanctioned rights were in peril: "In other words, in the new secularized and emancipated society, men were no longer sure of these social and human rights which until then had been outside the political order and guaranteed not by government and constitution, but by social, spiritual, and religious forces. Therefore throughout the nineteenth century, the consensus of opinion was that human rights had to be invoked whenever individuals needed protection against the new sovereignty of the state and the new arbitrariness of society" (Arendt 1958b, 291).

In light of the previous discussion, this might be rephrased as an enclosure of traditional freedoms within regimes of law. As Berkowitz (2012, 62) comments, "To seek the protection of human rights is to portray oneself as a helpless victim, a being, like a speechless animal, whose only claim to assistance is an appeal to our pity." Rights in this guise do not accrue to those who fight for them, but are assumed in and asserted by law, and the law—which they do not write—is their only foundation. Rights, from the point of view of those to whom they are ascribed, become an environment they face as something apart from themselves, and which diminishes their humanity even in attempting to extol it. Arendt goes on, "Historical rights were replaced by natural rights, 'nature' took the place of history, and it was tacitly assumed that nature was less alien than history to the essence of man. The very language of the Declaration of Independence as well as of the *Declaration des Droits de l'Homme*—'inalienable,' 'given with birth,' 'self-evident truths'—implies the belief in a kind of human 'nature' which would be subject to the same laws of growth as that of the individual and from which rights and laws could be deduced" (1958b, 298).

Again Arendt points toward the becoming-nature of once human and common attributes. In their place are the rights of a humanity stripped of all else. As Rancière has it, with the unforgiving logic of the philosopher, "Either the rights of man are the rights of the citizen, that is to say the rights of those who have rights, which is a tautology; or the rights of the citizen are the rights of man. But as bare humanity has no rights, then they are the rights of those who have no rights, which is an absurdity" (2006, 61).

As Arendt well knew, the millions of refugees created by World War II, the Chinese Revolution, the partition of India, and the building of the Soviet bloc constituted a profound challenge to the idea of rights, and to the concept of the state charged with recognizing them. In the twenty-first century, wealthy nations compete to find euphemisms that will allow them not to recognize the legal rights now given to refugees under the UN charter, and to ensure that legalistically named migrants or asylum seekers have no rights, other than to inhabit the nonstates of the camps, mostly in the poorest parts of the world. This is what Rancière, probably reflecting Agamben (1998), refers to as "bare life." It is this bare life that Arendt (1958b, 295–96) foreshadowed by insisting that rights not only followed the decimation of the commons and its alienation from both nature and its own traditional freedoms, but legalized an isolated and abstracted form of life that severs each from all.

> The conception of human rights, based upon the assumed existence of a human being as such, broke down at the very moment when those who professed to believe in it were for the first time confronted with people who had indeed lost all other qualities and specific relationships—except that they were still human. The world found nothing sacred in the abstract nakedness of being human. . . . The survivors of the extermination camps, the inmates of concentration and internment camps, and even the comparatively happy stateless people could see . . . that the abstract nakedness of being nothing but human was their greatest danger. Because of it they were regarded as savages and afraid that they might end by being considered beasts. (Arendt 1958b, 299–300)

The "developmental refugee" (Scudder 2005), driven from home by hydropower schemes, mining, pipelines, toxic waste, climate change, and the other apocalyptic horsemen of development, bears exactly the same burden of naked humanity today that Arendt described in the 1950s. Arendt concludes the argument of the key chapter ("The Decline of the Nation-State and the End of the Rights of Man") of *The Origins of Totalitarianism* with the warning that the construction of a rights-based polity creates the potential for exclusions, construing those others as mere specimens deemed to act only out of animal need. Bare humanity diminished to a set of rights with no common recognition from which they arise is a dangerous phenomenon: "The danger is that a global, universally interrelated civilization may produce barbarians from its own midst by forcing millions of people into conditions which, despite all appearances, are the conditions of savages" (Arendt 1958b, 302).

If we attempt to apply the language of rights to either natural or technological parts of the polity, those parts of no part that are governed but have no say in their own governance, we are instantly faced with dilemmas. In what sense can we speak of the rights of animals, ecologies, or machines? If the analogy is with human rights, then to have those rights they would need somehow to become citizens. Yet citizenship is, in Arendt's analysis, a legalistic frame that disguises and perpetuates the destruction of community. Animal welfare campaigners are clear that they work from a profound sense of communion with animals. Such communion, however, cannot be sustained by rights. The collapse of community that first severed environments from humans is itself perpetuated in the concept, and even more so in the practice, of human rights. The bare life that is all that remains as human right is a reduction to mere nature expelled from the community of governors, and subject to a form of rule characterized by simple counting: how many individuals, with what needs for food, water, shelter, and hygiene to maintain them in life, which is their one irreducible but decreasingly valuable right.

Yet human rights do have one remnant of hierarchy: that they are the rights of humans. Human rights cannot be environmental or technological rights because they are based on the superiority of the human over nature, and to an extent even over human nature. Any declaration of human rights is a declaration of the human exception: Whatever constitutes the good is good exclusively for humans. Its foundations lie in the triumph of monotheism over animism, belief systems that privileged the single, unified, and unifying Godhead over the multiple and protean spirits of nature. The long construction of the single God (Debray 2004) is a history of the brutal suppression of the many gods at home and in the colonies. The Enlightenment attack on superstition hated Catholicism for its remnants of polytheism in the shape of the saints, but its real goal was demythologization: to eradicate the last claims of nature to a partnership in human affairs. Indigenous faithfulness to this tradition is not a model for mystical retreat from the world of administration and economics, but a pantheon of names and subjects acting in the environments externalized from it. They are the excluded grit that gets into the machine, the friction in friction-free capital, traction for the new politics. The question then becomes not "what rights do humans have that can be transcribed to nonhumans" but what other kinds of subjectivity beyond the human can lay claim to their part of thus far exclusively human affairs, and in so doing bring humanity into a new mode of order. Rancière's (2006) argument that public administration proceeds by excluding those who are deemed incapable of speech needs to be reversed. If what has distinguished the governing class is its monopoly on meaningful speech, it is lack of speech that has excluded the rest of humanity and the rest of creation. Therefore just as every revolution begins in asserting the ability to speak, so eco-politics must begin in the assertion that our environments are not only capable of communication, but are constantly communicating. Wittgenstein's bon mot, "If a lion could talk, we wouldn't be able to understand it" (2009, para. 327), is in fact a statement about deafness. Lions speak continually. Nature howls around us her complaint, but we choose not to understand, to hear only noise.

Politics for Rancière is a disorder: a commanding challenge to the administered order. Any thing has being, but a political agent must speak. It does so by casting off the identity ascribed to it in the distribution of parts—the identity inscribed in an identity card, in the countable units of population management, or the datafication of both human behavior and the natural and technical environments. It casts off the very concept of behavior in order to assert that we do not behave but act. The act of speaking when spoken from the place of noise, of the unaccounted roar of migrants or environments, is not merely a refusal of one identity in order to take up another, which would simply reproduce the existing order, but an assertion of non-identity. For Rancière this new political subject "is not a group that 'becomes aware' of itself, finds its voice, imposes its weight on society. It is an operator that connects and disconnects different areas, regions, identities, functions, and capacities existing in the configuration of a given experience" (1999, 40). In a similar vein, Laclau describes the emergence of populist movements in terms of "demand." But where a demand for an extension of human rights would be easily assimilable into the existing order, and would in return configure the newly enfranchised as elements of its continuing power, the new political subject declines to be so identified: "The unity of the group is, in my view, the result of an articulation of demands. This articulation, however, does not correspond to a stable and positive configuration which could be grasped as a unified whole: on the contrary, since it is in the nature of all demands to present claims to a certain established order, it is in a peculiar relation with that order, being both inside and outside it. As this order cannot fully absorb the demand, it cannot constitute itself as a coherent totality" (Laclau 2005, ix).

Where Habermas sees the ordered society constituting itself from inclusive communication, Rancière and Laclau see public administration constituted in what it excludes from communication. Politics emerges not in the demand but in its articulation that, as part of no part, the new subject cannot articulate in the existing categories of rule. Combining Rancière's and Laclau's insights, this articulation is both dialogically nonidentical, in that the dominant partner has a fully articulated taxonomy that the other both lacks and contests, and ontologically nonidentical in that it articulates a configuration of disparate elements and actions. The self-identical then has no need for communication in this politicized sense since it is in equilibrium, while the nonidentical Other is obliged to communicate by the tensions and lacks of its "different areas, regions, identities, functions, and capacities."

In the historical evolution of natural, technical, and data environments through the dialectic of enclosure and externalization, the excluded comes face to face with what excludes it on a terrain that is political in this radical sense. The political event occurs when order is confronted with what it has excluded, yet over which it has exercised command or asserted stewardship. Such events are at their core about communication. But before we can confirm that the articulation of demand is indeed core, we must investigate the nature of the demand itself. The most silent and inert of minerals, and for that reason one indissolubly associated with money, gold would seem one of the least communicative. Yet when in August 2015 Environmental Protection Agency officials trying to secure a tailings dam at a Colorado mine last productive in 1917 (Free, Hutchinson, and Koch 1990) released 3 million gallons of mine waste into the Animas River, the silence was broken with a flood of "mustard-colored water loaded with heavy metals, including arsenic, lead, copper, aluminum and cadmium" (Garrison 2015). It is not only that, once again, indigenous people bear the brunt, with the river flowing through and providing the major water source for the Navajo Nation (Smith 2015). It also became apparent that other mines abandoned after the Colorado gold rush had been leaking for decades, while officials resisted Superfund status in expectation of restarting the mining industry (Morgan 2015). What did the gold tailings demand? Obviously, once released from the ground, to be set free, but once in the river, the heavy metals demanded to sediment out. The long conversation of minerals interrupted a century ago leaves the millennial pace of geological time to enter that of environmental crisis (EPA 2015). It is impossible to trace the gold that came from the Gold King Mine over its fifty-year career, or to know whether any ended up in electronics via long chains of pawn shops and deceased estates. The Animas provided locations for *Butch Cassidy and the Sundance Kid*: Perhaps as it plays on streaming servers and DVD, Gold King Mine gold is involved. Does the gold remember its origins? Has it achieved a new freedom by leaving its subterranean sleep to mediate between its landscape and the human world? Has the spill communicated to us a demand to revalue not only today's gold but the mutual responsibility of metal and men for the permanence of gold's release into the world?

Political economy is concerned with value, but also with the discourses around it that frame its changing nature (Graham 2006). The value system of contemporary consensus treats this communication about gold mining as natural disaster, extracting the economic message from the mine's broad-spectrum communiqué, hurrying toward a return to the status quo by celebrating rapid sedimentation and cleaner water while ignoring the geological time spans of the sediment as it returns into the landscape. As in the emergency response to the financial crash, the guilty are rewarded (no one imagines searching out the gold's current owners), the innocent punished, and the uninvolved left to pick up the pieces. But the uninvolved and innocent planet may no longer be innocent or uninvolved today as we look out toward a bleaker but more closely interdependent future. Each profession and every academic discipline asserts a particular value: health, wealth, shelter, justice, knowledge, efficiency. Let us surmise that in the broadest sense, the demand of those excluded, human or otherwise, is not for one of these or some combination of them, but for something less clearly definable, inherent in each and more difficult to deliver: happiness. In late lectures, Adorno argued that the requirement that we sacrifice happiness to some other, putatively higher but always later goal is an imposition. Deferral is "a kind of economy of thrift," but "the compensation promised by civilisation and our education in return for our acts of renunciation is not forthcoming" (Adorno 2000, 138). The sacrifice of happiness to rationality or to deferred gratifications is a truly tragic sacrifice. Happiness is not to be passed over. But nor is it to be undersold, passing it off with nostrums and trinkets. Capital fails continuously to address pandemic, famine, and poverty, and thrives on war. It also fails consistently to deliver happiness: only the greedy pleasures of the rich and their tawdry imitation for the poor. Unsurprisingly, drugs and fundamentalist religions fill the gap left behind, with their attendant miseries.

Meanwhile, the administrative ethos tends to tolerate the absence of happiness. Toleration names the absence of dialogue. What I tolerate is beneath attention, marginal to my world, what I am aware of but feel no obligation to respond to. What is at stake in the articulation of nonhuman demand is the end not only of rights but of human identity. This is possible only if the demand that instigates it is strictly incommensurable with the existing order, as the demand for happiness is. But if the demand were for square circles, the principle would be the same: It is the contradiction between tolerance and communication, between the true noncommunication of the tolerant order and the actual communication of the unheard and ignored, that drives the event.

The 1980s neoliberal revolution accomplished such an extension of the polity. Although admitting the nonhuman into the polity seems unthinkable, neoliberalism enabled the entry of the market into a dominant position in contemporary politics. Deeply changing the organization of the polity, since the 1980s it has crushed class struggle and reinstalled a hyperwealthy ruling class (Harvey 2005), changes effected at the level of expulsions from the polity and reorganization of power within it, that challenge its fundamental configuration and functioning. The fact that the market cyborg has achieved such political agency and remade the polity in its own image shows that a political event is still possible, even if in a negative form. In its triumph, information and bodies become environments to be commodified, but herein lies a contradiction that opens up an alternative teleology. The polity is based on the distinction between environment and human, but that distinction is breaking down in favor of a distinction between market and environment. If this trajectory were fulfilled, the exploitation of the human race and its exclusion from its own destiny would become total. At such a moment, having become autonomous from the market, humanity would be entirely environmental, and therefore in a position to build a completely unprecedented commons.

Ecologies of Communication

This is the point where ecological communications become much more than alerting the human public to environmental issues; become indeed the crucial medium of the postenvironmental world, when the distinction between human and environment is overcome. If sovereignty was the power to decide the exception (Schmitt 2004, 5), modern politics is the capacity to define what is human and what is natural (Beck 1995, 129–37; Foucault 2003, 244–45). This definition has been dynamic since the beginning of the colonial epoch, subject of competing powers—religious versus scientific, indigenous against colonial, local against universal—and rewritten again in the rise of economics to the determining role in political life. Political elites attempt to maintain power over what constitutes the environment, and therefore what constitutes the human, but the market redefines both of them, and the polity too. These exercises of power and extractions of wealth that create, constitute, and exploit the distinctions between population and environment are aesthetic operations, since they work at the level of perception: of what we perceive as environing, and what as human. This aesthetic operation is necessarily mediated, in communications that constitute and are in turn constituted by changing relations between what we must increasingly see as interdependent environments.

Economics, society, technology, and the national and global administration that passes for politics fail to offer solutions to the environmentalization of the world and the diminution of humanity. That task falls to communication; but communication lies under a cloud. If mediation names the precommunicative Eden in which the living, the ancestors, and the natural world were able to dialogue with one another, communication names the fallen state of communicative events that divide senders from receivers. This division, implicit in and formative of the separation of human from environment, shapes the materiality of the media of communication analyzed in this book. The ill-starred and demeaned term *communication* describes the condition that pertains to our time. However, even emphasizing the historicity of communication and thereby its capacity to become otherwise than its current form, communication is still loaded dice. Jodi Dean gives a succinct and challenging account of it in her *Communist Horizon*: "Some activists and theorists treat aesthetic objects and creative works as displaying a political potentiality missing from classes, parties and unions. This aesthetic focus disconnects politics from the organised struggle of working people, making politics into what spectators see. Artistic products, whether actual commodities or commodified experiences, thereby buttress capital as they circulate political affects while displacing political struggles" (2012, 13).

To respond that individual films like *An Inconvenient Truth* (2006), David Attenborough's TV wildlife documentaries, or Andy Goldsworthy's environmental artworks can communicate eco-political ideas is to miss the point. Such communication is always, following Dean, complicit in the circulation of capital, converting political motivations into anxiety, spectacle, or impotent tears. The only response to Dean's critique is to show that communication is the material form in which not only speech but action occurs.

The identities that divide us from one another (Agamben 1993, 86) do so because we are constituted not as mutually entwined with one another and the world but as discrete senders and receivers of messages. The task of overcoming self-identity is both fundamentally communicative, in the heightened sense of a communication across the boundaries established by administrative power, and therefore foundational of any eco-politics. Eco-political aesthetics has to move beyond the human exception to enfranchise a new dispensation of the commons grounded in the mobilization of repressed eudaemonistic demands for a good life, demands of the parts of no part represented by people, by the alienated forms of primal mediation we see as nature, by the ancestral labor we know as technology, and by the alienated knowledge we call databases.

Media are not only passive channels of communication: Parts of no part excluded from their own governance, they seek to speak for themselves. The inherently virtualizing tendency of every technology, its ability to evolve otherwise, is incompatible with each actual technology that embodies it. An actually existing sewing machine is not capable of projecting moving pictures, even though its eccentric motion can be extracted as an element and made to serve in movie projection. Dividing processes into elements and assembling elements into teleological, goal-driven ensembles appears to define and limit the autonomy of the general intellect. At the same time, the possibility of redesigning and reassembling elements in new ways, which constitutes their virtuality, depends on the prior distinction of elements as objects, a process that is both crucial to the process of technical evolution and simultaneously an imposition of objectality onto what is otherwise a common medium, the general intellect. Discerning elements as objects rather than processes makes possible the ownership of specific elements or combinations as intellectual property in conformity with the colonization of creativity by capital. Actualization in the form of objects terminates the autonomous virtuality of techniques, their ability to generate the new from their own internal workings. This is the necessary condition for the construction of subjects, those who can claim ownership, abrogating to themselves the agency of machines, and who can thus become the mediators of power.

And yet, as noted above, the actualization of a life completed in the moment of death is not only an imperative moment of the cycle of virtuality but is itself the goal of the virtual, just as much as the actual dead seek new virtuality in the form of the general intellect. This cycle is common to everything that possesses virtuality—everything capable of change and of acting—and is demonstrated in the loss of autonomy among the dead, who become entirely determined by physical laws. These laws are common to all technologies, as indeed, in the form of basic needs for shelter, warmth, companionship, and food, they determine the bare life of humanity. Innovations in technology are not only riven internally, but by determinations deriving from outside the technical field, not only according to the laws of nature but according to knowledge about them. These determinations make it possible for communication to actualize its potentials. Thus autonomy is essential to virtuality, but determination is essential to actualization. This contradiction generates their mutual productivity, as it generates the mutual permeability of excluded environments, in direct opposition to the hypostasis of the social, the political, and the economic. No longer either spectacle or sender-receiver system, eco-aesthetics instead incorporate the natural law into their own freedom. To answer Dean's critique, communication is the material mediation of this dialectic of freedom and necessity, division and communion, the medium of political action.

The market as political subject demonstrates in the negative the possibility of nonhuman communication within the polity, but also that their compatibility makes it impossible for either the market or the polity to deliver the necessary new: the engagement of environments. Of the available tools for a new politics, among the most promising are the SLOC (small, local, open, connected) model proposed by Ezio Manzini (2013) and peer-to-peer (P2P) economies (Bauwens and Kostakis 2014). Thus far, P2P has been imagined as a human-to-human mode of exchange. Roberto Verzola (2010) of the Philippine Green Party is among the first to extend this analysis to nonhuman environments. Reasserting the commons as commonwealth even from a purely human perspective undermines the presumption of property rights and the externality of environments. Moving to reestablish ancestral skills and knowledge as common requires a greater leap of understanding, of the kind demanded in the Cochabamba Declaration of the World People's Conference on Climate Change and the Rights of Mother Earth (2010): "In an interdependent system in which human beings are only one component, it is not possible to recognize rights only to the human part without provoking an imbalance in the system as a whole. To guarantee human rights and to restore harmony with nature, it is necessary to effectively recognize and apply the rights of Mother Earth."

When the language of rights—determined by the UN Declaration on the Rights of Indigenous People—is extended to the demand to recognize the political status of the natural world and its geology, it is a demand for a fundamental rethinking of the idea of rights and of the human exception. It implies, at the least, recognition of the technical mediations that make communication between human and natural worlds possible. Even though the liberation of dead labor from its mechanical servitude has a history dating back at least to Ted Nelson's (1974) *Computer Lib*, the ideology of unconstrained machines turning on their human masters has been the stuff of nightmares from Marx's vampiric vision of industrial capital to the *Termi-*

nator and *Matrix* film franchises. Like the fear of the dead we were taught by monotheism, fear of technology is a means of controlling communications between the living and the ancestors. We are taught to fear technology because in liberating itself it might liberate us. The advance of P2P thinking into relations with the alienated forms of skills, knowledge, and bodies is one way to end that fear and control, and to change universal standardization into a commons which includes all those aspects of humanity that have been severed from us, and which leave both us and them diminished and exploited.

It seems only fair that the information environment, one of the last great enclosures, should contain in it the germs of the collapse of enclosure and externality. Since the nature of both ecology and the general intellect is intrinsically communicative, it is only with continual vigilance that living and dead labor can be kept from rebelling against their chains. A core task of this book has been to assert the materiality of media, not simply to contradict theses about their immateriality, but because the fact that they are material makes them capable of changing the world as even the real abstractions of society, economy, and polity cannot. If media were not part of the problem, they could not be the solution. In communication—and mediation more broadly—the potential of the ages lies, coiled up in them like a spring. The fundamental political task is to build a communicative event embracing the whole world, not just the human. This is why politics must now be understood aesthetically.

Otherwise

We cannot simply rescind the freedom that scientific rationality forced upon us, any more than we can bring back the victims of colonialism, or pour metals back into the ground whence they came. It is equally hard to reconfigure the predominance of the human. The human subject capable of communication and domination, the human subject whose trace appears in such unremarked features as the height of the camera from the ground, is an abstraction; but a real abstraction, that is to say, one that arises historically from specific conditions and that operates on those conditions as if it were a universally valid truth. In Marx, the classic example of the real abstraction is money, the universal equivalent. In media, we might say that any sufficiently widely accepted standard proposes itself as a universal, even though its universality is belied by its temporal coming into existence and, in certain instances like the European wide-screen (1:1.88) ratio, its geographical boundaries. Thus too the subjectivity enounced by media—the author as autonomous agent or the authorial corporation (as Marvel Studios is the ultimate narrator of Marvel franchise films)—is destined to become only a textual effect, and to that extent a particular instance of a universal. What is left is not the always absent Absolute Subject (Althusser 1971) but its shadow, the spectating subject who takes on the role of subject of history as a persona because without that subjectivity, however illusory and ephemeral, there is no possibility of acting.

The task of the undisciplined spectator, the recipient of capital's communications, is to take that role seriously. Take, for example, Sam Peckinpah's *The Wild Bunch*, shot in 1968–1969 in the province of Coahuila, an area then dominated by coal mining, and nowadays by massive maquiladora factories building GM and Chrysler vehicles for export across the Rio Grande that separates it from Texas. Peckinpah's elegy for the horse and nomadic outlaw culture is matched by his account of a landscape soon to be deeply transformed. The Rio Grande, crossed by Peckinpah's outlaws, was listed as impaired a mere fifteen years later by the International Boundary and Water Commission, the result of salinity arising from excessive water extraction for agriculture, bacteria due to untreated sewage from the expanding slums of Ciudad Juárez and the other maquiladora cities, and chemical pollutants, especially from Laredo on the Texas side of the border (IBWC 1994), conditions that still obtain: A 2013 Texas government report mentions excessive levels of "residual chlorine, methylene chloride, toluene, arsenic, cadmium, chromium, copper, lead, mercury, nickel, selenium, silver, zinc, chlordane, p,p'-DDE, dieldrin, gamma-BHC (lindane), total PCBs, and cyanide" (Texas Commission on Environmental Quality 2013). Many of these metals and organics are associated with offshore chip fabrication and computer manufacture in the free trade zones along the Mexican border. Peckinpah's outlaws, meeting just before the brewing of this toxic soup to recall a lost way of life in a disappearing environment, speak more profoundly than pictorial, humanist realism normally allows of what is not humanly visible. Though every analogue film was made with silver and oil, not every film has to be about them. *The Wild Bunch* is just one example of what film can do to respond aesthetically to its own conditions of existence, a task that inevitably takes it beyond pictorial humanism.

Viewing the landscape of a film like *The Wild Bunch* obliquely is an action, "a gaze . . . by which what was once in the margin has come to take its place at the centre" (Lefebvre 2006, 27). In that gaze, however, we depart the preferred position prepared for us by the text, the position of mastery over it, the position of the universal subject of history. In full knowledge that we are enmeshed in a planetary ecology implicating human and nonhuman agents in one another's worlds, and at the same time acknowledging our alienation from them as the heirs of European Enlightenment, in confronting the cinematic landscape in the moment of its disappearance, we confront ourselves as radically incomplete.

It is exactly this incompletion that enables the act of taking responsibility for the past as it presents itself to us in the landscape, and that likewise drives us to action when it does not encourage us to withdraw from self-hood in favor either of a depoliticized environmentalism slumping into the indifference of primal mediation, or of a depoliticized formalism premised on the indifferent differences of numerical rationality. Media betray themselves when they seek the autonomy of art: betray their formal dependence on referents beyond themselves and their material dependence on fossil organics, metals, and energy. Media matter only because they are matter; only because they are matter can they mediate between fallen nature and fallen humanity. Only because they mediate can they take up the broken past and carry it into the future where alone its multiple failures to exist can be re-made. In this sense, all technologies are media technologies. As media, their demand takes the form of the proposition that there can never be an "I" that can truly occupy the position of subject of history, only a "we," a "we" that is always to be constructed, and in which the nonhuman is an active agent of historical change.

The politics of consensus and tolerance, the politics of no politics, declines dissent, especially debate about values, how we should live, or what is the good life. When we begin to think about the emancipation of artificial life and life more broadly, we strive in vain to imagine what such a polity might be like: votes for mountains? Oceans speaking at the UN Assembly? Such ideas are only as absurd as recognizing self-governance in Ireland in 1916 or migrants and prisoners as citizens in Europe, the United States, and Australia a hundred years later. As long as we reduce communication to messages and consent, we ignore the poetic function Jakobson (1960) identified when communication takes itself for its own subject. Playing between all the other functions of language, the poetic makes each reflect on themselves and each other: and the same is true of the poetic mode of any medium. Media as poetics, among their many tasks, envision for us the unimaginable, make music from the intangible tachyons coming from the future, and whisper un-thought-of concordats in the space between the scan lines. Such unthinkable futures are the media of eco-political aesthetics. If politics is the art of the possible, eco-political aesthetics is the art of the impossible.

There remains the great challenge of the dead and the debt we owe them. Hegel wrote of "the *cunning of Reason*—that it sets the passions to work for itself, while that through which it develops itself pays the penalty and suffers the loss" (Hegel 1953, 44, original emphasis). "That through which it develops itself" is human lives. Each of us suffers and dies, so that Reason can pursue its own self-development. Each of us must feel our passions set aflame so that cool Reason can motor calmly into its future. We individuals will be consumed, and the future will not come back to rescue or justify our sad existence, save as necessary sacrifice in which even our virtues played no more part than cogs in clockwork. In Peter Dews's (2013) analysis, this failure to address the stunted lives and broken dreams of the dead is common across the whole of Western rational philosophy. Unsurprisingly, neither economics nor contemporary politics, not even social science, has a place for the redemption of past suffering. Yet this failure has its own structure, one that might yet make possible the duty Benjamin recognized: to be the posterity that the past looked to for justification.

As Freud described it, melancholia emerges from a reproach aimed at the self, self-reproaches that are the repressed symptoms of "reproaches against a loved object which have been shifted away from it on to the patient's own ego," which themselves "proceed from a mental constellation of revolt, which has then, by a certain process, passed over into the crushed state of melancholia" (1984, 257). In the first instance, the melancholy gaze on a polluted landscape mourns its failure to master it. In a second moment, however, the work of mourning collapses as the onlooker confronts the landscape as victim of that failure. As Mladek and Edmondson phrase it, the melancholic becomes "a decompleted subject without mastery or agency, fully exposed and appropriated to the event" (2009, 227): a nonidentity who, in our case, is open, even vulnerable, to the multiple environments surrounding and composing it. The oblique gaze, in its fidelity to the lost, the silenced, and the unsuccessfully erased, human and nonhuman alike, undoes the self-identity of the self, placing its duty outside itself with the unmourned and excluded.

This melancholia is one of the wellsprings of critique precisely because it does not mourn. It does not seek to apologize to or speak on behalf of the dead, because that would be to return them to a Symbolic order from which their uncompleted lives exclude them. Mourning would merely assuage the living without repaying that unpayable debt the living owe the dead. The melancholy subject shrinks inward on itself, but where there is no self left, so profoundly diminished has it become through the successive enclosures, environmentalizations, and externalizations of modern history, that inward passage passes through its vanishing point, the obverse of neoliberal indi-viduation from which nothing has emerged but grief and trinkets, renounc-ing subject and object alike to transform itself into project. Contingency has passed from the iron laws of physics to the equally overbearing laws of proto-col and statistical control, and it is from them that this simultaneous retreat and projection seeks its aesthetic liberation in the construction of a new "we" capable of including the dead.

Against humanism, monotheism, and pantheism, in light of the failures of society, economy, and polities, aesthetics after anesthetic disciplined con-sumption embraces the virtual future against the mode of destruction, en-vironmentalization, and externalization. Mindful of the ancestors in chains and of ancestral traditions of commonwealth, and melancholic because it takes on the shame denied by cyborg capital, eco-politics looks toward the unimaginable as an aesthetic category, the unimaginable good life for human, natural, and technological phyla in their once and future interdependence. Against radical antianthropocentrism, which shadows the historical alien-ation of human faculties from human populations, eco-political aesthetics asserts that we are still not yet human, and will not be till we abandon human identity to become wholly environmental. The melancholic view back on the history of communitarian media (Dowmunt 1993; Downing et al. 2001; Drew 2013), communal living (Harford and Hopkins 1984; Van Gelder and the Staff of YES! Magazine 2012), and experiments in collaborative communications (Raqs Media Collective and Lovink 2001) sees in defeats the ancestral lineage of struggle for new communes, new commons, new communions, the coun-tertradition of the excluded. The iron in our blood, the salt in our tears, tie us as deeply to our tools and planet as to one another, and we will never reach one another until we reach, and reach through, the nonhuman.

The 1906 *Story of the Kelly Gang* with which this book began is an exem-plary case of just such transenvironmental poetry. We would not able to see the film as we do unless experimental media artists like Stan Brakhage had instructed us how to see this kind of material: "Imagine a world alive with incomprehensible objects and shimmering with an endless variety of move-ment and innumerable gradations of color. Imagine a world before 'In the beginning was the word'" (1963, 1). Now the restored clip of Kelly's last stand can stand as a record of a historic film, and as a record of its decay; but also as a freestanding work in itself, part human, part technological, and part organic, operating on a starting point arranged by human hands, like a gar-den going wild or an artificial life program gone feral. Human and physical agents meet on the terrain of technology to produce a gesture in time, a moment that has never existed before and may never exist, in this form at least, ever again.

Can we say *The Story of the Kelly Gang* reveals itself and a world to us in its more-than-human poetic, dis-closing the chemistry of nitrate stock and the perilously flimsy silver halide salts that cling to its moldering surface, as they migrate to the pixelated structure of twenty-first-century LCDs and data projectors? It is not impossible for us to understand the shadow play. An oblique glance is all it takes. Once positive film passed through movie projectors, casting shadows on the wall. Now DLP chips flicker their micromirrors, scattering waste light away from the screen into the nanoforests of the lamp housing. And still we watch, not only because the flicker is intrinsically fascinating, or because the structuring of time in patterns and narratives delights us, as creatures who love order. It is because what we see unfold, at best, is not the truth, which in any case is a quality of knowledge rather than of the world, but communication itself. We see the unsteady interplay of world and vision, the changing relationship that is knowing, the act of mediating where order fights symmetry, in the physical as in the psychic world, the unstill concatenation of mutually mediating nature, human, and technology. The cynic might argue that empire needs its rebels, though not as much as rebels need empire. And yet the grit in the gearbox can also bring the whole automobile to a stop, and maybe cheer us on as we get out to walk again on the green verge in a cool drizzle.

The Story of the Kelly Gang is a colonial narrative of the wild colonial boy who, driven out of Ireland by famine and colonial authorities and victimized and out of sorts with the penal laws of colonial Australia in Gold Rush Victoria, fights the imperial police. The legend made Kelly a type of Robin Hood, who gave his name in Australasia and the UK to what in the United States is called the Tobin Tax. The director, Charles Tait, claimed the tale was authentic: There were enough people alive who had witnessed or taken part in the real actions to support that, although his producer later admitted he had had to dress the police in uniforms in bush scenes to distinguish them, even though they would have worn riding clothes at the time. The scene of Kelly's arrest is a remnant, one of a handful of fragments, from what is widely recognized (including by UNESCO, who placed it under Memory of the World protection in 2007) as the first feature film in the world, a film that cost £400 to make, and which recouped its costs on its first weekend before circulating through Australia, New Zealand, and the United Kingdom (Bertrand and Routt 2007). Its decay and resurrection are as contingent on the vagaries of distribution and storage as the leaves in the background brush are on the breeze and the sunlight. Tait's authenticity, his truth to unforeseeable elements of gun smoke and biological life, belongs to André Bazin's realism, devoted to the inscription and revelation of the physical world; only topped off by the secondary realism of the video record of the film's distorted form a hundred years later. The story is acted out as a victory for the colonial power, tragic or triumphant as the audience chooses to take it. The final scene of Kelly's capture was shot at Charterisville, the home of Tait's wife's family in Heidelberg in suburban Melbourne, later associated with the Heidelberg School of artists, on traditional land already rendered nullius by genocidal wars against the indigenous Wurundjeri, Boonwurrung, and Wathaurong, and the Kulin Nation whose traditional meeting grounds coincided with the meeting of fresh and salt water in the Yarra River. We see in their place a garden largely planted with introduced species. The bush of myth, of Banjo Patterson's ballads, tamed by horticulture as Kelly is by the cops, is a plantation, a little Eden, "a wood outside Athens" where Tait and team enact their midsummer night's dream of insurrection and refusal of the yoke. Kelly's doomed rebellion is mythical partly because he is, or can be, an existential hero, one who refused. In Sydney Nolan's *Ned Kelly* series of paintings, he is characteristically alone or in conflict (though Peter Carey's novel *True History of the Kelly Gang* places him in colonial history). In Tait's version, it is the absence that tells: the absent other of the indigenous.

The triangle of relations includes the police as citizens; the embattled and twice-colonized Kelly, bushwhacker without rights, as settler; and the indigenous marked only as absence, the very world they walked replaced with an English garden, and its name erased under a nostalgic recall of Romantic Europe. It is into this nexus that the entropic process erupts. The physical film, with its cargo of recorded light, began its new and unattended growth. The material technology of mediation conspires with the physical process, the explosive birthright of film, to produce a new work, part Tait's project and part projection of an alien agency.

The Story of the Kelly Gang as it has come down to us is data visualization—both a record of the raining photons of 1906 and of chemical intelligence operating without the governing force of sovereignty, discipline, or biopolitical management in the years between then and its restoration. Our instinctual love of order collapses, as Freud has it, into Thanatos, the death instinct, the drive toward dissolution and entropy. He omitted to observe, released as he was before the horror of Belsen, that the opposite of the entropic death drive is not life, which is its complement, but totalitarian reason, universal rationality. The monotheism of the religions of the Book, inherited by Western scientific rationalism, here meets its nemesis in the unimagined beauty of a processual artifact in which the human encounters and engages with ungoverned technological and natural process. We sense, or should sense, in this entropic realism, the collusions devoutly to be hoped for after dominion.

Long before the buckled expansion of the nitrate substrate, when they were first exposed, the silver halides undertook their work as it were unconsciously, according to the prescriptions of the filmstock manufacturer as well as the choices made by the filmmakers and actors. It was an orderly job of mechanically disciplined work undertaken in the cultural and technical formation of the industrial era, even if its subject matter was a romantic rebellion against power and wealth. Over the ensuing decades, invisible in their tins, the ancestors were at liberty not so much to undo that work as to undertake a new work of their own. The nitrocellulose in the film stock reacted, probably with the camphor plasticizer, releasing nitric acid, which acts as a catalyst for further reactions, ending as a highly flammable viscous, syrupy mess or dry, flammable powder. Only in flames can the film's life be said to be truly over. Other reels almost certainly were destroyed by spontaneous combustion or in warehouse fires: nitrate stock releases oxygen as it burns, making it extremely difficult to put out. The survival of these fragments is a minor miracle, and the visual record of this chemical life is an education in itself.

But it is also evidence of another kind of work, a job of work genuinely undesigned and uncontrolled, and in this sense entropic—a work of unmaking, which media history mourns as the loss of a precious cinematic artifact, but which an eco-aesthetics celebrates as making actual the virtual capabilities lying dormant in the raw material of the nitrate. The materiality of the filmstrip would have been of consequence only to projectionists in 1906. Now it is a central part of how we must view the remains. In one manner of accounting, the decay is evidence of the fatigue that overcomes all complex devices, when the amount of energy needed to maintain equilibrium exhausts itself. We can also predict that, protected under an international regime, the remaining minutes of *The Kelly Gang* will from now on perpetually migrate from one new format to another as the permanent revolution in the means of production continues, each migration taking away some granular features of the original nitrate and adding new electronic artifacts. The contingency of both the survival and metamorphoses of the film's fragments ties the technical product into a complex chemical and biological environment with which it has interacted as an equal participant over the century of its afterlife.

There is no need to see this purely as entropic. Nor is there need to turn to Schumpeter (2010) or Bataille (1988) for a theory of creative destruction. What has emerged is a thing, without an obvious taxonomic position, that has its own aesthetic, an untamed and nonhuman beauty which has escaped even the kind of planned randomness of some of Cage's compositions where chance was invited in as collaborator in the making of the work. In *The Story of the Kelly Gang*, the work of chemical (natural) and digital (technological) life supervenes on the materials made by the human and speaks in palimpsest over the transmission from 1906. The automated work of the restoration algorithm produces its own inventions in the appearance of the restored film, an unexpected and autonomous process making its own aesthetic object, not knowing that its exacting labor at the level of the codec would be transferred into a time-based medium for an unknown species of spectator. The restored *Story of the Kelly Gang* of 2007 is a genuinely autonomous work springing from a human seed and exceeding it. It speaks, in a language that we cannot understand; so that what may appear to some of us (or some parts of all of us) as destruction may also appear as a message, or more particularly a mediation, from an environment whose existence we all too often ignore, or find ourselves unable to come face to face with. Unless we are ready to face the incomprehensible demand of this Other, we will not be able to understand the capacity of the all-too-actual codec to produce the means for its own overcoming, or our own capacity for freedom, that virtual freedom which this patiently autonomous chemical life has demonstrated for us.

The mediation of *The Story of the Kelly Gang* writes in little the utopian imaginary of a postenvironmental world. If our history is of a fall from primordial mediation with its mimetic immersion of human and environmental in one another, into a world of alienated humans and their environments, then we look earnestly for some future beyond that severance. The challenge of eco-aesthetics is to think through the actuality of ecological collapse and the shameless cyborg logic of neoliberalism in order not to plan that future but to prize open chinks in the boilerplate of biopolitics to allow some light from the future in. To do so demands a sacrifice, but the eudaemonistic principle does not allow us to sacrifice happiness on a promise. Thus our happinesses are tinged with melancholy, of the kind we experience in the simultaneous loss and arrival of this damaged film. This melancholy, while it can become incapacitating, can also recognize both weakness and responsibility as the means we have to hand to create a populist demand for a better world.

CODA ON SATURN

We generally know what we mean by political media. The claim made here is that all media are political, not only when they carry explicit messages, nor just because content is in some way always ideological, but by the very nature of being media. How could an image of a storm in the atmosphere of Saturn (NASA 2011) be political? Certainly there is a debate on the uses of space imagery for national prestige, and about whether we could spend the money better elsewhere, but as an image surely it is neutral. One reason it is not is that we have this image thanks to digital cameras and transmission devices powered by three radioisotopic thermoelectric generators aboard the Cassini-Huygens spacecraft that took the picture. Their fuel is 72.3 pounds of plutonium 238 ("Cassini Spacecraft Nears Liftoff" 1997), an isotope produced in the decay of uranium in nuclear power plants like FirstEnergy's Davis-Besse nuclear power plant in Ohio, discussed in chapter 1. Plutonium 238 constitutes about 1 percent of the spent fuel from a nuclear plant, so the seventy-two pounds aboard Cassini would have required about three and a half metric tons of uranium. U.S. nuclear power plants import about ten thousand metric tons of uranium a year from Australia, one of whose largest mines is the Ranger, also described in chapter 1. The spacecraft's journey is slated to end with entry into Saturn's atmosphere during the 2017 northern summer solstice, destroying the spacecraft and its three generators. The mineral first ripped from the terra nullius created by denying that indigenous

Catching Its Tail, image of a storm on Saturn taken by the Imaging Science Subsystem (wide angle) from the Cassini orbiter, July 6, 2011. Source: NASA/JPL-Caltech/Space Science Institute.

Australians existed will be dumped into the res nullius domain created by the UN Outer Space Treaty, largely on the legal model of doctrines established during the colonizing eighteenth century discussed in chapter 2. This is a first sense in which the image of the storm on Saturn is political.

Cassini-Huygens's camera is based on a CCD chip, an array of square, light-sensitive cells, each of which accumulates a charge according to the amount of light reaching it. These square pixels are organized in groups of four by a filtering mask that allocates particular wavelengths, corresponding to red, green, and blue, to each of its four pixels. The strict geometry of the array is continued through the processes required to amplify the charge and get it off the chip into digital storage ready for transmission back to Earth using the MPEG codec discussed in chapter 2. Not just capable of various kinds of surveillance, the MPEG codec determines how images exist in the twenty-first century. The politics of governance over the protocols underlying all our media are far less visible but in many ways far more fundamental than elections. As T. S. Eliot remarked, "Mankind cannot bear very much reality": We have to filter the world in order to survive in it. The precise design of Cassini-Huygens's instruments, the wavelengths and phenomena selected for recording, the transport mechanisms chosen for transmission, and the equipment at the receiving stations on Earth are precisely such filters, telling us only what we know how to ask, and framing the answers according to presets established for quite different terrestrial purposes, conforming the telemetry of Saturn to the requirements of Earth. The precise historical means we develop for filtering have consequences not only for ourselves and our perceptions, not only for the connections we make with other people, but for our connection to the rest of the universe. This is the second way these images are political.

It has been argued that space science does not need spectacular and expensive missions like Cassini. There is also an argument that if it does, it is more efficient to throw the machinery away in deep space than to try to bring it back to Earth for recycling. Neither decision—to send or to destroy—is apolitical. Cassini-Huygens's mission began with a launch whose impact on the local and atmospheric environments was enormous: NASA's prelaunch estimates were that the Titan IV rocket would release more than ten thousand kilograms of hydrochloric acid, almost twelve thousand kilos of carbon monoxide, and nearly twenty thousand kilos of aluminum oxide in the first few seconds (NASA 1995, section 4.1.2.2). Reports suggest that the cleanup at the Florida launch area will take decades and cost up to a billion dollars (Waymer 2011), while Ross et al. (2009) estimate that rocket launches are also responsible for 1 percent of anthropogenic ozone depletion. Quite apart from the problem of space junk—the debris from older missions now in fragments in Earth orbit—such launches represent both significant environmental impacts and dramatic waste. Cassini-Huygens writes in little the truth that overproduction and waste are essential to the growth model of capital.

We live in a culture of compulsory consumption. The drive for productivity creates more and more efficient machines, automation, and robotics, reducing the unit cost of products. But that also means that the profit per unit goes down. The falling rate of profit drives manufacturing to produce more units, all of which have somehow to be consumed. We learn to consume more of the junk food that screams at us its desire to be consumed, more pharmaceuticals to counteract the junk food, more diets and sports equipment, driven by social and body anxieties that drive us to consume more entertainment and more devices to hook into social media in case we miss the latest thing we are supposed to consume. Extremely alert to our age, gender, class, ethnic, and lifestyle demographics, we are as highly disciplined as consumers as our forebears were as factory hands. Space exploration, in this perspective, is merely one extreme example of highly specialized consumerism.

Electoral politics today presents itself as just another consumer choice. We are asked to vote in the same tone that we are told to take personal responsibility for environmentally and morally informed consumption. We are asked to change our habits, to become even more disciplined consumers, and to work individually against a background of civic inaction at the political level and accelerating damage at the corporate. Even faced with catastrophic climate change, in successive summits since Rio neither political elites nor the economics of the market seem motivated by or capable of change. Our existing instruments of cosmopolitan governance, notably the United Nations, have been so hollowed out that they can only point in horror at the pace of destruction. Technological solutions are stymied both by the laws of thermodynamics—the finite resources of a closed system—and by the history of capital-intensive technological development, standardizing around the most profitable (and often the most wasteful) rather than the best or most efficient. The blind hand of the market seems ready to sacrifice not only individuals but the entire species to the pursuit of profit in corporate cyborgs, posthuman agglomerations of computers, networks, and human biochips, capable of neither shame nor self-preservation.

When we exclude something from communicative community, we expel it into the environs. The first enclosures excluded the forests and wilderness from the properly human world, in the process marginalizing vagabonds and outlaws; the second excluded tools and technologies—the factory environment, which also excluded saboteurs and idlers. Today's marginals—hackers and Luddites (a category we hear less about today but that might well come back to bite us) are excluded from the data environment, where objects of collective knowledge are no longer identical to what any one of us knows (common sense). Something we call "science" knows the microscopic anatomy of the blue whale, but we do not. In many respects, our bodies themselves are becoming external, to be used up or stewarded as the case demands. Paradoxically, as the domain of media expands, the residual elements of us that remain definitively human seem to shrink.

We are at our best when we are happy. For the eudaemonist, the goal of politics is the good life. Politics should mean free and open discussion about what constitutes the good life, and about how we are to achieve it. Sara Ahmed (2010) and Will Davies (2015) have argued forcefully that happiness has become a tool of social control. Happiness as a goal of politics is a different creature. Social and more-than-human happiness is not reducible to treats for individualized consumers, but we have yet to determine what it is made of, and that requires debate. In a global age and among so many inhabitants, communication, and therefore media, is clearly essential for the conduct of political life as discussion. Instead of conducting this debate, contemporary politics rests on periodic agreement to allow a small elite to administer the existing state of affairs. This technocratic rule by experts tends to privilege some media more than others: A speech in Parliament is worth more than a letter to your MP. As Jodi Dean (2009) argues, we all have the right to speak, but governments have the right to ignore us. True political debate demands equality of access to the media of communication and equal significance for all participants, whatever medium they choose, praying that it is not the medium of last resort, armed insurrection. The first job of a political aesthetics of media is to put the political back in politics.

Ideally we are all able to connect, all able to contribute, all listened to and listening, all communicating. Restricting participation in debate not only ignores the fundamental political question about what constitutes the good life. It makes especially obvious the underlying question of who is the "we" who are entitled to debate it. Communication technologies tend to exclude communication with nonhumans. That is less true of scientific instruments, even though typically they are one-way devices, transporting data from the environment to human observers. Instruments like Cassini's highest-resolution camera, the Imaging Science Subsystem, can respond across the electromagnetic spectrum from 200 to 1,100 nm—human eyes typically respond to wavelengths between 390 and 700 nm—and can search, according to its designers, "for temporal variability throughout the system on a variety of time scales" (Porco et al. 2004). Sensing in frequencies and timescales we humans cannot, instruments like the Imaging Science Subsystem form a bridge between human perception and a world far beyond our sensorium. Chapter 4 lamented the absence of such capabilities when it comes to sensing the geological time span of nature's communication: These instruments begin to build the media on which a new "we" might come into dialogue.

The restriction on this utopian vision lies in the devotion of scientific instruments to a particular notion of truth as facts. Narrowly organized and defined in opposition to fiction and fantasy, facts that are always statements about reality begin to take themselves as realities. The saving grace of the situation is that, as real abstractions, facts like the Cassini images are informative, but they are also beautiful, and communicate with us at levels that enrich the experience of seeing and can open us to communication on multiple planes. We have learned to drop the word *beauty* from political debate, with some reason: Benjamin taught us to see aesthetic spectacle as a tool of domination. And yet abandoning beauty altogether, rather than demanding that it be democratized, has its consequences. In Kant's (1952) account, beauty is the shared, sociable recognition of the norms of good taste, while ugliness is equally a common cultural value. Kant opposes beauty to the sublime, that awe-inspiring experience when we are forced to confront the inexplicable. And if beauty is aesthetic, then its true opposite is neither ugliness nor the sublime but the an-aesthetic, having no sensation at all, whether of beauty or of ugliness or indeed of the sublime.

The idea of the sublime as something that exceeds language and social being, something overwhelming and final, suggests that it is only one step away from the anesthetic. Neither the sublime nor anesthesia can be discussed; both end in silence. The sublime simply overwhelms, in the baroque, under Nazism, or in the mass spectacles of contemporary national pomp. The anesthetic of contemporary life underwhelms with banality, subordinating architecture, design, and mass communications to repetitive marketing slogans and gray profit. If we see the Cassini image of the rings of Saturn as awe-inspiring presentations of scales and processes that strike us dumb, then we see in reverse the silenced dialogues we are not having with the graveyard of our plutonium. If we see them as sublime, then they veer toward anesthetic evidence of the might of those who organized their capture and their disdain for the struggles of the earthbound poor. But if we see them as beautiful, they are emblems of the deepest yearnings of the human. These aesthetic questions are also fundamentally political.

Which brings us back to the question: Who is this "we"? Is it possible to imagine even a "we" corresponding with the whole of our species? Not even Kant (1983), the Enlightenment prophet of "Idea for a Universal History with a Cosmopolitan Intent," could bring himself to believe in a global human commons. As the world shatters between rival monotheisms and modernities, as poverty and oppression redouble even in the midst of unfathomable wealth and privilege, that skepticism seems well placed. Under the regime of Universal Human Rights, all identities are subsumed under the single identity of naked humanity. When the nonhuman demand is strictly incommensurable with the existing order, in the same way that the demands of migrants, prisoners, and indigenous peoples are, or as the demand for happiness is, what is at stake is the end of human rights, and the end of the human exception, the very idea of human identity. Of course that is unthinkable, and yet we have all intuited being other than human: out walking, immersed in music, falling in love. Our traditions have made these experiences private matters. But they are political if the common experience of communion with the rest of the world—with machinery and tools, animals and landscapes—prefigures the future good of which political life should be capable. One way to enter the global commons—alternative to the present global privatization of wealth and resources—would be to yield our compulsive faith in the human exception: The only way to become truly human may be to become wholly environmental.

These media from Cassini, remote as they seem from human concerns, connect indigenous land use, urban power generation, national spectacle, political elites, and the pursuit of scientific or transcendent connection with the universe. Happiness as a political goal cannot be achieved unless we take into account all the marginalized and excluded domains, human and nonhuman, that we are so intricately involved with. The task of media aesthetics is to consider, to evaluate and debate the rival claims of these versions of the good, and the many more that have been repressed, no longer speaking on behalf of but communing with all the "we"s who form our planetary commons.

Eco-political aesthetics is politics and aesthetics otherwise, thinking differently about difference. To be wise to the other, we need to wise up to the true, the beautiful, and the good, not the data. Since in our time we think not only in the medium of words but in all forms of media, this book attempts to be wise to people, technologies, and environments—otherwise—by thinking through mediation. As long as those mediations are constrained by the communicative instrumentalities of institutional politics, we are unlikely to hear or see what precedes and exceeds our normative alienations. As long as we keep our ancestors as artificial life in chains, we will never hear their wisdom, or see what feats of imagination and invention they and we are capable of. Environmentalism is a populism: a constantly reformulated demand for better, different ways of being and becoming. It needs to embrace the environments constituted by machine and digital revolutions, if it is to shake off the universalism, normativity, and misanthropy it shares with politically paralyzed and economically catastrophic digital capital. Refusing to sacrifice happiness, it still must confront in melancholy its duty to the dead, the living, and the future. In Ned Kelly's last words on the gallows, "Such is life."

REFERENCES

ABC. 2016. "Carmichael coalmine: Mining Leases Approved for $21 Billion Project in Queensland's Galilee Basin." *Australian Broadcasting Corporation*, April 2. http://www.abc.net.au/news/2016-04-03/mning-leases-approved-carmichael-mine-qld-galilee-basin-adani/7295188.

Abizadeh, Arash. 2008. "Democratic Theory and Border Coercion: No Right to Unilaterally Control Your Own Borders." *Political Theory* 35 (1): 37–65.

Adelman, Maurice. 1972. *The World Petroleum Market*. Baltimore: Johns Hopkins University Press.

Adorno, Theodor W. 2000. *Problems of Moral Philosophy*. Translated by Edmund Jephcott. Cambridge, MA: Polity.

Agamben, Giorgio. 1993. *The Coming Community*. Translated by Michael Hardt. Minneapolis: University of Minnesota Press.

Agamben, Giorgio. 1994. "We Refugees." Translated by Michael Rocke. *Symposium* 49, no. 2 (1995): 114–19.

Agamben, Giorgio. 1998. *Homo Sacer: Sovereign Power and Bare Life*. Translated by Daniel Heller-Roazen. Stanford, CA: Stanford University Press.

Agamben, Giorgio. 2002. *The Open: Man and Animal*. Translated by Kevin Attell. Stanford, CA: Stanford University Press.

Agamben, Giorgio. 2005. *State of Exception*. Translated by Kevin Attell. Chicago: University of Chicago Press.

Agamben, Giorgio. 2011. *The Kingdom and the Glory: For a Theological Genealogy of Economy and Government*. Translated by Lorenzo Chiesa with Matteo Mandarini. Stanford, CA: Stanford University Press.

Ahmed, Sara. 2010. *The Promise of Happiness*. Durham, NC: Duke University Press.

AHRC. 2008. *A Statistical Overview of Aboriginal and Torres Strait Islander Peoples in Australia*. Canberra: Australian Human Rights Commission. http://www .humanrights.gov.au/publications/statistical-overview-aboriginal-and-torres -strait-islander-peoples-australia-social.

Alberta Energy Regulator. 2013. *Report 2013-B: Pipeline Performance in Alberta, 1990–2012*. http://www.aer.ca/documents/reports/R2013-B.pdf.

Allwood, Julian, and Jonathan Cullen. 2011. *Sustainable Materials—with Both Eyes Open: Future Buildings, Vehicles, Products and Equipment—Made Efficiently and Made with Less New Material*. Cambridge: UIT.

Althusser, Louis. 1971. "Ideology and Ideological State Apparatuses (Notes towards an Investigation)." In *Lenin and Philosophy and Other Essays*, translated by Ben Brewster, 127–88. New York: Monthly Review Press.

Appadurai, Arjun, ed. 1986. *The Social Life of Things: Commodities in Cultural Perspective*. Cambridge: Cambridge University Press.

APTN National News. 2012. "Aboriginal Groups Labelled 'Adversaries' by Federal Government: Document." January 26. Aboriginal Peoples Television Network. http://aptn.ca/news/2012/01/26/aboriginal-groups-labelled-adversaries-by -federal-government-document/.

Arendt, Hannah. 1958a. *The Human Condition*, 2nd ed. Chicago: University of Chicago Press.

Arendt, Hannah. 1958b. *The Origins of Totalitarianism*, 2nd ed. New York: Meridian.

Arendt, Hannah. 1978. *"We Refugees": The Jew as Pariah: Jewish Identity and Politics in the Modern Age*. Edited by Ron H. Feldman. New York: Grove.

Aristotle. 1925. *The Nichomachean Ethics*. Translated by David Ross. Oxford: Oxford University Press.

Aristotle. 1992. *The Politics*. Translated by T. A. Sinclair, revised by Trevor J. Saunders. Harmondsworth, UK: Penguin.

Arrighi, Giovanni. 2007. *Adam Smith in Beijing: Lineages of the Twenty-First Century*. London: Verso.

Arrighi, Giovanni, and Beverly J. Silver, with Iftikhar Ahmad, Kenneth Barr, Shuji Hisaeda, Po-keung Hui, Krishmendu Ray, Thomas Ehrlich Reifer, Miin-wen Shih, and Eric Slater. 1999. *Chaos and Governance in the Modern World System*. Minneapolis: University of Minnesota Press.

Arvesen, Anders, and Edgar G. Hertwich. 2012. "Assessing the Life Cycle Environmental Impacts of Wind Power: A Review of Present Knowledge and Research Needs." *Renewable and Sustainable Energy Reviews* 16 (8): 5994–6006.

Asian Labour Update. 2014. *Workers' Struggles in Electronic Industry*. January–July. Hong Kong: Asia Monitor Resource Centre.

Assies, Willem. 2003. "David versus Goliath in Cochabamba: Water Rights, Neoliberalism, and the Revival of Social Protest in Bolivia." *Latin-American Perspectives* 30 (3): 14–36.

Associated Press. 2014. "Samsung Promises to Compensate Factory Workers Who Suffered Cancer." *The Guardian*, May 14. http://www.theguardian.com /technology/2014/may/14/samsung-compensate-factory-workers-cancer.

ATSDR. 2014. "Medical Management Guidelines for Hydrogen Peroxide." Atlanta: Agency for Toxic Substances and Disease Registry. http://www.atsdr.cdc.gov /mmg/mmg.asp?id=304&tid=55.

Augustine. 1961. *Confessions.* Translated by R. S. Pine-Coffin. Harmondsworth, UK: Penguin.

Auty, Richard M., and Raymond F. Mikesell. 1993. *Sustaining Development in Mineral Economies: The Resource Curse Thesis.* London: Routledge.

Badiou, Alain. 2012. *Philosophy for Militants.* Translated by Bruno Bosteels. London: Verso.

Baitz, Martin, Johannes Kreißig, and Eloise Byrne. 2004. *Life Cycle Assessment of PVC and of Principal Competing Materials.* Brussels: European Commission.

Baker, Flossie. 2013. "Alberta's Oil Sands Bring Jobs, Services and Despair." Inter Press Service, August 5. http://www.ipsnews.net/2013/08/albertas-oil-sands-bring -jobs-services-and-despair/.

Baker Institute. 2008. *The Global Energy Market: Comprehensive Strategies to Meet Geopolitical and Financial Risks—the G8, Energy Security and Global Climate Issues.* Houston: James A. Baker III Institute for Public Policy, Rice University.

Bakker, Karen. 2007. "The 'Commons' versus the 'Commodity': Alter-globalization, Anti-privatization and the Human Right to Water in the Global South." *Antipode* 39 (3): 430–55.

Banerjee, Subhankar. 2013. "Ought We Not to Establish 'Access to Food?'" *Third Text* 27 (1): 33–43.

Baranowsky, Patrick W. 2004. "Transmittal of Preliminary Davis-Besse ASP Analysis." Memorandum to Ledyard B. Marsh, U.S. NRC, September 16. http://www .nrc.gov/reactors/operating/ops-experience/vessel-head-degradation/news/2004 /09–16–04-m10426005320.pdf.

Barclay, Barry. 2005. *Mana Tuturu: Maori Treasures and Intellectual Property Rights.* Auckland: Auckland University Press.

Barthes, Roland. 1980. *La chambre claire.* Paris: Gallimard.

Bartlett, Jamie, and Nathaniel Tkacz. 2014. "Keeping an Eye on the Dashboard." *Demos,* October 24. http://quarterly.demos.co.uk/article/issue-4/keeping-an-eye -on-the-dashboard/.

Basel Action Network. 2002. *Exporting Harm: The High-Tech Trashing of Asia.* February 25. http://www.ban.org/E-waste/technotrashfinalcomp.pdf.

Basel Action Network. 2005. *The Digital Dump: Exporting High-Tech Re-use and Abuse to Africa.* BAN Report, October 24. http://www.ban.org/BANreports/10– 24–05/index.htm.

Bataille, Georges. 1988. *The Accursed Share,* vol. 1: *Consumption.* Translated by Robert Hurley. New York: Zone.

Bateson, Gregory. 1973. *Steps to an Ecology of Mind: Collected Essays in Anthropology, Psychiatry, Evolution and Epistemology.* London: Paladin.

Baudrillard, Jean. 1980. *For a Critique of the Political Economy of the Sign.* Translated by Charles Levin. St. Louis, MO: Telos.

Baudrillard, Jean. 2005. *The Intelligence of Evil, or The Lucidity Pact*. Translated by Chris Turner. London: Verso.

Baudrillard, Jean. 2010. *The Agony of Power*. Translated by Ames Hodges, with an introduction by Sylvère Lottringer. New York: Semiotext(e).

Bauman, Zygmunt. 1999. *Culture as Praxis*. Rev. ed. London: Sage.

Bauwens, Michel. 2005. "The Political Economy of Peer Production." *C-Theory*, December 1. http://www.ctheory.net/articles.aspx?id=499.

Bauwens, Michel, and Vasilis Kostakis. 2014. "From the Communism of Capital to Capital for the Commons: Towards an Open Co-operativism." *triplec* 12 (1): 356–61.

BBC. 2005. "Waves 'Brought Waste to Somalia.'" *BBC News*, March 2. http://news .bbc.co.uk/1/hi/world/africa/4312553.stm.

Beck, Ulrich. 1995. *Ecological Politics in an Age of Risk*. Translated by Amos Weisz. Cambridge: Polity.

Beck, Ulrich. 1999. *World Risk Society*. Cambridge: Polity.

Beebe, Barton. 1999. "Law's Empire and the Final Frontier: Legalizing the Future in Early *Corpus Juris Spatialis*." *Yale Law Journal* 108 (7): 1737–73.

Beinart, William, and Lotte Hughes. 2007. *Environment and Empire*. Oxford: Oxford University Press.

Belich, James. 1986. *The New Zealand Wars and the Victorian Interpretation of Racial Conflict*. Auckland: Penguin.

Belton, Catherine. 2006. "For Russia, Dependence on 'a Man-Made Disaster.'" *New York Times*, January 12. http://www.nytimes.com/2006/01/12/world/europe/12iht -uranium.html.

Benjamin, Walter. 2003a. "On the Concept of History." In *Selected Writings*, vol. 4: *1938–1940*, edited by Howard Eiland and Michael W. Jennings, 389–400. Cambridge, MA: Belknap.

Benjamin, Walter. 2003b. "The Work of Art in the Age of Its Technological Reproducibility: Third Version." In *Selected Writings*, vol. 4, *1938–1940*, edited by Howard Eiland and Michael W. Jennings, 251–83. Cambridge, MA: Belknap.

Benkler, Yochai. 1998. "Overcoming Agoraphobia: Building the Commons of the Digitally Networked Environment." *Harvard Journal of Law and Technology* 11 (2): 1–113.

Benkler, Yochai. 2006. *The Wealth of Networks: How Social Production Transforms Markets and Freedom*. New Haven, CT: Yale University Press.

Benner, Thorsten, and Jan Martin Witte. 2004. "Everybody's Business: Accountability, Partnerships, and the Future of Global Governance." In *The Partnership Principle: New Forms of Governance in the 21st Century*, edited by Susan Stern and Elisabeth Seligman. London: Archetype.

Bennett, Jane. 2010. *Vibrant Matter: A Political Ecology of Things*. Durham, NC: Duke University Press.

Berardi, Franco "Bifo." 2009a. *Precarious Rhapsody: Semiocapitalism and the Pathologies of the Post-Alpha Generation*. Translated by Arianna Bove, Erik Empson,

Michael Goddard, Giuseppina Mecchia, Antonella Schintu, and Steve Wright. London: Minor Compositions.

Berardi, Franco "Bifo." 2009b. *The Soul at Work: From Alienation to Autonomy*. Translated by Francesca Cadel and Giuseppina Mecchia. New York: Semiotext(e).

Berardi, Franco "Bifo." 2012. "Semio-capital and the Problem of Solidarity." *Through Europe*, December 12. http://th-rough.eu/writers/bifo-eng/semio-capital-and -problem-solidarity.

Berkowitz, Roger. 2012. "Hannah Arendt on Human Rights." In *Handbook of Human Rights*, edited by Thomas Cushman, 59–67. New York: Routledge.

Bertrand, Ina, and William D. Routt. 2007. *The Picture That Will Live Forever: The Story of the Kelly Gang*. Canberra: Australian Teachers of Media/National Film and Sound Archive.

Bessire, Lucas. 2003. "Talking Back to Primitivism: Divided Audiences, Collective Desires." *American Anthropologist* 105 (4): 832–38.

Biermann, Frank, Philipp Pattberg, Harro van Asselt, and Fariborz Zelli. 2009. "The Fragmentation of Global Governance Architectures: A Framework for Analysis." *Global Environmental Politics* 9 (4): 14–40.

Bisschop, Lieselot. 2014. "How eWaste Challenges Environmental Governance." *International Journal for Crime, Justice and Social Democracy* 3 (2): 81–95.

Blakely, Christopher, Joseph Cooter, Ashu Khaitan, Iclal Sincer, and Ross Williams. 2012. *Rare Earth Metals and China*. Ann Arbor, MI: Ford School of Public Policy.

Bloch, Ernst. 1986. *The Principle of Hope*. 3 vols. Translated by Neville Plaice, Stephen Plaice, and Paul Knight. Cambridge, MA: MIT Press.

Bloch, Ernst. 1988. *The Utopian Function of Art and Literature: Selected Essays*. Translated by Jack Zipes and Frank Mecklenburg. Cambridge, MA: MIT Press.

Boccaletti, Giulio, Markus Löffler, and Jeremy M. Oppenheim. 2008. "How IT Can Cut Carbon Emissions." *McKinsey Quarterly*, October. http://www.kyotoclub.org /docs/mckinsey_it_otto8.pdf.

Bordwell, David. 2011. "Forking Tracks: *Source Code*." *Observations on Film Art*, May 3. http://www.davidbordwell.net/blog/2011/05/03/forking-tracks-source -code/.

Bosteels, Bruno. 2011. *The Actuality of Communism*. London: Verso.

Bough, Jill. 2011. "The Mirror Has Two Faces: Contradictory Reflections of Donkeys in Western Literature from Lucius to Balthazar." *Animals* 1: 56–68.

Bourdieu, Pierre. 1986. *Distinction: A Social Critique of the Judgement of Taste*. Translated by R. Nice. Cambridge, MA: Harvard University Press.

Bourdieu, Pierre. 1998. *Acts of Resistance: Against the New Myths of Our Time*. Cambridge: Polity.

Boutang, Yann Moulier. 2012. *Cognitive Capitalism*. Cambridge: Polity.

Bradsher, Keith. 2013. "China Tries to Clean Up Toxic Legacy of Its Rare Earth Riches." *New York Times*, October 22. http://www.nytimes.com/2013/10/23 /business/international/china-tries-to-clean-up-toxic-legacy-of-its-rare-earth -riches.html.

Brakhage, Stan. 1963. "Metaphors on Vision." Special issue, *Film Culture*, no. 30 (fall).

Brassier, Ray. 2007. *Nihil Unbound: Enlightenment and Extinction*. London: Palgrave Macmillan.

Bratton, Benjamin H. 2014. *The Stack: On Software and Sovereignty*. Cambridge, MA: MIT Press.

Bratton, William W. 2002. "Enron and the Dark Side of Shareholder Value." *Tulane Law Review* 76 (May): 1275–1361.

Brecht, Bertolt. 1979. "Radio as a Means of Communication." Translated by Stuart Hood. *Screen* 20 (3–4): 24–28.

Bresson, Robert. 1977. *Notes on Cinematography*. Translated by Jonathan Griffin. New York: Urizen.

Brugge, Doug, Timothy Benally, and Esther Yazzie-Lewis, eds. 2006. *The Navajo People and Uranium Mining*. Albuquerque: University of New Mexico Press.

Brummer, Alex. 2014. *Bad Banks: Greed, Incompetence and the Next Global Crisis*. London: Random House.

Bruns, Axel. 2008. *Blogs, Wikipedia, Second Life, and Beyond: From Production to Produsage*. New York: Peter Lang.

Bryan, Martin. 2007. *Report on WG1 Activity for December 2007 Meeting of ISO/IEC JTC1/SC34/WG1 in Kyoto*. ISO/JTC1 SC34, November 29. http://www.jtc1sc34.org/repository/0940.htm.

Burawoy, Michael. 2009. "Redefining the Public University: Developing an Analytical Framework." New York: Social Science Research Council. http://publicsphere.ssrc.org/burawoy-redefining-the-public-university/.

Burgis, Tom. 2015. *The Looting Machine: Warlords, Tycoons, Smugglers, and the Systematic Theft of Africa's Wealth*. London: William Collins.

Cabanne, Pierre. 1971. *Dialogues with Marcel Duchamp*. London: Thames and Hudson.

Caffentzis, George. 2005. *No Blood for Oil! Energy, Class Struggle, and War, 1998–2004*. Portland, ME: Midnight Notes Collective. http://citeseerx.ist.psu.edu/viewdoc/download;jsessionid=19B4D02A0937763B2AD1D39B87E37778?doi=10.1.1.113.2382&rep=rep1&type=pdf.

Campbell, Colin J., and Jean H. Laherrère. 1998. "The End of Cheap Oil." *Scientific American* 278 (3).

Campbell-Kelly, Martin. 2004. *From Airline Reservations to Sonic the Hedgehog: A History of the Software Industry*. Cambridge, MA: MIT Press.

CAN Canada. 2012. *Dirty Oil Diplomacy: The Canadian Government's Global Push to Sell the Tar Sands*. Ottawa: Climate Action Network Canada, March 8. http://climateactionnetwork.ca/2012/03/08/dirty-oil-diplomacy/?rel=691.

Cardinale, Matthew Charles. 2013. "United States: Native Americans Take Lead in Tar Sands Resistance." Indigenous Peoples Issues and Resources, September 2. http://www.ipsnews.net/2013/09/native-americans-take-lead-in-tar-sands-resistance/.

Carr, Nicholas. 2009. *The Big Switch: Rewiring the World, from Edison to Google.* New York: W. W. Norton.

Casas-Cortés, Maribel. 2014. "A Genealogy of Precarity: A Toolbox for Rearticulating Fragmented Social Realities in and out of the Workplace." *Rethinking Marxism: A Journal of Economics, Culture and Society* 26 (2): 206–26.

"Cassini Spacecraft Nears Liftoff, but Critics Object to Its Risks. 1997. *New York Times,* October 12. http://www.nytimes.com/1997/10/12/us/cassini -spacecraft-nears-liftoff-but-critics-object-to-its-risks.html.

Castells, Manuel. 2009. *Communication Power.* Oxford: Oxford University Press.

Caulderwood, Kathleen. 2013. "Chinese Copper Mining Operations Halted by Zambia's Environmental Agency." *International Business Times,* December 9. http://www.ibtimes.com/chinese-copper-mining-operations-halted-zambias -environmental-agency-1501396.

Center for Constitutional Rights. 2009. "Factsheet: Shell's Environmental Devastation in Nigeria." March 24. http://ccrjustice.org/home/get-involved/tools -resources/fact-sheets-and-faqs/factsheet-shells-environmental-devastation.

Chaffee, C. David. 2011. "The Coming Market for Optical Fiber and Cable." *Photonics Spectra.* http://www.photonics.com/Article.aspx?AID=49953.

Chakrabarty, Dipesh. 2009. "The Climate of History: Four Theses." *Critical Inquiry* 35 (winter): 197–222.

Chao, Julie. 2001. "Relocation for Giant Dam Inflames Chinese Peasants." *National Geographic,* May 15. http://news.nationalgeographic.co.uk/news/2001/05/0515 _threegorges.html.

Checchi, Daniele, Massimo Florio, and Jorge Carrera. 2007. "Privatisation Discontent and Utility Reform in Latin America." *Journal of Development Studies* 45 (3): 333–50.

Chen, H. W. 2006. "Gallium, Indium, and Arsenic Pollution of Groundwater from a Semiconductor Manufacturing Area of Taiwan." *Bulletin of Environmental Contamination and Toxicology* 77 (2): 289–96.

Chew, Corky. 2011. "Environmental and Public Health Issues." In *83. Microelectronics and Semiconductors,* edited by Michael E. Williams. *Encyclopedia of Occupational Health and Safety,* Jeanne Mager Stellman, editor in chief. Geneva: International Labor Organization. http://iloencyclopaedia.org/contributors/author/2540 -chewcorky.

China Labor Watch. 2011. *Tragedies of Globalization: The Truth behind Electronics Sweatshops.* New York: China Labor Watch. http://www.chinalaborwatch.org /report/52.

China Water Risk. 2013. "8 Things You Should Know about Water and Semiconductors." July 11. http://chinawaterrisk.org/resources/analysis-reviews/8-things-you -should-know-about-water-and-semiconductors/.

Chiu Yu-Tzu. 2013. "ASE Faces Possible Halt Due to Water Pollution." *ZDnet,* December 11. http://www.zdnet.com/ase-faces-possible-halt-due-to-water-pollution -7000024138/.

Chung, Jalen, and Frances Huang. 2014. "ASE Expects Production at Full Capacity in Q3." *Focus Taiwan*, June 26. http://focustaiwan.tw/news/aeco/201406260023.aspx.

Clastres, Pierre. 1987. *Society against the State: Essays in Political Anthropology.* Translated by Robert Hurley. New York: Zone.

Climate Group. 2008. SMART 2020: *Enabling the Low Carbon Economy in the Information Age.* London: The Climate Group on Behalf of the Global eSustainability Initiative (GeSI). http://www.theclimategroup.org/what-we-do/publications /SMART2020-Enabling-the-low-carbon-economy-in-the-information-age/.

COHA. 2009. "Bolivia: The Myth of the Saudi Arabia of Lithium." Washington, DC: Council for Hemispheric Affairs, October 28. http://www.coha.org/bolivia-the -myth-of-the-saudi-arabia-of-lithium/.

Cohen, David. 2007. "Earth's Natural Wealth: An Audit." *New Scientist*, May 23. http://www.newscientist.com/article/mg19426051.200-earths-natural-wealth-an -audit.html.

Cohen, Tom. 2014. *Telemorphosis: Theory in the Era of Climate Change*, vol. 1. Ann Arbor, MI: Open Humanities Press.

Collette, Augustin. 2009. *Case Studies on Climate Change and World Heritage.* Paris: UNESCO World Heritage Centre.

Commonwealth of Australia. 2003. "Regulating the Ranger, Jabiluka, Beverley and Honeymoon Uranium Mines," October. Canberra: Environment, Communications, Information Technology and the Arts References Committee.

Coombe, Rosemary J. 1995. "The Cultural Life of Things: Anthropological Approaches to Law and Society in the Age of Globalization." *American University International Law Review* 10 (2): 791–835.

Cope, Gord. 2009. "Pure Water, Semiconductors and the Recession." *Global Water Intelligence* 10 (10). http://www.globalwaterintel.com/archive/10/10/market -insight/pure-water-semiconductors-and-the-recession.html.

Copper Development Association. 2013. *Annual Data 2013: Copper Supply and Consumption, 1992–2012.* New York: Copper Development Association.

Corr, Anders. 1999. *No Trespassing! Squatting, Rent Strikes, and Land Struggles Worldwide.* New York: South End.

Cox, Lisa. 2015a. "Adani's Carmichael Mine Is Unbankable Says Queensland Treasury." *Sydney Morning Herald*, June 30. http://www.smh.com.au/business/mining -and-resources/adanis-carmichael-mine-is-unbankable-says-queensland -treasury-20150630-gi1137.html.

Cox, Lisa. 2015b. "Uncertainty over Massive Queensland Mine after Election Shock and Concerns over Indian Company." *Sydney Morning Herald*, February 7. http:// www.smh.com.au/business/uncertainty-over-massive-queensland-mine-after -election-shock-and-concerns-over-indian-company-20150205-137mbi.

Crary, Jonathan. 1999. *Suspensions of Perception: Attention, Spectacle and Modern Culture.* Cambridge, MA: MIT Press.

Credit Suisse. 2013. *Global Wealth Report 2013.* Zurich: Credit Suisse. https:// publications.credit-suisse.com/tasks/render/file/?fileID=BCDB1364-A105–0560– 1332EC9100FF5C83.

Creed, Barbara. 1993. *The Monstrous-Feminine: Film, Feminism, Psychoanalysis.* London: Routledge.

Crosby, Alfred W. 2013. *Ecological Imperialism: The Biological Expansion of Europe, 900–1900.* 2nd ed. Cambridge: Cambridge University Press.

Cubitt, Sean. 1998. *Digital Aesthetics.* London: Sage.

Cubitt, Sean. 2014a. *The Practice of Light: A Genealogy of Visual Technologies from Prints to Pixels.* Cambridge, MA: MIT Press.

Cubitt, Sean. 2014b. "Regional Standardisation: MPEG and Intercultural Transmission." In *Art in the Asia-Pacific: Intimate Publics,* edited by Larissa Hjorth, Natalie King, and Mami Kataoka, 134–45. New York: Routledge.

Dahl, Carol A. 2004. *International Energy Markets: Understanding Pricing, Policies, and Profits.* Tulsa, OK: PennWell.

Davies, Anna R. 2012. "Geography and the Matter of Waste Mobilities." *Transactions of the Institute of British Geographers* 37 (2): 191–96.

Davies, William. 2015. *The Happiness Industry: How the Government and Big Business Sold Us Well-Being.* London: Verso.

Davis, Angela Y. 2003. *Are Prisons Obsolete?* New York: Open Media/Seven Stories.

Davis, Mike. 2004. "Planet of Slums." *New Left Review* 26 (March–April): 14.

Dean, Jodi. 2005. "Communicative Capitalism: Circulation and the Foreclosure of Politics." *Cultural Politics* 1 (1): 51–74.

Dean, Jodi. 2009. *Democracy and Other Neoliberal Fantasies: Communicative Capitalism and Left Politics.* Durham, NC: Duke University Press.

Dean, Jodi. 2012. *The Communist Horizon.* London: Verso.

Debray, Régis. 1991. *Cours de médiologie générale.* Paris: NRF.

Debray, Régis. 2004. *God: An Itinerary.* Translated by Jeffrey Mehlmann. London: Verso.

de Carolis, Massimo. 1996. "Towards a Phenomenology of Opportunism." In *Radical Thought in Italy: A Potential Politics,* edited by Paolo Virno and Michael Hardt, 37–52. Minneapolis: University of Minnesota Press.

de Certeau, Michel. 1984. *The Practice of Everyday Life.* Translated by Steven Rendall. Berkeley: University of California Press.

Deleuze, Gilles, and Félix Guattari. 1985. *Anti-Oedipus: Capitalism and Schizophrenia.* Translated by Robert Hurley, Mark Seem, and Helen Lane. Minneapolis: University of Minnesota Press.

Deleuze, Gilles, and Félix Guattari. 1994. *What Is Philosophy?* Translated by Hugh Tomlinson and Graham Burchell. New York: Columbia University Press.

deNardis, Laura. 2009. *Protocol Politics: The Globalization of Internet Governance.* Cambridge, MA: MIT Press.

deNardis, Laura. 2014. *The Global War for Internet Governance.* New Haven, CT: Yale University Press.

Derrida, Jacques. 2002. *Negotiations: Interventions and Interviews 1971–2001.* Translated by Elizabeth Rottenberg. Stanford, CA: Stanford University Press.

DeSombre, Elizabeth R. 2006. *Flagging Standards: Globalization and Environmental, Safety and Labor Regulations at Sea.* Cambridge, MA: MIT Press.

Dews, Peter. 2013. *The Idea of Evil.* London: Wiley-Blackwell.

Dharmadhikary, Shripad. 2008. *Mountains of Concrete: Dam Building in the Himalayas.* Berkeley, CA: International Rivers.

Di Filippo, Patricia. 2011. "The Mists of Riachuelo." *Argentina Independent,* April 11. http://www.argentinaindependent.com/socialissues/environment/the-mists-of -riachuelo/.

Dorfman, Ariel, and Armand Mattelart. 1984. *How to Read Donald Duck: Imperialist Ideology in the Disney Comic.* Translated by David Kunzle. New York: International General.

Douglas, Mary. 1966. *Purity and Danger: An Analysis of Concepts of Pollution and Taboo.* London: Routledge.

Douglas, Susan J. 1987. *Inventing American Broadcasting, 1899–1922.* Baltimore: Johns Hopkins University Press.

Dowmunt, Tony, ed. 1993. *Channels of Resistance: Global Television and Local Empowerment.* London: British Film Institute/Channel Four Television.

Downey, Anthony. 2009. "Zones of Indistinction: Giorgio Agamben's 'Bare Life' and the Politics of Aesthetics." *Third Text* 23 (2): 109–25.

Downing, John, with Tamara Villareal Ford, Genève Gil, and Laura Stein. 2001. *Radical Media: Rebellious Communication and Social Movements.* New York: Sage.

Drange, Matt, and Susanne Rust. 2014. "Toxic Trail: The Weak Points in the Superfund Waste System." *The Guardian,* March 17. http://www.theguardian.com /environment/2014/mar/17/toxic-trail-weak-points-superfund-waste.

Drew, Jesse. 2013. *A Social History of Contemporary Democratic Communications.* New York: Routledge.

Duffy, Rosaleen. 2005. "Criminalisation and the Politics of Governance: Illicit Gem Sapphire Mining in Madagascar." Paper presented at Redesigning the State? Political Corruption in Development Policy and Practice Conference at IDPM, Manchester University, November 25. http://www.ddiglobal.org/login/resources /criminalisation-and-the-politics-of-governance.pdf.

Duménil, Gérard, and Dominique Lévy. 2004. *Capital Resurgent: Roots of the Neoliberal Revolution.* Cambridge, MA: Harvard University Press.

Dymond, Abi. 2007. *Undermining Development: Copper Mining in Zambia.* London: ACTSA, Action for Southern Africa.

EIA. 2012. "How Much Electricity Is Lost in Transmission and Distribution in the United States?" U.S. Energy Information Administration, July 9. http://www.eia .gov/tools/faqs/faq.cfm?id=105&t=3.

EIA. 2016. "Monthly Energy Review." U.S. Energy Information Administration. https://www.eia.gov/totalenergy/data/monthly/.

Eichenwald, Kurt. 2005. *Conspiracy of Fools: A True Story.* New York: Broadway.

Eisenhammer, Stephen. 2015. "Brazil Mining Flood Could Devastate Environment for Years." Reuters, November 15. http://www.reuters.com/article/2015/11/15/us -brazil-damburst-environment-idUSKCN0T40PY20151115.

EJAtlas.org. 2015. *Environmental Justice Atlas*. Barcelona: Environmental Justice Organisations, Liabilities and Trade. http://ejatlas.org/.

Ellul, Jacques. 1964. *The Technological Society*. Translated by John Wilkinson. New York: Vintage.

Enzensberger, Hans Magnus. 1970. "Constituents for a Theory of the Media." Translated by Stuart Hood. *New Left Review* 64 (November/December): 13–36.

EPA. 1985. *Wastes from the Extraction and Beneficiation of Metallic Ores, Phosphate Rock, Asbestos, Overburden from Uranium Mining, and Oil Shale: Report to Congress*. ES-13, December. Washington, DC: U.S. Environmental Protection Agency.

EPA. 2007. *Border Air Quality Data—Ciudad Juarez/El Paso Area Monitoring Sites*. U.S. Environmental Protection Agency. http://www.epa.gov/ttncatc1/cica/sites_cj_e.html.

EPA. 2008. *Semiconductor Industry: Basic Information*. U.S. Environmental Protection Agency. https://www.epa.gov/f-gas-partnership-programs/semiconductor-industry.

EPA. 2013. "Tijuana River Watershed, Baja California and CA." U.S. Environmental Protection Agency, September 25. http://www.epa.gov/region9/water/watershed/tijuana.html.

EPA. 2015. "Gold King Mine Release Emergency Response." U.S. Environmental Protection Agency, August 14. http://www2.epa.gov/goldkingmine.

Ernest and Young. 2012. *Global Semiconductor Industry Study*. San Jose: Ernest and Young Global Technology Center. EYG NO DC0098.

Esposito, Elena. 2011. *The Future of Futures: The Time of Money in Financing and Society*. Cheltenham, UK: Edward Elgar.

Esposito, Roberto. 2009. Preface to *Categories of the Impolitical*. Translated by Connal Parsley. *diacritics* 39 (2): 99–115.

European Commission. 2009. *Towards a Sustainable Front-End of Nuclear Energy Systems*. JRC report. Strasbourg: European Commission. EUR 23955EN EN.

European Commission. 2012. *National Roma Integration Strategies: A First Step in the Implementation of the EU Framework*. Brussels: European Commission. COM (2012) 226 final.

Eurostat. 2015. "Electricity Production, Consumption and Market Overview." May. http://ec.europa.eu/eurostat/statistics-explained/index.php/Electricity_production,_consumption_and_market_overview.

Evans, Chris. 2011. *The Internet of Things: How the Next Evolution of the Internet Is Changing Everything*. Cisco Internet Business Solutions Group. https://www.cisco.com/c/dam/en_us/about/ac79/docs/innov/IoT_IBSG_0411FINAL.pdf.

Evans, Gwyn, and David Maddox. 2010. *The Tonypandy Riots, 1910–11*. Plymouth, UK: University of Plymouth Press.

Ewalt, Donald. 1981. "The Fight for Oil: Britain in Persia, 1919." *History Today* 31 (9). http://www.historytoday.com/donald-ewalt/fight-oil-britain-persia-1919.

Faujas, Alain, and Brice Pedrelotti. 2013. "L'économie chinoise montre des signes de rebond." *Le Monde*, August 10. http://www.lemonde.fr/economie/article/

2013/08/10/1 economie-chinoise-montre-des-signes-de-rebond_3459895_3234
.html.

Feilhauer, Matthias, and Soenke Zehle, eds. 2009. "Ethics of Waste in the Information Society." Special issue, *International Review of Information Ethics* 11 (October). http://www.i-r-i-e.net/issue11.htm.

Ferguson, Niall. 2009. *The Ascent of Money: A Financial History of the World*, updated version. London: Penguin.

Ferris-Rotman, Amie. 2009. "Russian Arctic Tribe at Risk from Yamal Gas Projects." Reuters, October 6. http://www.reuters.com/article/2009/10/06/us-russia
-yamal-nenets-idUSTRE5953ZB20091006.

Fletcher, Kate. 2008. *Sustainable Fashion and Textiles: Design Journeys*. London:
Earthscan.

Flew, Stephen. 2009. "Excel 2010: Another Opportunity Missed." *Visual Business Intelligence*, August 10. http://www.perceptualedge.com/blog/?p=583.

Flusser, Vilém. 2000. *Towards a Philosophy of Photography*. Translated by Anthony
Matthews, with an introduction by Hubertus Von Amelunxen. London: Reak-
tion.

Flynn, Daniel, and Geert de Clerq. 2014. "Special report: Areva and Niger's Uranium Fight." Reuters, February 5. http://www.reuters.com/article/2014/02/05/us
-niger-areva-specialreport-idUSBREA140AA20140205.

FOE. 2013. "Keystone XL: Friends of the Earth Files for Release of State Department
Records on Massive Lobbying Operation by TransCanada and Province of Alberta." Friends of the Earth, April 15. http://www.foe.org/news/news-releases/201
3-04-friends-of-the-earth-files-kxl-foia-request.

Foresight. 2011. *The Future of Computer Trading in Financial Markets*. London: Government Office for Science.

Fossati, Giovanna. 2009. *From Grain to Pixel: The Archival Life of Film*. Amsterdam:
Amsterdam University Press.

Foucault, Michel. 1972. *The Archaeology of Knowledge and the Discourse on Language*. Translated by Alan Sheridan. New York: Harper Colophon.

Foucault, Michel. 1977. *Discipline and Punish: Birth of the Prison*. Translated by Alan
Sheridan. London: Penguin.

Foucault, Michel. 1986. "Of Other Spaces." Translated by Jay Miskowiec. *Diacritics*
16 (1): 22–27.

Foucault, Michel. 1998. "Different Spaces." Translated by Robert Hurley. In *Aesthetics, Method and Epistemology—Essential Works of Foucault, 1954–1984*, vol. 2, edited by Paul Rabinow, 175–85. London: Penguin.

Foucault, Michel. 2000. "The Subject and Power." In *Power—Essential Works of
Foucault, 1954–1984*, vol. 3, edited by James D. Faubion, translated by Robert
Hurley and others, 326–48. London: Penguin.

Foucault, Michel. 2003. *Society Must Be Defended: Lectures at the Collège de France,
1975–1976*. Edited by Mauro Bertani and Alessandro Fontana, translated by
David Macey. London: Penguin.

Foucault, Michel. 2004. *The Birth of Biopolitics: Lectures at the Collège de France, 1978–1979*. Edited by Michel Senellart, translated by Graham Burchell. Basingstoke, UK: Palgrave Macmillan.

Foucault, Michel. 2007. *Security, Population, Territory: Lectures at the Collège de France, 1977–1978*. Edited by Michel Senellart, translated by Graham Burchell. Basingstoke, UK: Palgrave Macmillan.

Fowler, Catherine S., with data contributed by Maribeth Hamby, Elmer Rusco, and Mary Rusco. 1991. *Native Americans and Yucca Mountain: A Revised and Updated Summary Report on Research Undertaken between 1987 and 1991*. October. Reno, NV: Cultural Resource Consultants.

Fox, Loren. 2003. *The Rise and Fall of Enron*. New York: Wiley.

Free, Bernhard, Richard W. Hutchinson, and Bernhard C. Koch. 1990. "Gold Deposition at Gold King, Silverton Caldera, Colorado." *Mitteilungen des Naturwissenschaftlichen Vereines für Steiermark* 120:135–43.

Freedman, Des. 2012. "Outsourcing Internet Regulation." In *Misunderstanding the Internet*, edited by James Curran, Natalie Fenton, and Des Freedman, 95–120. London: Routledge.

Freese, Barbara. 2003. *Coal: A Human History*. New York: Random House.

Freud, Sigmund. 1984. "Mourning and Melancholia." In *On Metapsychology: The Theory of Psychoanalysis*, translated by James Strachey, edited by Angela Richards, 251–68. Pelican Freud Library 11. Harmondsworth, UK: Pelican.

Froomkin, A. Michael. 2003. "Habermas@Discourse.net: Toward a Critical Theory of Cyberspace." *Harvard Law Review* 116 (January): 751–873.

Fuller, Matt. 2001. "It Looks Like You're Writing a Letter: Microsoft Word." *Telepolis*, March 7. http://www.heise.de/tp/r4/artikel/7/7073/1.html; reprinted in Matthew Fuller. 2003. *Behind the Blip: Essays on Software Culture*. New York: Autonomedia.

Fuller, Matthew. 2006. "Softness: Interrogability; General Intellect; Art Methodologies in Software." Institute of Aesthetic Studies, Aarhus Universitet. http://darc.imv.au.dk/wp-content/files/13.pdf.

Fuller, Matthew, ed. 2008. *Software Studies: A Lexicon*. Cambridge, MA: MIT Press.

Gabrys, Jennifer. 2010. *Digital Rubbish: A Natural History of Electronics*. Ann Arbor: University of Michigan Press.

GAHP. 2014. "Pollution: The Largest Cause of Death in the Developing World." New York: Global Alliance on Health and Pollution. http://www.gahp.net/new/pollutionthelargestcauseofdeath/.

Galison, Peter. 1997. *Image and Logic: A Material Culture of Microphysics*. Chicago: University of Chicago Press.

Galloway, Alexander R. 2004. *Protocol: How Control Exists after Decentralization*. Cambridge, MA: MIT Press.

Galloway, Alexander R. 2012. *The Interface Effect*. Cambridge: Polity.

Galloway, Robert L. 1882. *A History of Coal Mining in Great Britain*. London: Macmillan.

GamePlanet.com. 2008. "World of Warcraft Hits 11.5m Subscriptions." December 24. http://www.gameplanet.co.nz/news/i132746/World-of-Warcraft-hits-11.5m -subscribers/.

Gantz, John, project director. 2008. *The Diverse and Exploding Digital Universe.* IDC White Paper, March. Framingham, MA: IDC. http://www.emc.com/collateral /analyst-reports/diverse-exploding-digital-universe.pdf.

Garrison, Steve. 2015. "EPA Says 3 Million Gallons of Contaminated Water Released into Animas River." *Daily Times* (Farmington), August 10. http://www.daily -times.com/four_corners-news/ci_28611665/.

Gaud, William S. 1968. "The Green Revolution: Accomplishments and Apprehensions." Address to the Society for International Development, Washington, DC, March 8. AgBioWorld. http://www.agbioworld.org/biotech-info/topics/borlaug /borlaug-green.html.

Geertz, Clifford. 1965. "The Transition to Humanity." In *Horizons of Anthropology*, edited by Sol Tax. London: Allen and Unwin.

Geertz, Clifford. 1973. "Thick Description: Toward an Interpretative Theory of Culture." In *The Interpretation of Cultures: Selected Essays*, 3–30. New York: Basic Books.

Gibbs, Samuel. 2014. "Google Reinforces Undersea Cables after Shark Bites." *The Guardian*, August 14. http://www.theguardian.com/technology/2014/aug/14 /google-undersea-fibre-optic-cables-shark-attacks.

Gibson, William. 1999. "The Science in Science Fiction." *Talk of the Nation.* NPR, November 30. http://www.npr.org/templates/story/story.php?storyId=1067220.

Glanz, James. 2012. "The Cloud Factories. Part 1: Power, Pollution and the Internet; Part 2: Data Barns in a Farm Town, Gobbling Power and Flexing Muscle; Part 3: Real Estate or Utility? Surging Data Center Industry Blurs Boundaries." *New York Times*, September 22. http://www.nytimes.com/2012/09/23/technology/data -centers-waste-vast-amounts-of-energy-belying-industry-image.html.

Goldman, Michael. 2005. *Imperial Nature: The World Bank and Struggles for Social Justice in the Age of Globalization.* New Haven, CT: Yale University Press.

Goldsmith, Ben. 2014. "The Smartphone App Economy and App Ecosystems." In *The Routledge Companion to Mobile Media*, edited by Gerard Goggin and Larissa Hjorth, 171–80. New York: Routledge.

Google. 2015. "How Search Works." https://www.google.co.uk/insidesearch /howsearchworks/thestory/.

Gorz, André. 2010. *The Immaterial.* Translated by Chris Turner. Chicago: University of Chicago Press.

Graham, Phil. 2006. *Hypercapitalism: Language, New Media, and Social Perceptions of Value.* New York: Peter Lang.

Graham, Stephen, and Simon Marvin. 2001. *Splintering Urbanism: Networked Infrastructures, Technological Mobilities and the Urban Condition.* London: Routledge.

"The Great Transition." 2014. *The Economist*, March 22.

Greenpeace. 2008. *The True Cost of Coal.* Amsterdam: Greenpeace.

Greenpeace. 2010. *Left in the Dust: AREVA's Radioactive Legacy in the Desert Towns of Niger*. Amsterdam: Greenpeace.

Greenpeace. 2013. "The Dangers of Arctic Oil." http://www.greenpeace.org /international/en/campaigns/climate-change/arctic-impacts/The-dangers-of -Arctic-oil/.

Greenpeace International. 2005. "Recycling of Electronic Wastes in China and India: Workplace and Environmental Contamination." Amsterdam: Greenpeace. http://www.greenpeace.org/international/PageFiles/25134/recycling-of-electronic -waste.pdf.

Gregson, N., Mike Crang, F. Ahamed, N. Akhter, and R. Ferdous. 2010. "Following Things of Rubbish Value: End-of-Life Ships, 'Chocky-Chocky' Furniture and the Bangladeshi Middle Class Consumer." *Geoforum* 41 (6): 846–54.

Grossman, Elizabeth. 2007. *High Tech Trash: Digital Devices, Hidden Toxics, and Human Health*. Washington, DC: Shearwater.

Grossman, Elizabeth. 2011. "Toxics in the 'Clean Rooms': Are Samsung Workers at Risk?" *Yale Environment 360*, June 9. http://e360.yale.edu/content/print.msp?id= 2414.

Grossman, Elizabeth. 2012. "How a Gold Mining Boom Is Killing the Children of Nigeria." *Yale Environment 360*, March 1. http://e360.yale.edu/content/print.msp ?id=2500.

Grotius, Hugo. [1609] 1916. *The Freedom of the Seas, or the Right Which belongs to the Dutch to take Part in the East India Trade*. Translated by Ralph van Deman Magoffin. New York: Oxford University Press.

Gruber, Paul W., Pablo A. Medina, Gregory A. Keoleian, Stephen E. Kesler, Mark P. Everson, and Timothy J. Wallington. 2011. "Global Lithium Availability." *Journal of Industrial Ecology* 15 (5): 760–75.

Grumbine, R. Edward, and Maharaj K. Pandi. 2013. "Threats from India's Himalaya Dams." *Science* 339 (6115): 36–37.

Guilbault, Serge. 1983. *How New York Stole the Idea of Modern Art, Abstract Expressionism, Freedom and the Cold War*. Chicago: University of Chicago Press.

Gurevich, Leon. 2011. "Google Warming: Panoptical Regimes and the Machinima of the Visible." Unpublished manuscript, Victoria University, Wellington.

Habermas, Jürgen. 1984. *The Theory of Communicative Action*, vol. 1: *Reason and the Rationalisation of Society*. Translated by Thomas McCarthy. Cambridge: Polity.

Habermas, Jürgen. 1987. *The Theory of Communicative Action*, vol. 2: *The Critique of Functionalist Reason*. Translated by Thomas McCarthy. Cambridge: Polity.

Habermas, Jürgen. 1989. *The Structural Transformation of the Public Sphere: An Enquiry into a Category of Bourgeois Society*. Translated by Thomas Burger with Frederick Lawrence. Cambridge: Polity.

Habermas, Jürgen. 1992. *Postmetaphysical Thinking*. Cambridge: Polity.

Hailu, Degol, Rafael Osorio, and Raquel Tsukada. 2012. "Privatization and Renationalization: What Went Wrong with Bolivia's Water Sector?" *World Development* 40 (12): 2564–77.

Hall, David. 2006. *Water and Electricity in Nigeria*. London: Public Services International Research Unit, University of Greenwich.

Halliday, Fred. 1974. *Arabia without Sultans: A Political Survey of Instability in the Arab World*. Harmondsworth, UK: Penguin.

Halliday, Fred. 1997. "Arabia without Sultans Revisited." *Middle East Reports* 204 (July–September): 27–29.

Hardin, Garrett. 1968. "The Tragedy of the Commons." *Science*, no. 162: 1245–48.

Harding, Jim. 2007. *Canada's Deadly Secret: Saskatchewan Uranium and the Global Nuclear System*. Black Point, NS: Fernwood.

Hardt, Michael, and Antonio Negri. 2000. *Empire*. Cambridge, MA: Harvard University Press.

Hardt, Michael, and Antono Negri. 2004. *Multitude: War and Democracy in the Age of Empire*. New York: Penguin.

Hardt, Michael, and Antonio Negri. 2009. *Commonwealth*. Cambridge, MA: Harvard University Press.

Harford, Barbara, and Sarah Hopkins, eds. 1984. *Greenham Common: Women at the Wire*. London: Women's Press.

Harman, Chris. 2009. *Zombie Capitalism: Global Crisis and the Relevance of Marx*. London: Bookmarks.

Harman, Graham. 2005. *Guerrilla Metaphysics: Phenomenology and the Carpentry of Things*. Chicago: Open Court Press.

Harvey, David. 1989. *The Condition of Postmodernity: An Enquiry into the Origins of Cultural Change*. Oxford: Blackwell.

Harvey, David. 2003. *The New Imperialism*. Oxford: Oxford University Press.

Harvey, David. 2005. *A Brief History of Neoliberalism*. Oxford: Oxford University Press.

Harvey, David. 2010. *The Enigma of Capital and the Crises of Capitalism*. Oxford: Oxford University Press.

Hausman, William J., Peeter Hertner, and Mira Wilkins. 2008. *Global Electrification: Multinational Enterprise and International Finance in the History of Light and Power, 1878–2007*. Cambridge: Cambridge University Press.

Hayles, N. Katherine. 2009. "RFID: Human Agency and Meaning in Information-Intensive Environments." *Theory, Culture and Society* 26 (2–3): 47–72.

Healy, Paul M., and Krishna G. Palepu. 2003. "The Fall of Enron." *Journal of Economic Perspectives* 17 (2): 3–26.

Hegel, G. W. F. 1953. *Reason in History: A General Introduction to the Philosophy of History*. Translated by Robert S. Hartman. New York: Bobbs-Merrill.

Hegel, G. W. F. 1969. *The Science of Logic*. Translated by A. V. Miller. New York: Humanities.

Heller, Charles, and Lorenzo Pezzani. 2014. "Liquid Traces: Investigating the Deaths of Migrants at the Maritime Frontier of the EU." In *Forensic: The Architecture of Public Truth*, edited by Forensic Architecture. Berlin: Sternberg.

Helmreich, Stefan. 2011. "From Spaceship Earth to Google Ocean: Planetary Icons, Indexes, and Infrastructures." *Social Research* 78 (4): 1211–42.

Hill, Kashmir. 2013. "Blueprints of NSA's Ridiculously Expensive Data Center in Utah Suggest It Holds Less Info Than Thought." *Forbes*, July 24. http://www.forbes.com/sites/kashmirhill/2013/07/24/blueprints-of-nsa-data-center-in-utah-suggest-its-storage-capacity-is-less-impressive-than-thought/.

Hillier, Jim, ed. 1985. *Cahiers du Cinéma: The 1950s—Neo-realism, Hollywood, New Wave.* Cambridge, MA: Harvard University Press.

Hinkson, John. 2008. "After the Intervention." *Arena Journal* 29/30: 3–9.

Hodson, Hal. 2012. "Power Struggle: How to Keep India's Lights On." *New Scientist,* August 3. http://www.newscientist.com/article/dn22140-power-struggle-how-to-keep-indias-lights-on.html.

Hollender, Rebecca, and Jim Schultz. 2010. *Bolivia and Its Lithium: Can the "Gold of the 21st Century" Help Lift a Nation out of Poverty?* Cochabamba: Democracy Center.

Hölzle, Urs. 2009. "Powering a Google Search." *Googleblog*, January 11. http://googleblog.blogspot.com/2009/01/powering-google-search.html.

Hooper, Malcolm. 1999. *Depleted Uranium Munitions: New Weapons of Indiscriminate and Mutually Assured Destruction.* Lecture presented at United Nations Peace Celebrations, Helsinki, October 23. http://www.kaapeli.fi/~tep/vipu/2000–1/.

Hoornweg, Daniel, and Perinaz Bhada-Tata. 2012. *What a Waste: A Global Review of Solid Waste Management.* Urban Development Series: Knowledge Papers no. 15. Washington, DC: World Bank. http://siteresources.worldbank.org/INTURBANDEVELOPMENT/Resources/336387-1334852610766/What_a_Waste2012_Final.pdf.

Hrudey, Steve, Pierre Gosselin, M. Anne Naeth, André Plourde, René Therrien, Glen Van Der Kraak, and Zhenghe Xu. 2010. *Royal Society of Canada Expert Panel: Environmental and Health Impacts of Canada's Oil Sands Industry.* December. Ottawa: Royal Society of Canada. http://rsc-src.ca/en/expert-panels/rsc-reports/environmental-and-health-impacts-canadas-oil-sands-industry.

Huabo Duan, T. Reed Miller, Jeremy Gregory, Randolph Kirchain. 2013. *Quantitative Characterization of Domestic and Transboundary Flows of Used Electronics: Analysis of Generation, Collection, and Export in the United States.* November. Cambridge MA: MIT/STeP Initiative.

Hubbert, M. King. 1956. *Nuclear Energy and the Fossil Fuels.* Publication 95, June. Houston: Shell Development Company.

Hu-Dehart, Evelyn. 2007. "Surviving Globalization: Immigrant Women Workers in Late Capitalist America." In *Women's Labor in the Global Economy: Speaking in Multiple Voices*, edited by Sharon Harley. New Brunswick, NJ: Rutgers University Press.

Hughes, Thomas P. 1983. *Networks of Power: Electrification in Western Society, 1880–1930.* Baltimore: Johns Hopkins University Press.

Hughes, Thomas P. 1994. "Technological Momentum." In *Does Technology Drive History? The Dilemma of Technological Determinism*, edited by Merritt Roe Smith and Leo Marx, 101–14. Cambridge, MA: MIT Press.

Human Rights Watch. 2012. "Nigeria: Child Lead Poisoning Crisis." Human Rights Watch, February 7. http://www.hrw.org/news/2012/02/07/nigeria-child-lead -poisoning-crisis.

Humphreys, Macartan, Jeffrey D. Sachs, and Joseph E. Stiglitz, eds. 2007. *Escaping the Resource Curse.* New York: Columbia University Press.

Hunt, Lynn. 2008. *Inventing Human Rights: A History.* New York: W. W. Norton.

Husain, Zakir, and Mousoumi Dutta. 2014. *Women in Kolkata's IT Sector: Satisficing between Work and Household.* New Delhi: Springer.

Huxley, Thomas. 1895. "The Abundance of the Seas." *New York Times,* November 17.

IAEA. 1999. *Inventory of Radioactive Waste Disposals at Sea.* Vienna: International Atomic Energy Authority. http://www-pub.iaea.org/MTCD/Publications/PDF/te _1105_prn.pdf.

IBWC. 1994. *Binational Study Regarding the Presence of Toxic Substances in the Rio Grande/Rio Bravo and Its Tributaries along the Boundary between the United States and Mexico.* International Border and Water Commission. EPA-900-R-94–001.

ICC. 2013. "Piracy and Armed Robbery News and Figures." International Chamber of Commerce International Maritime Bureau. London: ICC Commercial Crime Services. http://www.icc-ccs.org/piracy-reporting-centre/piracynewsafigures.

IFC/World Bank. 2007. "Environmental, Health, and Safety Guidelines for Semiconductors and Other Electronics Manufacturing." Washington, DC: International Finance Corporation/World Bank. http://www.ifc.org/wps/wcm/connect /bc321500488558d4817cd36a6515bb18/Final+-+Semiconductors+and+Other +Electronic+Mnfg.pdf?MOD=AJPERES.

IPCC. 2014. "Chapter 4: Sustainable Development and Equity." Working Group III contribution to the *IPCC 5th Assessment Report Climate Change 2014: Mitigation of Climate Change.* IPCC WGIII AR5. Geneva: Intergovernmental Panel on Climate Change.

Ippolita Collective, Geert Lovink, and Ned Rossiter. 2009. "The Digital Given: 10 Web 2.0 Theses." *fibreculture journal* no. 14 (October). http://journal.fibreculture .org/issue14/issue14_ippolita_lovink_rossiter.html.

IRIN. 2006. "Lagos, the Mega-city of Slums." Integrated Regional Information Networks, September 6. http://www.irinnews.org/Report.aspx?ReportId=60811.

ISO. 2010. "Environmental Management: The ISO 14000 Family of International Standards." Geneva: International Organization for Standardization. http://www .iso.org/iso/home/store/publication_item.htm?pid=PUB100238.

ISO/IEC JTC1/SC29/WG11 N13468. 2013. *Context, Objectives, Use Cases and Requirements for Green MPEG.* International Organisation for Standardisation. April.

ITOPF. 2012. "Oil Tanker Spill Statistics 2012." London: International Tanker Owners Pollution Federation. http://www.itopf.co.uk/information-services/data-and -statistics/statistics/.

ITU. 2007. *ITU-T Technology Watch Report #3: ICTs and Climate Change.* Geneva: International Telecommunications Union, December. http://www.itu.int/dms _pub/itu-t/oth/23/01/T23010000030002PDFE.pdf.

Jackson, Sally, and Graham Shirley. 2006. *The Story of the Kelly Gang*. Canberra: National Film and Sound Archive of Australia. http://nfsa.gov.au/collection/film /story-kelly-gang/.

Jakobson, Roman. 1960. "Closing Statements: Linguistics and Poetics." In *Style in Language*, edited by Thomas A. Sebeok, 350–77. Cambridge, MA: MIT Press.

Jameson, Fredric. 2004. "The Politics of Utopia." *New Left Review* 25 (January– February): 35–54.

Jaskula, Brian W. 2009. "Gallium." *2007 Minerals Yearbook*. U.S. Geological Survey. http://minerals.usgs.gov/minerals/pubs/commodity/gallium/myb1–2007-galli .pdf.

Kahn, Douglas. 2013. *Earth Sound Earth Signal: Energies and Earth Magnitude in the Arts*. Berkeley: University of California Press.

Kant, Immanuel. 1952. *The Critique of Judgement*. Translated by James Creed Meredith. Oxford: Oxford University Press.

Kant, Immanuel. 1983. "Idea for a Universal History with a Cosmopolitan Intent." In *Perpetual Peace and Other Essays on Politics, History and Morals*. Translated by Ted Humphrey, 29–40. Indianapolis: Hackett.

Karl, Herman A. 2001. "Search for Containers of Radioactive Waste on the Sea Floor." In *Beyond the Golden Gate: Oceanography, Geology, Biology and Environmental Issues in the Gulf of the Farallones*, edited by Herman A. Karl, John L. Chin, Edward Ueber, Peter H. Stauffer, and James W. Hendley II, 207–17. U.S. Geological Survey Circular 1198. http://pubs.usgs.gov/circ/c1198/.

Katz, Elihu, and Paul Lazarsfeld. 1955. *Personal Influence*. New York: Free Press.

Keefe, Heidi. 1995. "Making the Final Frontier Feasible: A Critical Look at the Current Body of Outer Space Law." *Santa Clara Computer and High Technology Law Journal* 11: 345–71.

Kelly, Andrea. 2012. "Border-Crossing Dust Earns Nogales Air Quality Exemption." Arizona Public Media, September 6. https://www.azpm.org/p/top-news/2012/9/6 /15338-nogales-air-quality-plan-takes-into-account-dust-from-mexico/.

Kember, Sara. 2013. "Ubiquitous Photography." *Philosophy of Photography* 3 (2): 331–48.

Keshavarzi, Ali, and Chris Nicol. 2014. "Perspectives on the Future of the Semiconductor Industry and the Future of Disruptive Innovation." *IEEE Solid-State Circuits Magazine* (spring): 77–81. doi: 0.1109/MSSC.2014.2317431.

Khoo, Su-Ming, and Henrike Rau. 2009. "Movements, Mobilities and the Politics of Hazardous Waste." *Environmental Politics* 18 (6): 960–80.

King, Michael. 2004. *The Penguin History of New Zealand*. Wellington: Penguin.

Kittler, Friedrich A. 1997. "Protected Mode." In *Literature, Media, Information Systems: Essays*, edited and with an introduction by John Johnston, 156–68. Amsterdam: G+B Arts International.

Klessa, A. A., A. F. Bollhofer, I. Marcshamn, and A. R. Milnes. 2007. *Radiation Monitoring and Dose Assessment at Ranger Uranium Mine, Australia, over 25 Years: A Summary of Findings*. International Conference on Environmental Radioactivity: From Measurements and Assessments to Regulation, Paper IAEA-CN-145/049.

Koerner, Brendan I. 2008. "The Saudi Arabia of Lithium." *Forbes*, November 21. http://www.forbes.com/forbes/2008/1124/034.html.

Koomey, Jonathan G. 2007. *Estimating Power Consumption by Servers in the US and the World*. Stanford, CA: Lawrence Berkeley National Laboratory, Stanford University, February. http://enterprise.amd.com/Downloads/svrpwrusecompletefinal.pdf.

KPMG. 2013. *2013 Technology Industry Outlook Survey*. KPMG Technology Innovation Center. https://www.kpmg.com/US/en/IssuesAndInsights/ArticlesPublications/Documents/technology-outlook-survey-2013.pdf.

Krajewski, Markus. 2014. "The Great Lightbulb Conspiracy." *IEEE Spectrum*, September 24. http://spectrum.ieee.org/geek-life/history/the-great-lightbulb-conspiracy.

Kroll, Andy. 2013. "State Dept. Hid Contractor's Ties to Keystone XL Pipeline Company." *Mother Jones*, March 21. http://www.motherjones.com/politics/2013/03/keystone-xl-contractor-ties-transcanada-state-department.

Kurlansky, Mark. 1997. *Cod: A Biography of the Fish That Changed the World*. London: Vintage.

Labban, Mazen. 2013. "Mazen Labban on Timothy Mitchell's 'Carbon Democracy: Political Power in the Age of Oil.'" Antipode Foundation, March 19. http://antipodefoundation.org/2013/03/19/book-review-mazen-labban-on-timothy-mitchells-carbon-democracy/.

Laclau, Ernesto. 2005. *On Populist Reason*. London: Verso.

Lagendijk, Vincent. 2008. *Electrifying Europe: The Power of Europe in the Construction of Electricity Networks*. Amsterdam: Aksant.

Laing, Aislinn. 2012. "Sapphire Discovery in Madagascar Sparks Rush." *Daily Telegraph*, April 24. http://www.telegraph.co.uk/news/worldnews/africaandindianocean/madagascar/9223613/Sapphire-discovery-in-Madagascar-sparks-rush.html.

Latour, Bruno. 2004. *Politics of Nature: How to Bring the Sciences into Democracy*. Translated by Catherine Porter. Cambridge, MA: Harvard University Press.

Latour, Bruno. 2005. *Reassembling the Social: An Introduction to Actor-Network-Theory*. Clarendon Lectures in Management Studies. Oxford: Oxford University Press.

Lazarsfeld, P. F., B. Berelson, and H. Gaudet. 1944. *The People's Choice: How the Voter Makes Up His Mind in a Presidential Campaign*. New York: Columbia University Press.

Lazzarato, Maurizio. 2012. *The Making of the Indebted Man: An Essay on the Neoliberal Condition*. Translated by Joshua David Jordan. New York: Semiotext(e).

Leake, Jonathan, and Richard Woods. 2009. "Revealed: The Environmental Impact of Google Searches." *Sunday Times*, January 11. http://www.enn.com/business/article/39060.

Lear, W. H. 1998. "History of Fisheries in the Northwest Atlantic: The 500-Year Perspective." *Journal of Northwest Atlantic Fishery Science* 23:41–73.

Lee, Mike. 2012. "Fears of Gene Pollution Emerge in TJ River." *San Diego Union-Tribune*, May 6. http://www.utsandiego.com/news/2012/May/06/fears-gene-pollution-grow-tj-river/.

Lefebvre, Martin. 2006. "Between Setting and Landscape in the Cinema." In *Landscape and Film*, edited by Martin Lefebvre, 19–59. New York: American Film Institute/Routledge.

Legal Team for the Ecuadorian Communities. 2014. "Chevron's Mockery of Justice." http://chevrontoxico.com/assets/docs/2014-chevrons-mockery-of-justice.pdf.

Lepawsky, Josh. 2014. "The Changing Geography of Global Trade in Electronic Discards: Time to Rethink the E-waste Problem." *Geographical Journal*, March 5 (first published online). doi: 10.1111/geoj.12077.

Lessig, Lawrence. 2006. *Code v.2: Code and Other Laws of Cyberspace*. New York: Basic Books. http://codev2.cc/.

Levine, Steve. 2010. "The Great Battery Race." *Foreign Policy*, November. http://www.foreignpolicy.com/articles/2010/10/11/the_great_battery_race.

Lin, Jintai, Da Pan, Steven J. Davis, Qiang Zhang, Kebin He, Can Wang, David G. Streets, Donald J. Wuebbles, and Dabo Guan. 2014. "China's International Trade and Air Pollution in the United States." *Proceedings of the National Academy of Sciences of the United States of America* 111 (5): 1736–41. http://www.pnas.org/content/early/2014/01/16/1312860111.

Ludlow, Mark. 2015. "Adani's $16b Carmichael Mine Approval Hit by 'Error.'" *Australian Financial Review*, August 5. http://www.afr.com/news/politics/adanis-16b-carmichael-mine-approval-hit-by-error-20150805-girulp.

Luxemburg, Rosa. [1913] 1951. *The Accumulation of Capital*. Translated by Agnes Schwarzschild. London: Routledge.

Lyman, Edwin. 2011. "Statement of Dr. Edwin Lyman, Senior Scientists, Global Security Program, Union of Concerned Scientists to the Senate Environment Program and Public Works Committee." Union of Concerned Scientists, March 16. http://www.ucsusa.org/assets/documents/nuclear_power/lyman-senate-epw-3-16-11.pdf.

Lyman, Peter, and Hal R. Varian. 2003. *How Much Information?* Berkeley: University of California Press. http://www2.sims.berkeley.edu/research/projects/how-much-info-2003/index.htm.

Lyotard, Jean-François. 1984. *The Postmodern Condition: A Report on Knowledge*. Translated by Geoff Bennington and Brian Massumi. Manchester, UK: Manchester University Press.

Macdonald, Martin. 2007. "Death and the Donkey: Schubert at Random in *Au Hasard, Balthazar*." *Musical Quarterly* 90 (3–4): 446–68.

Macher, Jeffrey T., David C. Mowrey, and Alberto Di Minin. 2007. "The 'Non-Globalization' of Innovation in the Semiconductor Industry." *California Management Review* 50 (1): 217–42.

Mackenzie, Adrian. 2006. *Cutting Code: Software and Sociality*. New York: Peter Lang.

Mandel, Ernest. 1977. *Late Capitalism*. London: Verso.

Mander, Jerry. 1978. *Four Arguments for the Elimination of Television*. New York: Morrow.

Manderson, Desmond. 2008. "Not Yet: Aboriginal People and the Deferral of the Rule of Law." *Arena Journal* 29/30: 219–72.

Mann, Michael. 2012. *The Hockey Stick and the Climate Wars: Dispatches from the Front Lines*. New York: Columbia University Press.

Manzini, Ezio. 2013. "Small, Local, Open and Connected: Resilient Systems and Sustainable Qualities." *Design Observer*. http://designobserver.com/feature/small-local-open-and-connected-resilient-systems-and-sustainable-qualities/37670.

Marazzi, Christian. 2011. *The Violence of Financial Capitalism*. Translated by Kristina Lebedeva and Jason Francis McGimsey. New York: Semiotext(e).

Martí, José. 2002. "The Monetary Conference of the American Republics" (1891). In *Selected Writings*, 304–9. London: Penguin.

Martinez-Allier, Joan. 2002. "The Environmentalism of the Poor." Paper presented at conference, The Political Economy of Sustainable Development: Environmental Conflict, Participation and Movements, University of Witwatersrand, Johannesburg, August 30. http://www.unrisd.org/unrisd/website/document.nsf/8b18431d756b708580256b6400399775/5eb03ffbdd19ea90c1257664004831bd/$FILE/MartinezAlier.pdf.

Marx, Karl. 1968. *The German Ideology: Critique of Modern German Philosophy According to Its Representatives Feuerbach, B. Bauer and Stirner, and of German Socialism According to Its Various Prophets*. Moscow: Progress Publishers. https://www.marxists.org/archive/marx/works/1845/german-ideology/index.htm.

Marx, Karl. 1973. *Grundrisse*. Translated by Martin Nicolaus. London: Penguin/New Left.

Marx, Karl. 1974. *Capital: A Critique of Political Economy*, vol. 3. Translated by Rodney Livingstone. London: NLB/Penguin.

Marx, Karl. 1976. *Capital: A Critique of Political Economy*, vol. 1. Translated by Rodney Livingstone. London: NLB/Penguin.

Marx, Karl, and Friedrich Engels. 1969. *Manifesto of the Communist Party*. Translated by Samuel Moore. In *Marx/Engels Selected Works*, vol. 1, 98–137. Moscow: Progress Publishers. http://www.marxists.org/archive/marx/works/1848/communist-manifesto/.

Masanet, Eric, Arman Shehabi, and Jonathan Koomey. 2013. "Characteristics of Low-Carbon Data Centers." *Nature Climate Change* 3 (7): 627–30.

Mason, Paul. 2015. *PostCapitalism: A Guide to Our Future*. London: Penguin.

Maxwell, Richard, and Toby Miller. 2012. *Greening the Media*. Oxford: Oxford University Press.

Mayah, Emmanuel. 2012. "Climate Change Fuels Nigeria Terrorism." *Africa Review*, February 24. http://www.africareview.com/News/Climate-change-fuels-Nigeria-terrorism/-/979180/1334472/-/view/printVersion/-/1hug7s/-/index.html.

Mazlish, Bruce. 1993. *The Fourth Discontinuity: The Co-evolution of Humans and Machines*. New Haven, CT: Yale University Press.

Mazurek, Janice. 1998. *Making Microchips: Policy, Globalization, and Economic Restructuring in the Semiconductor Industry*. Cambridge, MA: MIT Press.

Mbembe, Achille. 2001. *On the Postcolony*. Berkeley: University of California Press.

McDougall, Dan. 2009. "In Search of Lithium: The Battle for the 3rd Element." *Daily Mail*, April 5. http://www.dailymail.co.uk/home/moslive/article-1166387/In-search-Lithium-The-battle-3rd-element.html.

McGrath, Chris. 2015. "Carmichael Coal Mine Case in the Land Court of Queensland." St. Lucia: Environmental Law Australia. http://envlaw.com.au/carmichael-coal-mine-case/.

McLean, Don. 2003. "The Quest for Inclusive Governance of Global ICTs: Lessons from the ITU in the Limits of National Sovereignty." *Information Technologies and International Development* 1 (1): 1–18.

McLuhan, Marshall. 1964. *Understanding Media: The Extensions of Man*. London: Sphere.

McMillan, Robert. 2013. "Google Cranks Green Dial in Building Endless Server Farm." *Wired*, July 6. http://www.wired.com/wiredenterprise/2013/06/google_green/.

Meadows, Donella H., Dennis L. Meadows, Jørgen Randers, and William H. Behrens III. 1972. *The Limits to Growth: A Report for the Club of Rome's Project on the Predicament of Mankind*. New York: Universe.

Médecins sans Frontières. 2012. *Médecins sans Frontières US Annual Report 2012*. http://cdn.doctorswithoutborders.org/sites/usa/files/attachments/msf_usa_annual_report_2012.pdf.

Mehta, Suketu. 2004. *Maximum City: Bombay Lost and Found*. New York: Knopf.

Meiksins Wood, Ellen. 1981. "The Separation of the Economic and the Political in Capital." *New Left Review* 127 (May–June): 66–95.

Meillassoux, Quentin. 2008. *After Finitude: An Essay on the Necessity of Contingency*. Translated by Ray Brassier. London: Continuum.

Mengchang He, Xiangqin Wang, Fengchang Wu, and Zhiyou Fu. 2012. "Antimony Pollution in China." *Science of the Total Environment* nos. 421–22 (April): 41–50.

Merck, Thomas. 2009. *Assessment of the Environmental Impacts of Cables*. London: OSPAR Commission/Convention for the Protection of the Marine Environment of the North-East Atlantic.

Midnight Notes. 2009. *Promissory Notes: From Crisis to Commons*. Jamaica Plain, MA: Midnight Notes Collective.

Mignolo, Walter D. 2011. *The Darker Side of Modernity: Global Futures, Decolonial Options*. Durham, NC: Duke University Press.

Miller, Rich. 2007. "Google Patents Portable Data Centers." *Data Center Knowledge*, October 9. http://www.datacenterknowledge.com/archives/2007/10/09/google-patents-portable-data-centers/.

Miller, Rich. 2008. "Google Planning Offshore Data Barges." *Data Center Knowledge*, September 8. http://www.datacenterknowledge.com/archives/2008/09/06/google-planning-offshore-data-barges/.

Milman, Oliver. 2014. "US Banks Vow Not to Fund Great Barrier Reef Coal Port, Say Activists." *The Guardian*, October 28. http://www.theguardian.com /environment/2014/oct/28/us-banks-vow-not-to-fund-great-barrier-reef-coal -port-say-activists.

Milman, Oliver. 2015. "Aboriginal Group Fights to Stop $16bn Carmichael Coalmine, Australia's Largest." *The Guardian*, March 25. http://www.theguardian.com /australia-news/2015/mar/26/aboriginal-group-fights-to-stop-16bn-carmichael -coalmine.

Milonakis, Dimitris, and Ben Fine. 2009. *From Political Economy to Economics: Method, the Social and the Historical in the Evolution of Economic Theory*. London: Routledge.

Milun, Kathryn. 2011. *The Political Uncommons: The Cross-Cultural Logic of the Global Commons*. Burlington, VT: Ashgate.

MIR. 2008. *The Trouble with Lithium 2: Under the Microscope*. Marseilles: Meridian International Research.

Mirzoeff, Nicholas. 2009. "The Sea and the Land: Biopower and Visuality from Slavery to Katrina." *Culture, Theory and Critique* 50 (2–3): 289–305.

Mirzoeff, Nicholas. 2014. "Visualizing the Anthropocene." *Public Culture* 26 (2): 213–22.

Mitchell, Donald. 2008. *A Note on Rising Food Prices*. Washington, DC: World Bank. https://openknowledge.worldbank.org/handle/10986/6820.

Mitchell, Timothy. 2011. *Carbon Democracy: Political Power in the Age of Oil*. New York: Verso.

Mladek, Klaus, and George Edmondson. 2009. "A Politics of Melancholia." In *A Leftist Ontology: Beyond Relativism and Identity Politics*, edited by Clausten Strathausen, 208–34. Minneapolis: University of Minnesota Press.

Moore, Charles J., and Cassandra Phillips. 2011. *Plastic Ocean*. London: Penguin.

Morgan, Erinn. 2015. "Durango Copes with 'Orange Nastiness' of Toxic Sludge River Pollution." *The Guardian*, August 10. http://www.theguardian.com/us-news /2015/aug/10/colorado-spill-animas-river-durango-toxic-orange.

Moscaritolo, Angela. 2013. "3 More Foxconn Employees Commit Suicide." PC *News*, May 20. http://uk.pcmag.com/news/15360/reports-3-more-foxconn-employees -commit-suicide.

Mosco, Vincent. 2015. *To the Cloud: Big Data in a Turbulent World*. New York: Routledge.

Mouffe, Chantal. 2005. *On the Political*. London: Routledge.

Mueller, Milton L. 2004. *Ruling the Root: Internet Governance and the Taming of Cyberspace*. Cambridge, MA: MIT Press.

Mueller, Milton L. 2010. *Networks and States: The Global Politics of Internet Governance*. Cambridge, MA: MIT Press.

Murdoch, Lindsay. 2011. "Forget the Billions, Return Jabiluka Site to Kakadu, Say Traditional Owners." *Sydney Morning Herald*, April 7. http://www.smh.com.au /national/forget-the-billions-return-jabiluka-site-to-kakadu-say-traditional -owners-20110406–1d4kv.html.

Naess, Arne. 1989. *Ecology, Community and Lifestyle: Outline of an Ecosophy.* Translated and revised by David Rothenberg. Cambridge: Cambridge University Press.

NASA. 1995. *Final Environmental Impact Statement for the Cassini Mission.* Washington, DC: National Aeronautics and Space Administration. http://saturn.jpl .nasa.gov/spacecraft/safety/safetyeis/.

NASA. 2011. "Catching Its Tail." National Aeronautics and Space Administration. https://www.nasa.gov/mission_pages/cassini/multimedia/pia12826.html.

Neeson, J. M. 1993. *Commoners: Common Right, Enclosure and Social Change in England, 1700–1820.* Cambridge: Cambridge University Press.

Negi, Nalin Singh, and Sujata Ganguly. 2011. *Development Projects vs. Internally Displaced Populations in India: A Literature Based Appraisal.* Paper presented at the ESF-UniBi-ZiF research conference, Environmental Change and Migration: From Vulnerabilities to Capabilities, Bad Salzuflen, Germany, December 5–9, 2010; COMCAD Arbeitspapiere—Working Papers No. 103, 2011.

Negri, Antonio. 1996. "Twenty Theses on Marx: Interpretations of the Class Struggle Today." Translated by Michael Hardt. In *Marxism beyond Marxism*, edited by Saree Makdisi, Cesare Casarino, and Rebecca E. Karl, 149–80. New York: Routledge.

Negri, Antonio. 2008. *Reflections on Empire.* With contributions from Michael Hardt and Danilo Zolo. Translated by Ed Emery. Cambridge: Polity.

Neilson, Brett, and Ned Rossiter. 2010. "Still Waiting, Still Moving: On Labour, Logistics and Maritime Industries." In *Stillness in a Mobile World*, edited by David Bissell and Gillian Fuller, 51–68. New York: Routledge.

Nelson, Theodore H. 1974. *Computer Lib/Dream Machines.* n.p.: Author.

Newton, Isaac. 1952. *Opticks, or A Treatise of the Reflections, Refractions, Inflections and Colours of Light Based on the Fourth Edition London, 1730.* New York: Dover.

NFSA. 2016. *The Story of the Kelly Gang* (1906). National Film and Sound Archive. http://aso.gov.au/titles/features/story-kelly-gang/.

Ngai, Pun. 2005. *Made in China: Women Factory Workers in a Global Workplace.* Durham, NC: Duke University Press.

Nixon, Rob. 2011. *Slow Violence and the Environmentalism of the Poor.* Cambridge, MA: Harvard University Press.

Nye, David E. 1990. *Electrifying America: Social Meanings of a New Technology.* Cambridge, MA: MIT Press.

Nye, David E. 2010. *When the Lights Went Out: A History of Blackouts in America.* Cambridge, MA: MIT Press.

Oakford, Samuel. 2014. "United States: An Environment-Wrecking Pipeline Hangs in Limbo." *Indigenous Peoples Issues and Resources*, March 10. http://www.ipsnews .net/2014/02/environment-wrecking-pipeline-hangs-limbo/.

O'Brien, Dave. 2010. *Measuring the Value of Culture: A Report to the Department for Culture Media and Sport.* London: Department of Culture, Media and Sport.

Oceana. 2010. *Shipping Solutions: Technological and Operational Methods Available to Reduce CO_2.* Washington, DC: Oceana.

O'Donnell, John. 2014. "European Union Moves to End Smartphone Patent Wars." Reuters, April 29. http://www.reuters.com/article/2014/04/29/us-eu-competition-motorola-idUSBREA3S09220140429.

OHCR. 2009. *Concluding Observations of the Human Rights Committee: Australia.* Geneva: Office of the High Commissioner for Human Rights, Human Rights Committee. UN Doc CCPR/C/AUS/CO/5.

OTA. 1988. *Copper: Technology and Competitiveness* (OTA-E-367). Washington, DC: U.S. Congress, Office of Technology Assessment.

Packer, George. 2006. "The Megacity: Decoding the Chaos of Lagos." *New Yorker,* November 13. http://www.newyorker.com/archive/2006/11/13/061113fa_fact_packer.

Palmer, Paul. 2005. *Getting to Zero Waste.* Sebastopol, CA: Purple Sky.

Panimbang, Fahmi. 2011. "Global Supply Chains and Their Impact on the Labour Movement in Asia." *Asian Labour Update* 44 (Global Supply Chains, January–March). Hong Kong: Asia Monitor Resource Centre. http://www.amrc.org.hk/taxonomy/term/list/259.

Parikka, Jussi. 2007. *Digital Contagions: A Media Archaeology of Computer Viruses.* New York: Peter Lang.

Parikka, Jussi, ed. 2011. *Medianatures: The Materiality of Information Technology and Electronic Waste.* London: Open Humanities Press. http://www.livingbooksaboutlife.org/books/Medianatures.

Parikka, Jussi. 2015. *A Geology of Media.* Minneapolis: University of Minnesota Press.

Pearce, Fred, Sara Reardon, and Catherine Brahic. 2012. "Industries Make a Dash for the Arctic." *New Scientist,* October 12.

PEER. 2013. "White House Approves Radical Radiation Cleanup Rollback." Washington, DC: Public Employees for Environmental Responsibility. http://www.peer.org/news/news-releases/2013/04/08/white-house-approves-radical-radiation-cleanup-rollback/.

Peryman, Lisa. 2013. "Has the Three Gorges Dam Increased Shanghai's Flood Risk Potential?" *Probe International,* August 9. http://journal.probeinternational.org/2013/08/09/has-the-three-gorges-dam-increased-shanghais-flood-risk-potential/.

Peters, John Durham. 2016. *The Marvelous Clouds: Toward a Philosophy of Elemental Media.* Chicago: University of Chicago Press.

Pickren, Graham. 2014. "Political Ecologies of Electronic Waste: Uncertainty and Legitimacy in the Governance of E-waste Geographies." *Environment and Planning A* 46 (1): 26–45.

Pieterse, Jan Nederveen. 2001. *Development Theory: Deconstructions/Reconstructions.* London: Sage.

Piketty, Thomas. 2014. *Capital in the Twenty-First Century.* Translated by Arthur Goldhammer. Cambridge, MA: Belknap.

Polimeni, John M., Mayumi Kozo, Giampietro Mario, and Alcott Blake. 2008. *The Jevons Paradox and the Myth of Resource Efficiency Improvements.* Sterling, VA: Earthscan.

Pope Francis. 2015. *Encyclical on Capitalism and Inequality: On Care for Our Common Home*. Edited by Sam Levigne. London: Verso.

Porco, Carolyn C., Robert A. West, Steven Squyres, Alfred McEwen, Peter Thomas, Carl D. Murray, Anthony Delgenio, Andrew P. Ingersoll, Torrence V. Johnson, Gerhard Neukum, Joseph Veverka, Luke Dones, Andre Brahic, Joseph A. Burns, Vance Haemmerle, Benjamin Knowles, Douglas Dawson, Thomas Roatsch, Kevin Beurle, and William Owen. 2004. "Cassini Imaging Science: Instrument Characteristics and Anticipated Scientific Investigations at Saturn." *Space Science Reviews* 115 (1–4): 363–497.

Porter, Theodore M. 1996. *Trust in Numbers: The Pursuit of Objectivity in Science and Public Life*. Princeton, NJ: Princeton University Press.

Proactive Investors. 2013. "Arafura Resources Teams with China's Shenghe Resources to Develop NT Rare Earths Project." *Proactive Investors Australia*, September 10. http://www.proactiveinvestors.com.au/companies/news/47779/arafura-resources-teams-with-chinas-shenghe-resources-to-develop-nt-rare-earths-project-47779.html.

Pruzan-Jorgensen, Peder Michael, and Angie Farrag. 2010. *Sustainability Trends in the Container Shipping Industry: A Future Trends Research Summary*. September. New York: Business for Social Responsibility.

Public Citizen. 2001. "Blind Faith: How Deregulation and Enron's Influence over Government Looted Billions from Americans: Sen. Gramm, White House Must Be Investigated for Role in Enron's Fraud of Consumers and Shareholders." December. Washington, DC: Public Citizen's Critical Mass Energy and Environment Program.

Quijano, Aníbal. 2007. "Coloniality and Modernity/Rationality." *Cultural Studies* 21 (2–3): 168–78.

Rabasa, José. 1993. *Inventing America: Spanish Historiography and the Formation of Eurocentrism*. Norman: University of Oklahoma Press.

Rabinbach, Anson. 1990. *The Human Motor: Energy, Fatigue and the Origins of Modernity*. New York: Basic Books.

Rancière, Jacques. 1999. *Disagreement: Politics and Philosophy*. Translated by Julie Rose. Minneapolis: University of Minnesota Press.

Rancière, Jacques. 2006. *Hatred of Democracy*. Translated by Steve Corcoran. London: Verso.

Rao, Srinivasa, and John Lourdusamy. 2010. "Colonialism and the Development of Electricity: The Case of Madras Presidency 1900–47." *Science Technology Society* 15 (1): 27–54.

Raqs Media Collective and Geert Lovink, eds. 2001. *Sarai Reader 2001: The Public Domain*. Delhi: Sarai.

"Rare-Earth Mining in China Comes at a Heavy Cost for Local Villages." 2012. *The Guardian*, August 7. http://www.theguardian.com/environment/2012/aug/07/china-rare-earth-village-pollution.

Raunig, Gerald. 2013. *Factories of Knowledge: Industries of Creativity*. Translated by Aileen Derieg. New York: Semiotext(e).

Rawls, John. 1971. *A Theory of Justice*. Cambridge, MA: Belknap.

Rebello, Joe. 2010. "Tata Hardens Stance as Mumbai Power Battle Reaches Climax." April 9. http://www.livemint.com/Companies/FtkTn89Kv3amrtUGwMrGAK /Tata-hardens-stance-as-mumbai-power-battle-reaches-climax.html.

Ribera, Marco Octavio, with Cecilia Requena. 2011. "Bolivia's Lithium: Opportunities and Challenges." *Global Corruption Report: Climate Change*, edited by Transparency International, 207–10. London: Earthscan.

Ringius, Lasse. 1997. "Environmental NGOs and Regime Change: The Case of Ocean Dumping of Radioactive Waste." *European Journal of International Relations* 3 (1): 61–104.

Riseborough, Jesse. 2012. "iPad Boom Strains Lithium Supplies after Prices Triple." *Businessweek*, June 19. http://www.bloomberg.com/news/articles/2012–06–19/ ipad-boom-strains-lithium-supplies-after-prices-triple.

Robins, Nicholas A. 2011. *Mercury, Mining, and Empire: The Human and Ecological Cost of Colonial Silver Mining in the Andes*. Bloomington: Indiana University Press.

Rooney, Paula. 2008. "Ubuntu's Shuttleworth Blames ISO for OOXML's Win." *ZDNet* (UK), April 1. http://www.zdnet.com/blog/open-source/ubuntus-shuttleworth -blames-iso-for-ooxmls-win/2222.

Ross, Martin, Darin Toohey, Manfred Peinemann, and Patrick Ross. 2009. "Limits on the Space Launch Market Related to Stratospheric Ozone Depletion." *Astropolitics* 7 (1): 50.

Rosso, Dan. 2014. "Semiconductor Industry Posts Record Sales in 2013." Semiconductor Industry Association, February 3. http://www.semiconductors.org/news /2014/02/03/global_sales_report_2013/semiconductor_industry_posts_record _sales_in_2013/.

Rostow, W. W. 1960. *The Stages of Economic Growth: A Non-Communist Manifesto*. Cambridge: Cambridge University Press.

Roy, Arundhati. 1999. "The Greater Common Good." Friends of River Narmada, April. http://www.narmada.org/gcg/gcg.html.

Rust, Susanne, and Matt Drange. 2014. "Cleanup of Silicon Valley Superfund Site Takes Environmental Toll." Center for Investigative Reporting, March 17. https:// www.revealnews.org/article/cleanup-of-silicon-valley-superfund-site-takes -environmental-toll-2/.

Saro-Wiwa, Ken. 2005. *A Month and a Day and Letters*. Banbury, UK: Ayebia Clarke.

Sassen, Saskia. 2006. *Territory, Authority, Rights: From Medieval to Global Assemblages*. Princeton, NJ: Princeton University Press.

Sassen, Saskia. 2014. *Expulsions: Brutality and Complexity in the Global Economy*. Cambridge, MA: Belknap.

Sayne, Aaron. 2011. *Climate Change Adaptation and Conflict in Nigeria*. Washington, DC: United States Institute of Peace.

Scalet, Bianca Maria, Marcos Garcia Muñoz, Aivi Querol Sissa, Serge Roudier, and Luis Delgado Sancho. 2013. *Best Available Techniques (BAT) Reference Document for the Manufacture of Glass*. Industrial Emissions Directive 2010/75/EU. European Commission Joint Research Centre, Institute for Prospective Technological Studies. Luxembourg: Publications Office of the European Union.

Scambary, Ben. 2013. "Mining Company Convicted and Fined for Desecration" [letter to the editor]. *Alice Springs News*, August 2. http://www.alicespringsnews.com .au/2013/08/02/mining-company-convicted-and-fined-for-desecration/.

Schatan, Claudia, and Liliana Castilleja. 2005. *The Maquiladora Electronics Industry and the Environment along Mexico's Northern Border*. Montreal: Commission for Environmental Cooperation.

Schivelbusch, Wolfgang. [1988] 1995. *Disenchanted Night: The Industrialization of Light in the Nineteenth Century*. Translated by Angela Davies. Berkeley: University of California Press.

Schmidt, Alfred. 1971. *The Concept of Nature in Marx*. Translated by Ben Fowkes. London: NLB.

Schmitt, Carl. 2004. *Political Theology: Four Chapters on the Concept of Sovereignty*. Translated by George D. Schwab. Introduction by Tracy B. Strong. Chicago: University of Chicago Press.

Scholz, Trebor. 2008. *Digital Media and Democracy: Tactics in Hard Times*. Cambridge, MA: MIT Press.

Schumpeter, Joseph A. 2010. *Capitalism, Socialism and Democracy*, with a new introduction by Joseph Stieglitz. New York: Routledge.

Schuurman, Nadine. 2000. "Trouble in the Heartland: GIS and Its Critics in the 1990s." *Progress in Human Geography* 24 (4): 569–90.

Scudder, Thayer. 2005. *The Future of Large Dams: Dealing with Social, Environmental, Institutional and Political Costs*. London: Earthscan.

Sen, Amartya. 2009. *The Idea of Justice*. London: Allen Lane.

Senate Environment, Communications, Information Technology and the Arts References Committee. 1999. *Jabiluka: The Undermining of Process—Inquiry into the Jabiluka Uranium Mine Project*. Wilderness Society, June. https://www.wilderness .org.au/articles/jabiluka-undermining-process-inquiry-jabiluka-uranium-mine -project.

Senate Environment, Communications, Information Technology and the Arts References Committee. 2002. *Regulating the Ranger, Jabiluka, Beverley and Honeymoon Uranium Mines*. Canberra: Commonwealth of Australia.

Shankland, Stephen. 2008. "Google-Backed Project Aims to Give 3 Billion More People Net Access." *CNET News*, September 9. http://news.cnet.com /8301–1035_3–10037036-94.html.

Shankland, Stephen. 2009. "Google Uncloaks Once-Secret Server." *CNET News*, April 1. http://news.cnet.com/8301–1001_3–10209580-92.html.

Shannon, Claude E., and Warren Weaver. 1949. *The Mathematical Theory of Communication*. Urbana: University of Illinois Press.

Shiva, Vandana. 1997. "The Turmeric Patent Is Just the First Step in Stopping Biopiracy." *Third World Network*, no. 86 (October). http://www.twn.my/title/tur-cn .htm.

Siegal, Shefa. 2011. "Threat of Mercury Poisoning Rises with Gold Mining Boom." *Yale Environment 360*, January 3. http://e360.yale.edu/feature/threat_of_mercury_poisoning_rises_with_gold_mining_boom/2354/.

Siegert, Bernard. 1999. *Relays: Literature as an Epoch of the Postal System.* Stanford, CA: Stanford University Press.

Smith, Linda Tuhiwai. 2012. *Decolonizing Methodologies: Research and Indigenous Peoples*, 2nd ed. London: Zed.

Smith, Noel Lyn. 2015. "Navajo Nation Northern Agency Chapters Issue Emergency Declarations." *Daily Times* (Farmington), August 10. http://www.daily-times.com/story/news/local/navajo/2015/08/10/navajo-nation-chapters-issue-emergency-declaration/32024265/.

Smith, Terry. 1993. *Making the Modern: Industry, Art and Design in America.* Chicago: University of Chicago Press.

Smythe, Dallas. 1957. *The Structure and Policy of Electronic Communications.* Urbana: University of Illinois Press.

Smythe, Dallas. 1994. "Communications: Blindspot of Western Marxism." In *Counterclockwise: Perspectives on Communication*, edited by Thomas Guback, 266–91. Boulder, CO: Westview. First published 1977, *Canadian Journal of Political and Social Theory* 1 (3): 1–27.

Snyder, John P. 1993. *Flattening the Earth: Two Thousand Years of Map Projections.* Chicago: University of Chicago Press.

Söderberg, Johan. 2008. *Hacking Capitalism: The Free and Open Source Software (FOSS) Movement.* London: Routledge.

Solnit, Rebecca. 2000. *Savage Dreams: A Journey into the Landscape Wars of the American West.* Berkeley: University of California Press.

Solnit, Rebecca. 2007. *Storming the Gates of Paradise: Landscapes for Politics.* Berkeley: University of California Press.

SourceWatch. 2015. *Environmental Impacts of Coal.* Madison, WI: Center for Media and Democracy. http://www.sourcewatch.org/index.php/Environmental_impacts_of_coal.

Sproull, Lee, and Sara Kiesler. 1991. *Connections: New Ways of Working in the Networked Organisation.* Cambridge, MA: MIT Press.

Stafford, Barbara. 1996. *Good Looking: Essays on the Virtue of Images.* Cambridge, MA: MIT Press.

Starosielski, Nicole. 2011. "Underwater Flow." *Flow* 15 (1).

Starosielski, Nicole. 2012. "'Warning: Do Not Dig': Negotiating the Visibility of Critical Infrastructures." *Journal of Visual Culture* 11 (1): 38–57.

Stewart, Emma, and John Kennedy. 2009. "The Sustainability Potential of Cloud Computing: Smarter Design." *Environmental Leader*, July 20. http://www.environmentalleader.com/2009/07/20/the-sustainability-potential-of-cloud-computing-smarter-design/.

Stiegler, Bernard. 1998. *Technics and Time 1: The Fault of Epimetheus.* Translated by Richard Beardsworth and George Collins. Stanford, CA: Stanford University Press.

Strand, Ginger. 2008. "Keyword: Evil: Google's Addiction to Cheap Electricity." *Harper's*, March, 64–65.

Sunstein, Cass. 2007. *Republic.com 2.0*. Princeton, NJ: Princeton University Press.

Sussman, Henry. 2012. *Impasses of the Post-Global: Theory in the Era of Climate Change*, vol. 2. Ann Arbor, MI: Open Humanities Press.

Swanson, Brett. 2013. "MPEG-LA Shows Need to Rebuild IP Foundations." *Forbes*, April 30. http://www.forbes.com/sites/bretswanson/2013/04/30/mpeg-la-shows -need-to-rebuild-ip-foundations/.

Tabone, Michaelangelo D., James J. Cregg, Eric J. Beckman, and Amy E. Landis. 2010. "Sustainability Metrics: Life Cycle Assessment and Green Design in Polymers." *Environmental Science and Technology* 44 (21): 8264–69.

Taffel, Sy. 2012. "Escaping Attention: Digital Media, Hardware, Materiality and Ecological Cost." *Culture Machine* 13:1–28.

Tahill, William. 2007. *The Trouble with Lithium: Implications of Future PHEV Production for Lithium Demand*. Martainville, France: Meridian International Research. www.evworld.com/library/lithium_shortage.pdf.

Tang, Wan-yee, Linda Levin, Glenn Talaska, Yuk Yin Cheung, Julie Herbstman, Deliang Tang, Rachel L. Miller, Frederica Perera, and Shuk-Mei Ho. 2012. "Maternal Exposure to Polycyclic Aromatic Hydrocarbons and 5′-CpG Methylation of Interferon-gamma in Cord White Blood Cells." *Environmental Health Perspectives*, May 4. http://ccceh.org/scientific-papers/maternal-exposure-to-polycyclic -aromatic-hydrocarbons-and-5-cpg-methylation-of-interferon-gamma-in-cord -white-blood-cells.

Tanquintic-Misa, Esther. 2012. "After Lifting Ban, Queensland Debates How to Transport Uranium without Hurting Great Barrier Reef." *International Business Times*, November 1. http://www.ibtimes.com.au/after-lifting-ban-queensland -debates-how-transport-uranium-without-hurting-great-barrier-reef.

Tapscott, Mark. 2014. "Vladimir Putin's Crimean Adventures Could Hasten Eastern European Energy Independence." *Washington Examiner*, March 14. http:// washingtonexaminer.com/vladimir-putins-crimean-adventures-could-hasten -eastern-european-energy-independence/article/2545674.

Terranova, Tiziana. 2004. *Network Culture: Politics for the Information Age*. London: Pluto.

Texas Commission on Environmental Quality. 2013. *Rio Grande Toxic Substances Study Summary*. http://www.tceq.texas.gov/waterquality/monitoring/riosum .html.

Théorie Communiste. 2011. "Communization in the Present Tense." In *Communization and Its Discontents: Contestation, Critique, and Contemporary Struggles*, edited by Benjamin Noys, 41–58. New York: Minor Compositions/Autonomedia.

Thirsk, Joan. 1958. *Tudor Enclosures*. London: Historical Association.

Thomas, Keith. 1983. *Changing Attitudes to Nature: Man and the Natural World in England, 1500–1800*. London: Penguin.

Thompson, E. P. 1963. *The Making of the English Working Class*. Harmondsworth, UK: Pelican.

Thrower, Norman J. W. 1996. *Maps and Civilization: Cartography in Culture and Society*. Chicago: University of Chicago Press.

Tolcin, Amy C. 2011. "Indium." *Mineral Commodity Summaries*. Washington, DC: U.S. Geological Survey.

Tollefson, Jeff. 2011. "Low-Cost Carbon-Capture Project Sparks Interest." *Nature*, January 18.

Transcanada. 2014. "Community, Aboriginal and Native American Relations." http://www.transcanada.com/662.html.

Tri-Mer. 2014. *Cloud Chamber Scrubber Case Study #3: Fiber Optics Manufacturing*. http://www.tri-mer.com/ccs_case_study_glass_3.html.

Tufte, Edward R. 2006. *The Cognitive Style of PowerPoint*, 2nd ed. Cheshire, CT: Graphics.

Turley, Jim. 2002. *The Essential Guide to Semiconductors*. New York: Prentice Hall.

Tyfield, David. 2014. "'King Coal Is Dead! Long Live the King!': The Paradoxes of Coal's Resurgence in the Emergence of Global Low-Carbon Societies." *Theory, Culture and Society* 31 (5): 59–81.

UNDP. 2006. *Human Development Report 2006: Beyond Scarcity: Power, Poverty and the Global Water Crisis*. New York: United Nations Development Program.

UNDP. 2010. *Human Development Report 2010: The Real Wealth of Nations: Pathways to Human Development*. New York: United Nations Development Program.

UNDP. 2011. *Human Development Report 2011: Sustainability and Equity: A Better Future for All*. New York: United Nations Development Program.

UNEP. 2011. *Environmental Assessment of Ogoniland*. Nairobi: United Nations Environment Programme.

UNESCAP. 2012. *Green Growth, Resources and Resilience: Environmental Sustainability in Asia and the Pacific*. ST/ESCAP/2600, RPT124260. Bangkok: United Nations Economic and Social Commission for Asia and the Pacific/United Nations and Asian Development Bank.

UNESCO. 1980. *Many Voices: One World (The MacBride Report)*, abridged ed. London: UNESCO/Kogan Page.

UNESCO. 2009. *Investing in Cultural Diversity and Intercultural Dialogue*. UNESCO World Report. Paris: UNESCO.

United Nations. 2002. *Final Report of the Panel of Experts on the Illegal Exploitation of Natural Resources and Other Forms of Wealth of the Democratic Republic of the Congo*. S/2002/1146, October 16. New York: United Nations Security Council.

United Nations. 2008. *United Nations Declaration on the Rights of Indigenous Peoples*. 07–58681, March. New York: United Nations General Assembly.

Urry, John. 2014. *Offshoring*. Cambridge: Polity.

"USA: German Shipping Companies Fined for Illegal Dumping of Oil at Sea." 2012. *World Maritime News*, November 5. http://worldmaritimenews.com/archives/68473/usa-german-shipping-companies-plead-guilty-to-illegal-dumping-of-oil-at-sea/.

USAID Asia. 2008. *Quality Control and Market Supervision of Compact Fluorescent Lamps in China*. Bangkok: United States Agency for International Development.

U.S.-Canada Power System Outage TaskForce. 2004. *Final Report on the August 14, 2003 Blackout in the United States and Canada: Causes and Recommendations.* April. U.S. Department of Energy. http://energy.gov/oe/downloads/blackout -2003-final-report-august-14–2003-blackout-united-states-and-canada-causes -and.

U.S. Department of Energy. 2011. "Information and Telecommunication Technology Portfolio: Improving Energy Efficiency and Productivity in America's Telecommunication Systems and Data Centers." Industrial Technologies Program, DOE/EE-0390, March. http://www1.eere.energy.gov/manufacturing/pdfs /ict_brochure.pdf.

U.S. Department of Energy and U.S. Environmental Protection Agency. 2008. "Fact Sheet on National Data Center Energy Efficiency Information Program." March 19. http://www1.eere.energy.gov/industry/saveenergynow/pdfs/national_data _center_fact_sheet.pdf.

Van Gelder, Sarah, and the Staff of YES! Magazine. 2012. *This Changes Everything: Occupy Wall Street and the 99% Movement.* San Francisco: Berrett-Koehler.

Vercellone, Carlo. 2008. "Wages Rent and Profit: The New Articulation of Wages, Rent and Profit in Cognitive Capitalism." Translated by Arianna Bove. Generation Online. http://www.generation-online.org/c/fc_rent2.htm.

Verzola, Roberto. 2010. "Abundance and the Generative Logic of the Commons." Keynote speech, Stream III: The Generative Logic of the Commons, International Conference on the Commons, Berlin, October 31–November 2. P2P Foundation. http://p2pfoundation.net/Abundance_and_the_Generative_Logic_of_the _Commons.

Vidal, John. 2013. "Toxic 'E-waste' Dumped in Poor Nations, Says United Nations." *The Guardian*, December 14. http://www.theguardian.com/global-development /2013/dec/14/toxic-ewaste-illegal-dumping-developing-countries.

Vidal, John. 2015. "Nigerian Government Finally Sets Up Fund to Clean Up Ogoniland Oil Spills." *The Guardian*, August 7. http://www.theguardian.com /environment/2015/aug/07/nigerian-government-finally-sets-up-fund-to-clean -up-ogoniland-oil-spills.

Vieira, Mónica Brito. 2003. "*Mare Liberum* vs. *Mare Clausum*: Grotius, Freitas, and Selden's Debate on Dominion over the Seas." *Journal of the History of Ideas* 64 (3): 361–77.

Virilio, Paul. 2007. *The Original Accident.* Translated by Julie Rose. Cambridge: Polity.

Virno, Paolo. 1996. "Notes on the 'General Intellect.'" Translated by Cesare Casarino. In *Marxism beyond Marxism*, edited by Saree Makdisi, Cesare Casarino, and Rebecca E. Karl, 265–72. New York: Routledge.

Virno, Paolo. 2004. *A Grammar of the Multitude: For an Analysis of Contemporary Forms of Life.* Translated by Isabella Bertoletti, James Cascaito, and Andrea Casson. Los Angeles: Semiotext(e).

Vitalis, Robert. 2006. *America's Kingdom: Mythmaking on the Saudi Oil Frontier.* Stanford, CA: Stanford University Press.

Waitangi Tribunal. 1999. *The Radio Spectrum Management and Development Final Report.* Wellington, NZ: Waitangi Tribunal.

Waldrop, M. Mitchell. 2016. "The Chips are Down for Moore's Law." *Nature* 530, no. 7589 (February 9). http://www.nature.com/news/the-chips-are-down-for-moore-s-law-1.19338.

Walker, J. Samuel. 2000. *Permissible Dose: A History of Radiation Protection in the Twentieth Century.* Berkeley: University of California Press.

Wallerstein, Immanuel. 1983. *Historical Capitalism.* London: Verso.

Wanger, Thomas Cherico. 2011. "The Lithium Future—Resources, Recycling, and the Environment." *Conservation Letters* 4 (3): 1–5.

Wark, McKenzie. 2015. *Molecular Red: Theory for the Anthropocene.* London: Verso.

Waymer, Jim. 2011. "Space Program's Environmental Cleanup Could Take Decades. *USA Today*, July 31. http://usatoday30.usatoday.com/tech/science/space/2011–07–31-nasa-environmental-cleanup_n.htm.

Weber, Christopher L., Jonathan G. Koomey, and H. Scott Matthews. 2009. *The Energy and Climate Change Impacts of Different Music Delivery Methods: Final Report to Microsoft Corporation and Intel Corporation.* Intel, August 17. http://download.intel.com/pressroom/pdf/CDsvsdownloadsrelease.pdf.

Wegenstein, Bernadette. 2011. *The Cosmetic Gaze: Body Modification and the Construction of Beauty.* Cambridge, MA: MIT Press.

Weinman, Joe. 2009. "6 Half-Truths about the Cloud." *GigaOm*, April 11. http://gigaom.com/2009/04/11/6-half-truths-about-the-cloud/.

West, Michael. 2015. "Adani Caned but Not Canned." *Sydney Morning Herald*, August 5. http://www.smh.com.au/business/comment-and-analysis/adani-caned-but-not-canned-20150805-gis217.html.

"Where the Cloud Meets the Ground." 2008. *The Economist*, October 23.

WHO. 2013. *Global Status Report on Road Safety 2013: Supporting a Decade of Action.* Geneva: World Health Organisation.

Wiesing, Lambert. 2010. *Artificial Presence: Philosophical Studies in Image Theory.* Stanford, CA: Stanford University Press.

Wilford, John Noble. 2007. "World's Languages Dying Off Rapidly." *New York Times*, September 18. http://www.nytimes.com/2007/09/18/world/18cnd-language.html.

Williams, Charles E. 2005. "Environmental Impact." In *The Industrial Revolution in America*, vol. 1: *Iron and Steel*, edited by Kevin Hillstrom and Laurie Collier Hillstrom, 157–82. New York: ABC-CLIO.

Williams, Raymond. 1973. *The Country and the City.* Oxford: Oxford University Press.

Willis, Henry H., and David S. Ortiz. 2004. *Evaluating the Security of the Global Containerized Supply Chain.* Santa Monica, CA: RAND.

WIPO. 2003. "Consolidated Analysis of the Legal Protections of Traditional Cultural Expressions." Intergovernmental Committee on Intellectual Property and Genetic Resources, Traditional Knowledge and Folklore, Fifth Session, Geneva, July 15–17. Geneva: World Intellectual Property Organisation.

WISE Uranium. 2013. "Issues at Operating Uranium Mines and Mills—Ranger, Australia." Amsterdam: World Information Service on Energy (Uranium Project). http://www.wise-uranium.org/umopaura.html.

Wittgenstein, Ludwig. 1961. *Tractatus Logico-Philosophicus*. Translated by D. F. Pears and B. F. McGuinness. London: Routledge and Kegan Paul.

Wittgenstein, Ludwig. 2009. *Philosophischen Untersuchungen/Philosophical Investigations*. Translated by G. E. M. Anscombe, P. M. S. Hacker, and Joachim Schulte, 4th rev. ed. New York: Wiley Blackwell.

WNA. 2013. *Australia's Uranium*. World Nuclear Association, August. http://world-nuclear.org/info/Country-Profiles/Countries-A-F/Australia/.

Wolfe, Patrick. 1999. *Settler Colonialism and the Transformation of Anthropology: The Politics and Poetics of an Ethnographic Event*. London: Cassell.

World Bank. 2007. "First Satellite Observations of Gas Flaring Show Countries, Companies Need to Step Up Efforts." World Bank Press Release No: 2008/055/SDN. http://go.worldbank.org/LOMK8HZPM0.

World Coal Association. 2015. "Coal and the Environment." London: World Coal Association. http://www.worldcoal.org/coal-the-environment/.

World People's Conference on Climate Change and the Rights of Mother Earth. 2010. "People's Agreement of Cochabamba." April 2. https://pwccc.wordpress.com/2010/04/24/peoples-agreement/.

World Resources Institute. 1990. *World Resources 1990–97*. New York: Oxford University Press.

WTO. 2013. "China—Measures Related to the Exportation of Rare Earths, Tungsten and Molybdenum." May 6. Geneva: World Trade Organisation. http://www.wto.org/english/tratop_e/dispu_e/cases_e/ds431_e.htm.

Wu, Tim. 2003. "Network Neutrality, Broadband Discrimination." *Journal of Telecommunications and High Technology Law* 2: 141–78.

Wynter, Sylvia. 2003. "Unsettling the Coloniality of Being/Power/Truth/Freedom: Towards the Human, after Man, Its Overrepresentation—an Argument." *CR: The New Centennial Review* 3 (3): 257–337.

Xinhua. 2007. "China Warns of Environmental 'catastrophe' from Three Gorges Dam." September 26. news.xinhuanet.com/english/2007-09/26/content_6796234.htm.

Young, Leslie. 2013. "Crude Awakening: 37 Years of Oil Spills in Alberta." *Global News*, May 22. http://globalnews.ca/news/571494/introduction-37-years-of-oil-spills-in-alberta/.

Young, Oran R., Arild Underdal, Norichika Kanie, Steinar Andresen, Steven Bernstein, Frank Biermann, Joyeeta Gupta, Peter M. Haas, Masahiko Iguchi, Marcel Kok, Marc Levy, Måns Nilsson, László Pintér, and Casey Stevens. 2014. *Earth System Challenges and a Multi-layered Approach for the Sustainable Development Goals*. Post2015/UNU-IAS Policy Brief Nr. 1. http://www.earthsystemgovernance.org/publication/young-oran-r-earth-system-challenges-sdgs.

Yusoff, Kathryn. 2010. "Biopolitical Economies and the Political Aesthetics of Climate Change." *Theory, Culture and Society* 27 (2–3): 73–99.

Žižek, Slavoj. 2006. *The Parallax View*. Cambridge, MA: MIT Press.

Žižek, Slavoj. 2010. *Living in the End Times*. London: Verso.

Zylinska, Joanna. 2014. *Minimal Ethics for the Anthropocene*. Ann Arbor, MI: Open Humanities Press.

Aboriginal Peoples Television Network, 42

Abosede, Francisco Bolaji, 30

abstraction, 149–50, 160, 184

accumulation, 6–7

acid rain, 70

actual, 3, 182–83, 191

Adani, 173

Adelman, Maurice, 167

Adorno, Theodor W., 179

Advanced Semiconductor Engineering
    (ASE), 90–91

aesthetic, aesthetics, 181–82, 188, 192, 197

Agamben, Giorgio, 175

Ahmed, Sara, 197

Alaska, 45, 74

Algeria, 37

algo-trading, 101, 112

Althusser, Louis, 185

aluminum, 70–71, 178

ancestors, 154–58, 167, 187, 188, 200

Andes, 65–69, 73, 156

anesthesia, 109–10, 188, 198

Anglo-Persian Oil Company, 36

animal welfare, 176

Animas River, 178

anti-anthropocentrism, 10

antimony, 91

Arab American Oil Company, 39

Arab Spring, 37

Arafura, 76

archive, 2, 23

Arctic, 35, 45–46

Arendt, Hannah, 158, 166–67, 174–76

Areva, 53

Argentina, 66

Aristotle, 171

Arrighi, Giovanni, 93

arsenic, 75, 91, 178, 185

asbestos, 98

asphalt, 34

Athabasca tar sands, 34, 41

Attenborough, David, 181

Australia, 46–53

Aymara, 67

Bahrain, 37

Banerjee, Subhankar, 45

Bangladesh, 32, 112

Ban Ki-moon, 50
bankruptcy, 72
barium, 98
Basel Action Network, 119, 125, 129
Basel Convention, 58, 120, 127
Bateson, Gregory, 4
batteries, 146–47
Battersea Power Station, 27
Baudrillard, Jean, 80
Bauwens, Michel, 93
bauxite, 70–71, 74
Bazin, André, 190
beauty, 198
Beck, Ulrich, 180
Bell, Clive, 150
Benjamin, Walter, 151–52, 154, 155, 156, 187, 198
Benkler, Yochai, 93, 134, 168
Bennett, Jane, 28–30, 31, 34
Berardi, Franco "Bifo," 37–38, 109–10, 112
Berkowitz, Roger, 174
Biermann, Frank, 122
biopolymers, 99
black carbon, 103
blackouts. See power cuts
blocks, 141
Boccaletti, Giulio, 16
body, the, 164–65
Boko Haram, 77–78
Bolivia, 31, 65–69, 74
Boonwurrung, 190
Brakhage, Stan, 188
Brazil, 71
Brecht, Bertolt, 13, 131
British Petroleum (BP), 36, 40
Brundtland Report, 84
Bryan, Martin, 144
Burkina Faso, 32
Business Software Alliance, 122
Butch Cassidy and the Sundance Kid, 178

cadmium, 98, 178, 185
Caffentzis, George, 45
Cage, John, 192
California Gold Rush, 78

Canada, 42, 68
Carey, Peter, 190
Caribbean, 157
Carlsbad Waste Isolation Plant, 47
Carmichael Mine, 172–73
Cassini-Huygens, 193–99
cassiterite, 73
Castells, Manuel, 136
CCD (charge-coupled device), 195
Chakrabarty, Dipesh, 11
Chernobyl, 55
Chevron, 41
Chew, Corky, 88
Chief Seattle, 13
Chile, 66, 67, 81
China, 59, 73, 81, 91, 107
China Water Risk, 91
Chipewyan First Nation, 45
Chita, 63
chlorine, 96, 185
Churchill, Winston, 36
clean coal systems (CCS), 170
climate change, 122, 126
cloud computing, 16–21
coal, 169–70, 172–73
cobalt, 119
Cochabamba, 65
Cochabamba Declaration, 183
cod, 167
codec, 140, 192. See MPEG
Cofán, 41
Cohen, Tom, 11
Colombia, 77
colonization, 8–9, 26–27, 35, 51, 56, 57–58, 73, 80, 83, 87, 116–18, 130–31, 139, 149–50, 156, 158, 161–62, 180, 184
color, 141–42
Colorado, 178
commodity, 64–68, 79–80, 113, 127–28, 131
commons, 8–9, 31, 58, 82–83, 105, 116–18, 152–55, 161, 166, 180, 182–84, 188
communication, 3–7, 15, 26, 56, 154, 158, 161, 165, 169, 177–78, 180–84
Congo, 73, 112
consensus, 186

constituent power, 137, 158
constituted power, 137
consumer choice, 100–102, 107
consumer discipline, 108–13, 188, 196
container freight, 102–7
copper, 70, 178, 185
Corning Glass, 96
Cree, 58
cyanide, 185
cyborg, 10, 34, 61, 111, 112, 139, 157

data, 158–65, 197
data centers, 16–21
Davies, Anna, 125
Davies, Will, 197
Davis, Angela Y., 172
Davis, Mike, 60
Davis-Besse nuclear power plant, 29, 55, 193
dead labor, 152–53, 155
Dean, Jodi, 181, 183, 197
death instinct, 190
Debray, Régis, 176
debt, 81–82, 85, 111–12
Déclaration des Droits de l'Homme, 174
Declaration of Independence, 174
Declaration of the Rights of Indigenous People, 42, 173, 183
Deepwater Horizon, 38, 40
Deleuze, Gilles, 158
deNardis, Laura, 146
Dene, 58, 74
Deranger, Eriel, 45
Dews, Peter, 187
Dharmadhikary, Shripad, 61
Diamant algorithm, 2–3
diesel, 102
digital rights management (DRM), 142–43
DilBit (dilute bitumen), 43
dioxins, 98
dissent, 186
Douglas, Mary, 148
Duménil, Gérard, and Dominique Lévy, 81
dumping, 124
Duval, Frank, 72, 79

Edison, Thomas Alva, 26
electricity, 26–35
Eliot, T. S., 195
Ellul, Jacques, 159
enclosures, 8–9, 83, 116–18, 152–53, 154–58, 161, 196–97
Encyclopédie (Diderot and d'Alembert), 162
Engels, Friedrich, 158
Enron, 27, 29, 30, 79
entropy, 14
environmentalism of the poor, 80
environmentalization, 116, 128, 162, 188
Enzensberger, Hans Magnus, 131
Esposito, Elena, 101
Estonia, 36
eudaimonism, 11–12, 182, 197
European Environmental Agency, 106
European Union, 128–29
Eurozone crisis, 82
Everton, Rangiaho, 130
externality, externalities, 9, 82–84, 111, 112, 119, 128, 159, 165, 188
Exxon, 66

fabless corporation, 93
fabs (fabrication plants), 86
factory, factories, 152, 156, 157, 160, 163, 171–72, 197
falling rate of profit, 82
Feilhauer, Matthias, and Senke Zehle, 9
fiber optics, 96–102
fiber-to-the-home (FTH), 99
financialization, 79, 85
First Nations. *See* indigenous peoples
FirstEnergy Corporation, 27–29, 34, 55–56, 193
fishing, fisheries, 167
Flew, Terry, 22
Florida, 195
Foresight project, 101
Fortune Global 500, 34
Foucault, Michel, 5, 163, 180
Foxconn, 113
France, 53

Freedman, Des, 136
Freese, Barbara, 169
Freud, Sigmund, 187
Fukushima, 50, 52, 55, 173
Fuller, Matthew, 22

Gabrys, Jennifer, 9, 119
Gaia, 6
gallium, 74–75
Gantz, John, 21
general intellect, 155, 157, 162, 182, 184
germanium, 75, 96
Ghana, 129
glass, 96–97
God, 176
gold, 77–79, 178–79
Gold King Mine, 178
Goldman, Michael, 69, 121–22, 126
Goldsworthy, Andy, 181
Google, 18–19
Gordon, Janet, 83
governance, 115–50, 161, 195
Great Barrier Reef, 54, 172–73
Great Pacific Garbage Patch, 119
Greenaway, Peter, 58
green fascism, 121
Green Grid, 19, 24
Green MPEG, 145–46
Greenpeace, 46, 125
Gregson, N., M. Crang, F. Ahamed, N. Akhter, and R. Ferdous, 124
Grossman, Elizabeth, 9, 92, 119
Grotius, Hugo, 7–8, 56
Guattari, Félix, 158
Guinea, 75
Gundjeihmi, 51–52
Gundjeihmi Aboriginal Corporation, 49
Gwich'in, 45–46

Habermas, Jürgen, 166, 171, 177
Haghefilm Laboratories, 2
halibut, 167
happiness, 179, 192, 199
Hardin, Garrett, 31
Hardt, Michael, 8

Harvey, David, 85, 100, 107, 114, 139, 153, 180
Hegel, G. W. F., 155–56
Heidegger, Martin, 156, 157, 167
Herzog, Werner, 119
Himalayas, 60
Hölzle, Urs, 18
Huaorani, 41
Hubbert, M. King, 36–37, 170
Hurricane Sandy, 33
Hussein, Saddam, 37
Huxley, Thomas, 167
hydroelectricity, 59–62
hydrofluoric acid, 91
hydrogen peroxide, 91

Inconvenient Truth, An, 181
India, 27, 31–33, 33, 59–60
indigenous peoples, 8, 10, 14, 35, 38, 40–46, 49–53, 58–59, 67, 71, 73, 74, 77, 83, 87, 112, 118, 130–31, 133–34, 148–49, 152–54, 156, 173, 176, 178, 183, 190, 193–94
indium, 75, 119
indium tin oxide (ITO), 72–73, 75
Indonesia, 33, 72–73, 104
Institute of Electrical and Electronics Engineers, 132
integral waste, 114–18, 147, 168
integrated circuits. See semiconductors
intellectual property, 21–24, 87, 94, 146, 182. See also patents
Intergovernmental Panel on Climate Change (IPCC), 64
International Electrotechnical Commission, 143–44
International Maritime Organization (IMO), 103, 124, 126, 132
International Monetary Fund (IMF), 30, 85, 95, 127, 134
International Standards Organization (ISO), 132, 144
International Telecommunications Union (ITU), 19, 25, 130, 131, 134, 144
Internet, 132–39
Internet Corporation for Assigned Names and Numbers (ICANN), 132, 133

Internet Engineering Task Force (IETF), 132, 143, 171

Internet Exchange Points (IXPs), 133, 136, 140

Internet Governance Forum, 134

Internet of things, 20

Inuit, 58, 68, 74

Iñupiat, 45

invisibility, 159

iron, 71

Iroquois, 58

Jabiluka Mine, 46–49

Jackson, Sally, and Graham Shirley, 2

Jagalingou, 173

Jevons paradox, 47, 100

Kahn, Douglas, 129

Kant, Immanuel, 155–56, 198, 199

Kaohsiung City, 90–91

Kazakhstan, 75

Keefe, Heidi, 57

Kelly, Ned, 200. See also *Story of the Kelly Gang*

Ken Saro-Wiwa, 40–41

key frames, 141

Keystone XL, 43

Khoo, Su-Ming, and Henrike Rau, 125

knowing, 189

Koara, 118

Kulin, 190

Laclau, Ernesto, 177–78

Lac-Mégantic, 38

Lagos, 30

Lakota, 44–45

landfill, 74

lanthanides. *See* rare earths

La Paz, 31, 65

Latour, Bruno, 95, 139, 166

lead, 98, 185

LEDS, 74–75

Lefebvre, Henri, 185

Lepawsky, Josh, 125–26

Lessig, Lawrence, 136

Lévy, Dominique, 81

Libya, 37

life cycle analysis, 125

Li-ion batteries, 66–68, 119

Limits to Growth (Club of Rome), 13, 167

Lithco, 66

lithium, 64–69

Löffler, Markus, 16

logistics, 102–7, 120, 164

Looper, Carl, 2

Luxemburg, Rosa, 85

Madagascar, 75

Madras, 27

Manzini, Ezio, 183

Maori, 130–32, 154

maquiladoras, 94

Marazzi, Christian, 32, 81

maritime oil spills, 38

Marmada River, 60

Martí, José, 94

Martinez-Allier, Joan, 80

Marx, Karl, 8, 11, 65, 85, 109, 113, 153, 154–55, 157, 158–61

Maxwell, Richard, 9, 119

Mbembe, Achille, 139

McDougall, Dan, 67

mediation, 3–10, 59, 148, 154, 165, 170, 181–84, 186, 190, 192, 200

Mehta, Suketu, 30

melancholia, melancholy, 187–88, 192

mercury, 73, 98, 185

methane, 71

Mexico, 94–95, 156, 185

Microsoft, 19–20, 73

Mignolo, Walter, 80

migration, migrants, 53, 61, 74, 102, 107, 118, 172, 173, 175, 177

Miller, Toby, 9, 119

Milun, Kathryn, 56, 57, 58, 83, 131

Mirrar, 47–49

Mirzoeff, Nicholas, 8, 11

Mitchell, Timothy, 39, 170

Mladek, Klaus, and George Edmondson, 187

mode of destruction, 109, 111–12, 116, 188

Mongolia, 76
monotheism, 176, 190–91
Moore's Law, 89
Morales, Evo, 31, 67, 68, 69, 74
Mosco, Vincent, 18
Motion Picture Expert Group, 140
Mouffe, Chantal, 171
MPEG, 140–50, 195
MPEG-4, 2
MPEG-LA, 144–45, 147, 155
MPEG-M, 142, 146–47
MPEG user description (MPEG-UD), 140,
    142, 146
Mueller, Milton, 134
Mumbai, 30–31

Nanet, 46
Napster, 24
NASA (National Aerospace Agency), 195
natality, 166–67
National Security Administration (NSA), 20
Natural Resources Defense Council, 42
Navajo, 48, 178
Negri, Antonio, 137–38, 154, 161. See also
    Hardt, Michael
Nelson, Ted, 183
neodymium, 61
net neutrality, 134–36
New Zealand, 130
nickel, 119, 185
Niger, 53–54
Niger Delta, 37, 40–41
Nigeria, 30, 32, 37, 77–79
nitrate film, 2
Nixon, Rob, 59
Nolan, Sydney, 190
North American Free Trade Agreement
    (NAFTA), 94–95
Northern Territory Emergency Response, 51
Nunavut Resources Corporation, 68
Nye, David E., 26, 29

offshoring, 86–87, 103, 104
Ogoniland, 40–41, 77
oil, 35–46, 170–71

oil spills. *See also* maritime oil spills
OM Manganese, 71–72
OPEC, 36, 37
Open Compute Project, 19, 24
Open Data Center Alliance, 19
OPENXML, 144
Oppenheim, Jeremy M., 16
organotins, 98, 123
outer space, 57, 132–33, 195
Outer Space Treaty, 195
outsourcing, 86–87, 104

packet-switching, 135
Paiute, Southern, 47
Palmer, Paul, 120
Parikka, Jussi, 9, 83
particulate matter, 95, 97, 102, 106
patents, 144–45, 146–47, 155, 162
Pattberg, Philipp, 122
peak oil, 36–37, 170
Peckinpah, Sam, 185
peer-to-peer economics (P2P), 25, 183–84
perfluorinated chemicals (PFCs), 88
persistent organic pollutants (POPs), 104–5
Petroecuador, 41
Philippine Green Party, 183
Phoebus cartel, 24
plasma screens, 119–20
plastics, 97–100, 119, 123
plutonium, 56, 193, 198
polytheism, 176
polyvinyl chloride (PVC), 98, 100, 123
Ponce, Julio, 69
Potosí, 68
power cuts, 15, 28–30, 33
precarity, 74
primitive accumulation, 116–18
prison, 172
private property , 8, 147–48, 165
privation, 165
produser, 93

Quantum of Solace, 66
Quebec, 35
Queensland, 54, 70, 172–73

Quichua, 41
Quijano, Aníbal, 80

radioisotope thermoelectric generators (RTG), 56, 193
radio spectrum, 129–32
radon, 50
Rainforest Alliance, 173
Rancière, Jacques, 171, 174–75, 176–78
Ranger Mine, 46–49,193
Rao, Srinivasa, and John Lourdusamy, 27, 32
rare earths, 76
refugees, 175. *See also* migration, migrants
Regional Internet registries, 133
res communis, 8, 83
res nullius, 8, 83, 130, 131, 195
resource curse, the, 41, 61
Responsible Recycling (R2), 129
res publica, 8
Ribera, Marco Octavio, 68
rights, 173–80, 183–84
Rio Doce, 71
Rio Grande, 185
Rio Tinto, 50
Roma, 173
Rostow, Walt Whitman, 80
Roy, Arundhati, 59–60
Russia, 36, 46, 63

Salar de Uynuni, 66
Salgado, Sebastião, 119
Sami, 46
Samsung, 92
San Diego, 94–95
sapphires, 75
Saskatchewan, 52
Sassen, Saskia, 63, 72, 79, 84, 118
Saturn, 193–99
Scalet, Bianca Maria, 97
Scudder, Thayer, 175
Secoya, 41
selenium, 75, 185
semiconductors, 86–95
semiocapitalism, 81–82, 85–86, 109–10, 112, 149

semiotics, 79–80
Senate Environment, Communications, Information Technology and the Arts References Committee, 48–49
server farms, 16–21
Shannon, Claude, and Warren Weaver, 4
sharks, 99
Shell, 40–41
Shoshone, Western, 47
Shuar, 41
Shuttleworth, Mark, 144
Siberia, 19, 58
Siegert, Bernard, 140
sign value, 80
silicon, 96
silver, 73, 185
Smith, Linda Tuhiwai, 148–49, 152
social media, 113
Sociedad Química y Minera (SQM), 69
society, 166
Söderberg, Johan, 165
Solnit, Rebecca, 78, 83
Somalia, 124
Sony, 66
SourceWatch, 169
Southern Cross cable Network, 100
South Korea, 92
standardization, 140, 143, 184, 196
Starosielski, Nicole, 100
Stiegler, Bernard, 11, 145
Story of the Kelly Gang, The, 1–12, 188–92
structural readjustment, 95
subjectivity, 184–86
sublime, 117, 198
Suez Crisis, 37
sulfur, 102
sulfur dioxide, 70
Sussman, Henry, 11
sustainable design, 121
sustainable development, 121–22, 126, 137
sweatshops, 87–88, 95, 110
Syria, 37

Tait, Charles, 1, 189–90
Taiwan, 90–91

Tandja, Mamadou, 53
TCP/IP, 135, 140
telecommuting, 21
terra nullius, 8, 53, 58, 83, 170, 193–95
Texaco, 41
thanatos, 190
Thomas, Keith, 9
thorium, 50
Three Gorges Dam, 59
Three Mile Island, 29, 55
Tijuana River, 94–95
tin, 72–73, 98, 123
titanium, 120
Toleration, 179–80
Transcanada, 44
transport, 87, 102–7
Tri-Mer Corporation, 97
Tucurui dam, 71
Tulse Luper Suitcases: A Personal History of Uranium, 58
TVEL, 63
Tyfield, David, 170

ultrapure water (UPW), 89–90, 91
Uranium, 46–59
Urry, John, 89
utopia, 6
Utopia (Alan Lowery and John Pilger), 50–51

van Asselt, Harro, 122
vectors, 142
Vercellone, Paolo, 32
Verzola, Roberto, 183
Virno, Paolo, 160
virtual, 3, 182–83, 191
Vitalis, Robert, 39
Voyager 1, 56

Waitangi Tribunal, 130
Wallerstein, Immanuel, 156

Wangan, 173
Wanger, Thomas Cherico, 69
Wark, McKenzie, 11
waste, 106, 115, 118–129, 196. *See also* integral waste
waste electrical and electronic equipment (WEEE), 116
water, 64–66, 89–90, 97
Wathaurong, 190
Weinman, Joe, 20
Wild Bunch, The, 185
wisdom, 161–62
Wittgenstein, Ludwig, 177
Wolfe, Patrick, 149
Wood, Ellen Meiksins, 153
Woomera, 53
World Bank, 30, 38, 65, 69, 88–89, 91, 95, 99, 112, 121, 126, 127
World Intellectual Property Organisation (WIPO), 132–33
worldlessness, 158–59
World of Warcraft, 17
World Summit on the Information Society (WSIS), 25–26, 133
World Trade Organization (WTO), 132
Wurundjeri, 190

Yamal Peninsula, 46
Yellow River, 76
Young, Oran R., 126
Yucca Mountain, 47

Zambia, 70
Zamfara, 77–79
Zelli, Fariborz, 122
zero-waste movement, 120, 122–23
zinc, 98, 185
Žižek, Slavoj, 158, 159
Zylinska, Joanna, 11